EVENTS OF THE YEAR

TIME CAPSULE/1929

A HISTORY OF THE YEAR CONDENSED FROM THE PAGES OF TIME

TIME INCORPORATED, NEW YORK

TIME / 1929

EDITOR *Henry R. Luce*
MANAGING EDITOR *John S. Martin*
ASSOCIATES *John Shaw Billings, Niven Busch Jr.,
Laird S. Goldsborough, E. D. Kennedy,
Parker Lloyd-Smith, Myron Weiss*
WEEKLY CONTRIBUTORS *Elizabeth Armstrong,
Russel Crouse, Washington Dodge III, Mary Fraser,
Wilder Hobson, David W. Hulburd Jr., Alan Jackson,
Peter Mathews, T. S. Matthews, Elizabeth Moore,
Carl J. Mueller, Frank Norris, John O'Hara,
Frances deN. Schroeder, S. J. Woolf*

EDITOR *Maitland A. Edey*
EXECUTIVE EDITOR *Jerry Korn*
TEXT DIRECTOR *Martin Mann*
ART DIRECTOR *Sheldon Cotler*
CHIEF OF RESEARCH *Beatrice T. Dobie*

SERIES EDITOR *John Dille*
RESEARCHER *Don Nelson*
ASSISTANT ART DIRECTOR *Arnold Holeywell*
COPYREADER *Rosalind Stubenberg*

PUBLISHER *Rhett Austell*

COVER ILLUSTRATION *Lou Lomonaco*

Editors' Note

This was the year of the great Stock Market Crash. Among financial experts, there had been intimations of trouble. But for most of the year Americans in general were blissfully unaware of impending disaster; there was much more public concern over a variety of matters: the government was having trouble enforcing Prohibition (innocent people were getting shot); the Congress was fretting about more cruisers for the Navy and whether to raise or lower tariffs; Al Capone was going to jail; Charles Lindbergh was courting—and marrying—pretty Anne Morrow; and in baseball, the fabulous Babe Ruth was leading both leagues with a batting average of .404.

One of the remarkable things about reading the news of the stock market crash is that even after the event took place, much of the nation did not know quite what had happened. Life went on, and there was even much optimism in the air. It was not until months later that the nation awoke to the fact that it was in the midst of a catastrophic depression.

This is one of a series of volumes, each adapted and condensed from a year's contents of TIME, the Weekly Newsmagazine. The words, except for a few connecting passages, are those of the magazine itself, and therefore reflect the flavor, the attitudes and the state of knowledge of the day—sometimes innocent, sometimes opinionated, sometimes prescient. The book is divided, like the magazine, into departments, and is organized so that each department forms a chronological chapter for the entire year. The dates in the margin are the issue dates of the magazine.

NATIONAL AFFAIRS

The Presidency

In the national elections of 1928, Governor Alfred Emanuel Smith of New York, an anti-Prohibition Roman Catholic, was defeated for the Presidency by Herbert Clark Hoover, a one-time mining engineer. In 1914, at age 40, already a wealthy man, Hoover turned to a career of public service. He administered Belgian relief and directed the U.S. Food Administration during World War I. He then served as an able and energetic Secretary of Commerce under Presidents Harding and Coolidge. When Calvin Coolidge decided that he did not choose to run for re-election in 1928, Hoover's reputation as an enlightened administrator made him a natural choice of the Republican Party. He defeated Smith by a popular vote of 21,392,190 to 15,016,443, and prepared to take office in what appeared to be a time of booming and limitless prosperity.

JAN. 14 **HOOVER ELECTED:** Last week the next President of the U.S. was chosen by electors voting in each state capital. In 40 states they voted for Herbert Hoover. When he becomes President his age will be 54 years, seven months. He will be three months older than the average of all Presidents at the time of their inaugurations.

FEB. 18 **COMMANDER:** Mr. Hoover was fretful. He had drawn Cabinet lists, rearranged them, scratched them, interlined them, thrown them away and locked his decisions in the secret vault of his mind. His hands itched to grip the Presidency.

But Mr. Hoover was not too busy to go through a ceremony close to the heart of many a small boy. He became, last week, a tenderfoot Boy Scout. As President, he will be Commander-in-Chief Scout.

FEB. 25 **THE COOLIDGE WEEK:** The clean aromatic smell of raw pine wood spread through the White House. Excelsior littered the floors. Mrs. Coolidge was packing. Eight Coolidge trunks entered the White House in 1923; 16 trunks will go back to Northampton, Mass., not to mention all the boxes, barrels and crates of china, books, whittling knives, stag antlers—symbols of a free people's affection for their President. "It is," President Coolidge remarked, "easier to get into the White House than out of it."

THE COOLIDGE ERA: With Herbert Hoover already in Washington, the Coolidge era seemed to hurry to its close. Who but the historian recalls an August night among the Vermont hills less than six years ago—reporters in automobiles rushing over country roads; a knock on the door of a white farmhouse; oil lamps lit; telegrams read by their glow; a brief statement of mourning; an oath of office administered at 2:30 A.M. by a country notary public to his son, the thirtieth President of the U.S. Surely no one can have forgotten the slogan that carried the day in the next election, "Keep cool with Coolidge." Calvin Coolidge will forget neither these things nor more—including that hot summer when his younger son, Calvin Coolidge, Jr., overcome by a deadly infection, passed away.

He was called upon to be an Indian, a cowboy. There were several incidents that caused him, frayed as he was, to speak sharply to Mrs. Coolidge. She was glad when he made up his mind "I do not choose to run."

Farmer Coolidge. He also dresses like an Indian and a cowboy.

President Coolidge. In a great era of yes-men he is a no-man.

¶ Work Done. The Coolidge era has seen three great reductions in taxes, about five and a quarter billion dollars lopped off the public debt, the war debts refunded, adoption of the multilateral treaty renouncing war, the appropriation of 325 million dollars for Mississippi flood control, the 275-million dollar Federal buildings' program, the civil air program, the implanting of a tradition of economy in government.

¶ Work Not Done. The World Court has not been joined; the farmer has not been "relieved"; railroads are still unconsolidated; the coal industry is still bogged; prohibition remains a mess. All these were Coolidge projects.

¶ No-Man. In a great day of yes-men, Calvin Coolidge was a great no-man. He sought to be an astringent to his prosperity-swollen country. He took credit for Coolidge prosperity because it was expedient to do so, but he kept repeating that Coolidge economy was the priceless ingredient. He carried this thought to the picayune extreme of giving away only the pen *nib*, and not the pen *holder*, after signing important bills. "Peace and prosperity are not finalities," he said in his curt closing message to the country. "It is too easy under their influence for a nation to become selfish and degenerate. This test has come to the United States."

MARCH 4 **HOW TO BE PRESIDENT:** Getting elected President is a five-month job. Learning to *be* President is a much longer job. Luckily for him, President Hoover will have at his elbows two oldtime White House technicians, one for social, one for executive, routine. The social assistant is Irwin Hood Hoover, who came to the White House as plain "Ike" Hoover, a tall, long-nosed electrician to superintend a wiring job. He stayed on and on until he became major domo, chief usher and master of protocol. He has a little office off the main foyer, to the right as you enter. Is the new Peruvian Ambassador calling to present his credentials? Major Domo Hoover will warn President Hoover what time to go upstairs and wait, will escort the Ambassador into the Green Room, go aloft to bring the President down to the Blue Room, open the Green Room door, bow in the Peruvian, wait, lead the Peruvian out to his motor, bow him away.

In the executive offices, the connecting link between all administrations since McKinley's is Clerk Rudolph Forster. President Hoover will never have to say, "What do I do

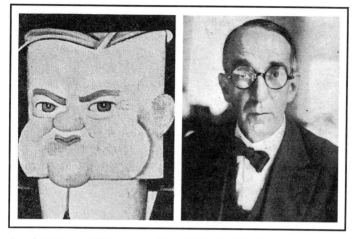

President Hoover: "We are steadily building a new civilization."

Clerk Rudolph Forster, suggesting, reminding, educating the President.

now?" because Clerk Forster will be there at his elbow, anticipating, suggesting, reminding, educating. And whom does the President wish to appoint Collector of the Port of New Orleans? Here is the man's name, all in proper form for submission to the Senate. And here is a recommendation from the Tariff Commission for 50% duty on cheesecloth. Mr. Forster will prepare the customary order and proclamation. Would the President blow up a bridge in California tomorrow? Mr. Forster will arrange for the connection. What flowers does the President like on his desk? An humble cog, it is Mr. Forster, largely, who keeps the big wheel revolving.

THE CHIEF: Boris cast an anxious eye out of the S Street MARCH 11 window. It looked like rain. Boris is a Serbian who lost his last name in the war. He works as valet for a big, friendly-faced engineer whose friends and helpers all call him The Chief. Today was to be The Chief's big day. As Boris helped The Chief into a pair of grey pin-striped trousers and a formal morning coat, he felt like giving little adjusting pats to the broad shoulders.

On the dais, the Chief moved up to the rose-decked reading stand among the microphones. Chief Justice William Howard Taft, in black robes and skullcap, moved to his side. The Chief Justice began the Presidential oath—he knew it well; he swore it once himself. Then the Bible was turned back to Proverbs 29:18 and President Hoover stooped and kissed the proverb: "Where there is no vision, the people will perish; but he that keepeth the law, happy is he."

A new-sworn President's first words are usually "My Countrymen." Excerpts from what new-sworn President Hoover said next:

"We are steadily building a new race—a new civilization great in its own attainments. . . . Crime is increasing. Confidence in speedy justice is decreasing. . . . We must critically consider the entire Federal machinery of justice. . . . There would be little traffic in illegal liquor if only criminals patronized it. . . . If citizens do not like a law . . . their right is openly to work for its repeal. . . . Regulation of private enterprise and not government ownership or operation is the course rightly to be pursued in our relation to business. . . . I have no fears for the future of our country. It is bright with hope. I beg your tolerance and cooperation. I ask the help of Almighty God in this service to which you have called me."

MARCH 18   **THE HONOR OF A CALL:** On his second day in office Mr. Hoover received 809 callers—including Chief Spotted Crow of the Sioux tribe, three squaws in paint and feathers and a five-months-old papoose—and decided that he would probably eschew noontime receptions. For the first time in many years a cradle was set up in the White House. It accommodates Herbert Hoover III, the President's grandson. After four nights in the bed provided at the White House, Mr. Hoover ordered his own bed to be brought from his S Street house.

MARCH 25   **MEN OF LAW:** A trained engineer about to sink a new shaft in quest of buried facts, the President plotted his operation cautiously. Six or nine worthy men had first to be found, men without passion or prejudice to advise him on prohibition enforcement. Youngest of the legal technicians was Dean Robert Maynard Hutchins, 30, Brooklyn-born, fair of face. Dean Hutchins may find himself a Hoover missionary spreading the gospel of abstinence. Next, to the White House, came Charles Evans Hughes, back from a bask in Bermuda. From his rangeful knowledge of courts, prosecutions, procedure, he drew much solemn counsel. Last and most august came Chief Justice Taft to discuss the U.S. Courts and their relation to the problem of law enforcement.

TELEPHONE: That President Hoover would bring Efficiency APRIL 8 to the White House no one ever doubted. First he had removed the old student's lamp, the ornate paper weights. Last week he had a telephone placed at his elbow. All other Presidents had gone to an adjoining room to telephone.

MESSAGE NO.1: "I have called this special session of Con- APRIL 22 gress to redeem two pledges given in the last election—farm relief and limited tariff revision. . . . There should be no fee or tax imposed upon the farmer. No government agency should engage in the buying or selling or price-fixing of production. The difficulties of agriculture cannot be cured in a day; they cannot be cured by the federal government alone. . . . Seven years of experience have proved the principle of the flexible tariff to be practical."

To the House and Senate last week President Hoover sent these and some 2,500 other words—his first Message—to be droned by clerks. He urged legislators to legislate: 1) Farm relief through a Federal Farm Board with "adequate working capital" to reorganize marketing, to assist cooperatives to handle surplus crops. 2) Tariff revision in the form of increased rates for agriculture and industries in which "there had been a substantial slackening of activity."

Vice President Curtis, a widower, got into a noisy squabble with Washington officialdom when it failed to treat his sister, Mrs. Gann, as his official hostess and seat her at banquets as if she were his wife.

PRECEDENCE: Many a suggestion flooded into Washington. The Vice President was called upon to marry again. Others suggested buffet dinners at which the question of precedence would be avoided by everybody standing up. "A bull-headed Vice President goaded by an ambitious woman," said the New York *Evening Post,* "can stir up all kinds of a mess."

PROHIBITION: Many were the visitations of great and near- JUNE 3 great at the White House last week. Henry Ford discussed prohibition with President Hoover, then stepped in front of the White House to announce: "Prohibition is here to stay.

Absolute enforcement must come. Nobody wants to fly with a drunken aviator.''

JUNE 10 **ACTION!:** Like the sea's ebb and flow, the spirit of naval disarmament rises and falls with the coming and going of governments. Last week President Hoover sent it billowing up the beach with fresh momentum. His argument: The Kellogg treaty for the renunciation of war is a ''declaration'' of ''faith'' which must be followed by ''action.'' It must mean ''all armament shall be used only for defense.'' ''Limitation upward is not our goal,'' he added, ''but actual reduction to lowered levels.''

Henry Ford on drinking: "Nobody wants to fly with a drunken aviator."

William R. Hearst demands a "reassuring utterance" on stocks. Page 17.

JULY 8 **DAM:** Toiling along, happy though hot, President Hoover derived immense personal satisfaction when he proclaimed effective the water-rights compact on the Colorado River, agreed to by six out of seven of the interested states. The proclamation cleared away the last obstacle to construction of a giant dam near Boulder or Black Canyons. [It eventually became Hoover Dam.] A 25-year-old interstate stalemate which blocked the river's development had been broken by Herbert Hoover as Secretary of Commerce. "It opens the avenue," he said, "for some hope of the settlement of other regional questions between states rather than the imposition of those problems on the federal government."

HATS: The Hoover headgear has been put under study. JULY 22 Results: The 31st President wears a $7\frac{1}{4}$ hat, $\frac{1}{8}$ larger than Lincoln's, $\frac{1}{8}$ smaller than Grant's. President Hayes had the smallest head ($7\frac{1}{16}$), President Garfield the largest ($7\frac{3}{4}$).

DEATH SENTENCE: Two years ago Rumrunner James Horace AUG. 12 Alderman killed two coast guardsmen in Florida. Last week President Hoover was asked to commute Alderman's death sentence to life imprisonment. This he declined to do.

WORLD COURT: The most foreign-policied President since SEPT. 16 Woodrow Wilson is Herbert Hoover. In six months in office he has stirred up a new naval disarmament to-do, and last week he opened up another question, discarded not so long ago: U.S. adherence to the World Court. In 1925 President Coolidge asked the Senate to let the U.S. join the Court. The Senate's answer was to tack five reservations to its approval. The reservations were of such a kind that only seven lesser nations out of 47 adhering to the Court agreed to them.

Last spring Elihu Root, grey Elder Statesman of U.S. diplomacy, good friend of Herbert Hoover, went to Geneva— quite unofficially—and began to draw up another set of reservations which would suit both foreign diplomats and the U.S. Last week more than 40 nations had approved the Root formula. So Henry Lewis Stimson, Hoover's Secretary of State, announced that he had notified the Secretary General of the League of Nations that the draft protocol met with his approval and that if other nations accepted it he would recommend to the President of the U.S. that it be signed and submitted to the Senate.

THE HOOVER WEEK: The President (so the story went): There SEPT. 23 is one law I should like to see passed. The President ought to be allowed to hang two men every year without giving any reason or explanation.

An Old Friend: Would two be enough?

The President: Perhaps not, but I could get word to 20 or 30 that they were being considered for the honor.

NO PARDON: The President made a brief announcement that SEPT. 30 he would issue no pardon to Oilman Harry F. Sinclair, in jail for contempt of Senate [for refusing to answer questions concerning the Teapot Dome oil scandal, which had started during the Harding Administration. He had been jailed May 6, 1929]. Sinclair must wait until November, in spite of his plea that his weight has fallen from 200 to 185 lbs., that stockholders are suffering from his absence.

OCT. 14 **NAVAL TALKS:** The White House telephone tinkled. The President's secretary answered it. His Chief was calling from the Blue Ridge Mountains of Virginia. Now, said the President, it could be told: he and British Prime Minister James Ramsay MacDonald, who was conferring with him, had agreed to have the latter issue invitations to France, Italy and Japan to discuss naval reductions with Britain and the U.S. in London on Jan. 20.

OCT. 28 **LIGHT:** President Hoover last week was all aglow as he boarded a special train, wound his way up along the Potomac, zigzagged through the Alleghenies and rolled down across level country to Dearborn, Mich. There he was met by Henry Ford, Thomas Alva Edison. His mission was important: to help celebrate the invention of Mr. Edison half a century ago of the incandescent electric lamp. That night the President spoke in tribute to Mr. Edison. His vein was reminiscent of his famed, mellow essay on fishing. Said he:

"The electric lamp enables us to postpone our spectacles a few years longer; it has made reading in bed infinitely more comfortable; by merely pushing a button we have introduced the element of surprise in dealing with burglars; the goblins that lived in dark corners and under the bed have now been driven to the outdoors."

NOV. 25 **"ACTION COUNTS":** President Hoover had a chance to compare himself with Theodore Roosevelt and Woodrow Wilson. Both those great men were mentioned in an open letter to the White House from long-nosed William Randolph Hearst, who said he wanted President Hoover to make "some reassuring utterance" at this time of "sudden and unjustifiable collapse of (stock) values." Publisher Hearst advised the President:

"The people expect as much from you as they would have expected from Mr. Theodore Roosevelt under similar circumstances. Surely your Administration could assemble the banking and financial leaders of the nation and insist that they cooperate with the government in reviving confidence and restoring normal prices."

Publisher Hearst was just 24 hours late. President Hoover had already made a move no less Hooveresque than Rooseveltian.

The first outward sign of what the President had done was three figures leaving a private door of the Treasury Department early in the morning. A thick grey mist enfolded them as they skirted the back of the White House and entered by a rear door used only by the President himself. Secretary of the Treasury Mellon—for he was one of the three—removed his coat and laid it on a messenger's desk. Undersecretary Ogden Mills tossed his coat into a chair. So did Roy Archibald Young, governor of the Federal Reserve Board. President Hoover cheerfully greeted his three visitors, led them into the Cabinet room, closed the door.

Thirty minutes later the four men arose with one thing definitely settled: There should be immediate tax reduction. That evening Secretary Mellon announced the President's plan to lop 1% from the 1929 income and corporation taxes [as a demonstration of the Government's confidence in the stability and future prosperity of U.S. business].

Two days after the tax news, the President read this announcement to assembled newsmen: "I am calling a small preliminary conference of representatives of industry, agriculture and labor to develop certain steps. In market booms we develop over-optimism with a corresponding reverse into over-pessimism. They are equally unjustified. Any lack of confidence in the economic future of the U.S. is foolish."

The Cabinet

KELLOGG ON CREST: As they must to all men of strong, JAN. 14 successful growth, completion and fulfillment came, last week, to Secretary of State Frank Billings Kellogg. The boy from Potsdam, N.Y. and the St. Paul lawyer of national prestige are now merged into the benign peace pact man. As 20 nations signed two Pan-American peace pacts under the chairmanship of Secretary Kellogg and as the U.S. Senate seemed disposed to ratify the Kellogg-Briand pact (for the renunciation of war) it could be fairly said that Frank Billings Kellogg rode the crest. Therefore, this week is an appropriate time to stroll into the large, comfortable home of Mr. and Mrs. Kellogg, on 19th Street, Washington, D.C. If a joyous, woolly dog comes bounding down the stair, call, "Bodger! Here Bodger!"

A white butler (odd in Washington) will serve tea in the library or dinner in the second floor dining room. There is one maid and one cook. Always the master dines frugally and sips sparingly, but he is no total teetotaler. Purring from the garage comes either Mr. Kellogg's own Pierce Arrow or the official Packard. The small man who steps briskly in always carries a cane, and wears a dark suit or morning clothes—but without a valet the clothes seldom seem newly pressed.

MARCH 11 **EIGHT NEW, TWO OLD:** After much secret and uncertain picking up and putting down, Herbert Hoover fitted ten pegs into ten holes and finally made up his Cabinet. It had been a brain-bullying task and the result, somehow, failed to produce the striking design of supermen which Mr. Hoover —and the U.S.—had hoped for last November. Viewed as men instead of as pegs, the Hoover Cabinet was seen as follows:

Secretary of State Simpson: 23 years of crossing the water. Page 20.

Treasury Secretary Mellon: shy little rich man. Page 20.

¶ Secretary of State. Henry Lewis Stimson of New York began crossing water at the behest of Presidents 23 years ago when he was a former U.S. District Attorney in Manhattan. He was serving as Governor General of the Philippines when President Hoover recalled him to sit at his right hand.

¶ Secretary of the Treasury. Andrew William Mellon's name was politically meaningless when President Harding chose him in 1921. But in eight years the shy little man, who for so long had ruled industrial empires from behind a Pittsburgh bank desk, has spread that name into every crack and cranny of the business world. No Republican President could function without his endorsement. He is third richest man in the U.S.

¶ Secretary of War. James William Good, pink and grey, smiling-eyed, is Iowa born and bred. His life carried him from City Attorney of Cedar Rapids to the Hoover Cabinet in two decades. He took command of the Hoover pre-convention campaign, doing a miraculous job of amalgamating the heterogeneous Hoover following. Mr. Hoover wanted him in his Cabinet as congressional contactman.

¶ Attorney-General. William DeWitt Mitchell, as a Minnesota boy, yearned to be an electrical engineer. Fishing in the Mississippi, he carried screws, wire and switches in his jeans as well as worms and tackle. But he became a lawyer. Hoover picked him for his legal talents. Mitchell boasts that he is an "old-fashioned independent Democrat."

¶ Postmaster-General. Walter Folger Brown of Ohio studied politics at the knee of Mark Hanna. He has improved considerably upon the Master. He is slick, suave, smooth, poker-faced. Foods fascinate him. He refuses to eat a strawberry that has touched water. He is an expert on patronage.

¶ Secretary of the Navy. Charles Francis Adams of Boston fits the sea as snugly as a well-made yachting cap. The Adams family has sailed far and famously in U.S. history. His great-grandfather was John Quincy, sixth U.S. President. His great-great-grandfather was John, second U.S. President. At 62 he is the greatest of U.S. amateur skippers. In 1920 he piloted the International Cup Defender *Resolute* to victory. His eyes are clear-water blue; his hands are hard and veined. His manner to strangers is austere.

¶ Secretary of the Interior. Ray Lyman Wilbur, Mr. Hoover's

friend since undergraduate days at Stanford. Mr. Hoover went out into the world to slay the Jabberwock. Dr. Wilbur stayed behind to become president of the university.

¶ Secretary of Agriculture. Arthur M. Hyde of Missouri was picked by Mr. Hoover over his own protest and set down to hoe one of the hardest rows in the Administration's patch of troubles. Mr. Hyde has three farms of his own, is a lawyer, a former governor of Missouri. On the stump Mr. Hyde is loud and noisy.

¶ Secretary of Commerce. Robert Patterson Lamont of Chicago, a trained engineer, a business man with a world outlook, an old friend, was chosen at the last minute. He is no politician.

¶ Secretary of Labor. James John Davis of Pennsylvania, a hold-over from Coolidge, holds a Cabinet position hard to fill. Labor is divided into many jealous factions. Mr. Davis' personal history is the G.O.P.'s conventional bid for labor support—immigrant boy, tin mill worker, economic and political rise to fortune and power.

SEPT. 2 **NO. 3 MAN:** It does not take a war to keep a Secretary of War busy. Though it was Washington's slack season and many a Cabinet member was out of town, the present occupant of the Cabinet's No. 3 post—James William Good —was more than usually occupied. It costs $454,000,000 per year to run the Army. Army pay is high ($21 to $126 per month plus subsistence) because the Army must compete with Industry for recruits. Scientific development has brought expensive new weapons which do not replace old ones.

Last week Mr. Good dissolved five infantry battalions and transferred their 1,960 men into the growing Air Corps. He untangled a badly snarled wharf problem for Kansas City (inland navigation is one of his responsibilities). Others include the Panama Canal, Porto Rico, the Philippines, flood control, waterpower, the Smithsonian Institution.

SEPT. 9 **3¢?:** The Post Office Department last week made sounds like a 3¢ postage stamp. From Capitol Hill, echo answered: "Pooh Pooh!" Mounting postal deficits have caused President Hoover much anxiety. This year's loss is estimated at $100,000,000. The President instructed Postmaster General Brown to discover the causes of, to devise remedies for, these

James W. Good. The Secretary of War dies after an operation.

Patrick Hurley, the new Secretary, failed to salute Pershing.

deficits. Quickly spread the firm belief that the Department would recommend an increase in first-class postage from 2¢ to 2½ or 3¢. Argument for the increase: Citizens pay the deficit anyway, either in higher postage rates or U.S. taxes.

PASSING OF GOOD: "You can't expect sympathy from NOV. 25 us. You look too healthy," bantered Cabinet colleagues when the Secretary of War complained, at Cabinet meeting last week, of a pain in his abdomen. By the next morning the pain was a stabbing torment. A cluster of doctors including Secretary of the Interior Dr. Ray Lyman Wilbur, sent James William Good to have his appendix out. The appendix was gangrenous. Doctors shook their heads gravely.

Mr. Good emerged favorably from the anesthetic, gave his wife lucid instructions about pressing War Department business. Two days later he began to sink. At night President Hoover went to the sickroom at Walter Reed Hospital. "How are you, my dear friend?" he said. The Secretary mumbled, slumped back unconscious. Oxygen failed to revive him as he slipped further and further away from life. Finally, as it must to all men, Death came, quietly.

HURLEY OF WAR: Out of an office labeled "Assistant Sec- DEC. 16 retary of War" strode a tall, straight, handsome man from

Tulsa, Okla. Briskly he paced a hundred feet, turned sharply into another office labeled "Secretary of War." Such last week was the promotion of Patrick Jay Hurley to replace Iowa's James William Good. In the War he was commissioned a Major. On one occasion, near the front, Major Hurley failed to salute General Pershing. Six years later, Mr. Hurley burst jovially in upon the general in his Washington office, defied being made to salute again. General Pershing was amused.

Hurley is not altogether popular in Tulsa, where small minds cavil that it is his personality, not real ability, which has carried him so far. The Tulsa *World* once openly charged that Col. Hurley was trying to rise to political heights purely on his good looks. He is the first Oklahoman to sit in a cabinet.

The Congress

The Congress that went into office with President Hoover was, like its predecessors of the past 10 years, heavily Republican; the count was 267 Republicans as against 167 Democrats in the House, 56 Republicans to 39 Democrats in the Senate. Unlike President Harding, Hoover got along fairly well with his Congress, despite the presence in both houses of some strong men of independent mind like Nebraska's Senator George Norris and Idaho's Senator William Borah.

JAN. 14 **THE SENATE WEEK:** Reconvening after the holidays, the Senate last week: Debated ratification of the Kellogg peace treaty, already signed by some 60 of the world's nations. As Chairman of the Senate Committee on Foreign Relations, Senator William Borah, fighting-man from Idaho, had steered it through legislative tangles, had secured for it the right of way. Crowds gathered in the galleries. The Kellogg treaty was ready to go over in bursts of Borahtorical splendor. Yet, as the debate progressed, Senator Borah's position appeared to grow hourly more on the defensive. The bill was being "pounded," the Senator was being "heckled." Relatively in the background remained Senator James

A. Reed of Missouri, big anti-treaty gun still to be shot off. The Senator from Idaho began somewhat to resemble an Horatius at the bridge.

Frequent discussion has made the treaty familiar enough —by it the signatory powers "condemn recourse to war" and "renounce it as an instrument of national policy." They agree to settle disputes "by peaceful means." Furthermore, as Senator Borah stated last week, the treaty should not be regarded as affecting in any manner the right of any signatory to go to war in what it considers self-defense. Inasmuch as virtually all modern wars are theoretically wars of self-defense, the question immediately arose as to what would prevent a war between two nations, each going to battle under a self-defense plea. Senator Borah admitted that the treaty in no way prevented such a possibility.

Senator Hiram Johnson of California asked whether the U.S. could have gone to war over the *Maine* [in the Spanish-American War] had the Kellogg Pact been in effect in 1898. Senator Borah replied that the U.S. could then have gone to war, since its ship had been blown up, its sailors killed. Connecticut's Senator Bingham asked whether, under the treaty, the U.S. could have sent an expedition into Mexico under General Pershing. Replied Senator Borah: "We would have a perfect right to send an expedition anywhere to protect the lives and property of our citizens." When

Hiram Johnson: would the Kellogg Pact have stopped war in '98?

Joseph Grundy: in one jump, from archlobbyist to Senator. Page 28.

Minnesota's Senator Shipstead asked how the treaty could have prevented the World War, Senator Borah answered that he did not know how it *could* have.

Thus the debate, with Senator Borah's defense easily twisted into an admission that the treaty did not mean very much of anything anyhow.

JAN. 28 **THE TREATY PASSES:** The Senate of the U.S. passed the Kellogg-Briand Multilateral Treaty for the Renunciation of War as an Instrument of National Policy by a vote of 85 to 1; sent it to the President.

Senator Carter Glass said: "I am unwilling to have anybody in Virginia suppose that I am simple enough to imagine that this treaty is worth a postage stamp in bringing about peace . . . but it would be psychologically bad to defeat it. I am going to be simple enough to go along and vote for this thing."

MORE CRUISERS?: Off Panama Canal, last week, the U.S. Battle Fleet held its Winter maneuvers. The grey, lowering ships formed precise patterns on the rolling waters. Now the vessels drove ahead in files, now they spread out in phalanges. Twenty airplanes were catapulted from the decks, droned ahead to find the "enemy." Certain formations meant probable success, others probable disaster. This was the mathematics of conflict, the grim study of warfare by men trained to stand on vibrating decks. Physical bravery and knowledge of strategy are already possessed by these men, but it is the function of their government to provide them with ships. Did the U.S. need more light cruisers? In view of the passage of the Kellogg treaty, should the U.S. feel that appropriating more money for more armament would be a belligerent act?

FEB. 11 **OLD SHIPS AND NEW:** The bill on which the Senate was trying to act was, on its face, quite simple. As passed by the House it authorized the Navy to build five cruisers each year for the next three years, and one small aircraft carrier. The Navy has argued that it needs this new fleet to replace obsolete vessels, some of them 30 years old. The President favored the new cruisers, but he objected to the three-year "time-limit." His objections, he said, were budgetary.

According to Senate debaters, the time-limit would mean ships of steel; its removal, ships of paper.

15 CRUISERS, NOW: To build or not to build was not the FEB. 11 question. *When* to build quite overshadowed all. The Senate remained deaf to all the President's pleas to space the ship program out. It passed the cruiser-building bill (68 to 12) *with* the three-year time-limit. The House shouted its approval. Observers noticed that, as is usually the case with Navy bills, the opposition was mostly composed of hinterlanders like Senator George W. Norris of Nebraska.

LIGHT ON LOBBYING: Senator Norris, grey and cadaverous, NOV. 11 was on his feet at his Senate desk. The chamber, emptied by an hour-long tariff speech, began filling up. In his rear-row seat Senator Hiram Bingham of Connecticut kept shifting his long legs nervously. Senator Norris explained: The Lobby Committee had developed the fact that Senator Bingham had hired Charles L. Eyanson (a Manufacturers' Association representative and high-tariff lobbyist), had put him on the Senate pay roll. Subsequently Senator Bingham in "discourteous language" on the Senate floor had assailed the Lobby Committee. Therefore, he, Senator Norris offered the following resolution: "That the action of the Senator from Connecticut . . . is contrary to good morals and senatorial ethics . . . and is hereby condemned." Thus was the stage set for a scene rare in Senate annals. Senator Norris would have dropped his resolution if Senator Bingham had consented to do "honestly and manfully" two things: 1) Admit his mistake; 2) Apologize to the Lobby Committee. Senator Bingham, despite the pleading of his friends, refused.

Two legislative days later the resolution came before a gravely hushed Senate. Insisted Senator Bingham: "Nothing dishonorable was attempted. . . . My motives were based on my wholehearted zeal for a protective tariff." The Senate was unconvinced. Senator Gillett of Massachusetts, pleading for his Connecticut neighbor, revealed that when he was House Speaker he "frequently saw Congressmen drunk on the floor" but he never "considered it necessary to censure them publicly." One concession was made by Senator Norris. He accepted an amendment that Bingham's action was "not the result of corrupt motives." Thus softened, the resolution was adopted, 54 to 22, old guard Republicans supporting their Connecticut colleague.

Meanwhile the Lobby Committee continued on its way after undercover legislative agents. Recalled to the witness stand was Joseph R. Grundy, archlobbyist from Pennsylvania. A minor political war developed between him and committee members (Arkansas' Senator Thaddeus Horatius Caraway, Idaho's Borah, Montana's Thomas J. Walsh, Wisconsin's John J. Blaine.)

Grundy: "It was a great mistake each State was given two Senators."

Caraway: "When it comes to interests of Pennsylvania, the people of Idaho ought not to say anything?"

Grundy: "They ought to talk darned small."

Walsh: "How would you silence Borah and myself?"

Grundy: "Your own intelligence would suggest silence on such matters [as the tariff]."

Blaine: "What do you think of Wisconsin?"

Grundy: "Oh, Senator, I'd hate to tell you!"

Blaine: "You think Pennsylvania would be better off if it seceded from the Union?"

Grundy: "In the Civil War we contributed more than any other state to keep the Union together—"

Caraway: "You contributed more people who stole everything they could get their hands on than any other five States!"

DEC. 2 **SINE DIE:** Into President Hoover's office at the White House last week marched two Senators—Jones of Washington, Walsh of Montana; and two Representatives—Tilson of Connecticut, Garner of Texas [later, Franklin D. Roosevelt's Vice President]. They came to perform a traditional ceremony—notification that Congress was about to adjourn. When Senator Jones' turn came to speak for the Senate, he repeated the historic phrase: "Mr. President, the Senate has completed its work—" Then he qualified: "—as far as possible." It was all the others present could do to keep from outright laughter.

The comedy of the scene was furnished by the fact that the Senate had defaulted on the tariff bill by voting to end the special session with this major legislation still uncompleted. The first session of the 71st Congress cost the country $177,000,000, exclusive of legislators' salaries which must be paid anyway. Of this amount $151,500,000, for example, was voted to start the Federal Farm Board; $4,500,000 for the eradication of the Mediterranean fruit fly in Florida; $1,000,000 for pay increases to legislative employees.

Statistician Roger Babson who had declared that Congress had fiddled like Nero while the stockmarket broke, who had urged it to "stop bickering, adjourn and stay adjourned," was loudly denounced by Senator Borah. Cried the Idaho Senator: "Utterly false and malicious statement! Who is this Babson? A man who has no responsibility, who could not carry a precinct!"

OPENING: Perfunctory was the opening last week of the DEC. 9 first regular session of the 71st Congress. The Senate sat only seven minutes. Because of bad weather, elder legislators did not bother to attend.

"A STRANGE GARRET": For the first time since March 4, 1927, DEC. 23 all 96 seats in the U.S. Senate were last week legally filled. Governor John S. Fisher of Pennsylvania rounded out the roster by appointing Joseph R. Grundy in place of William Scott Vare, rejected [by a vote of the Senate itself because he and his friends had spent $785,000 to win the primary].

The transformation of Mr. Grundy from a tariff archlobbyist to a full-fledged Senator caused some of his more volatile colleagues to gag and splutter furiously. He heard himself called a "corrupt lobbyist," his appointment an "insult to decency," his Governor an "ass." The essence of the complaint against Grundy: He had raised large amounts of cash to help elect Governor Fisher in 1926 and therefore his hands were as "soiled" as Senator-Reject Vare's.

Senator Nye of North Dakota framed a resolution designed to bar Senator Grundy from his seat and said the election had been an "auction sale." But a majority of the Senate recognized that it had no constitutional right to question the selection of a Governor, that it lacked legal grounds to bar Mr. Grundy. After he had taken his oath, Senator Grundy remarked cheerfully: "I feel like a cat in a strange garret. I have not yet got accustomed to looking from the floors to the galleries"—where he had sat for 20 years as a lobbyist.

Tariff

A serious and complex problem affecting many Americans was what to do about tariffs. In general, the U.S. was in a protectionist mood. The Republicans, who controlled the Congress, were committed by political tradition to support high protective tariffs to cut down competition of imports from abroad —especially farm produce. The Democratic Party, on the other hand, was committed to lowering tariffs wherever possible in order to increase competition and lower the price of goods for the average consumer. This set the stage in Congress for some of the era's trickiest logrolling, political oratory and backstage maneuvering.

FEB. 18 **THE TARIFF-MAKERS:** Senator Reed Smoot of Utah, regent of the Smithsonian Institution, President of the Provo (Utah) Commercial and Savings Bank, Apostle of the Church of Jesus Christ of Latter Day Saints and Chairman of the Senate Finance Committee, is a man of substance and consistency. Last week, as he arrived in Florida to see Mr. Hoover, he declared for "general and upward revision of the tariff to maintain Republican prosperity."

Three days later, emerging from conference with Mr. Hoo-

Senator Smoot: high tariffs "maintain Republican prosperity."

Senator Simmons: a tariff bill in two weeks? "Preposterous!" Page 36.

ver, Senator Smoot felt obliged to say that there would be "no general revision of the tariff law at the extra session." Thus did Mr. Smoot show consistency. He supported his President—future as well as present. Mr. Smoot's summary conversion showed plainly that Mr. Hoover had made up his mind. He wants a higher tariff for agriculture and a few specific industries which are now in poor condition.

One of the modists who have drawn the old-style plans is Mr. Joseph R. Grundy of Pennsylvania. "Who is Mr. Grundy?" ask the ill-informed. "We have heard of Mrs. Grundy—but who is MISTER Grundy?" Mr. Grundy is a man who raised $700,000 to elect Mr. Coolidge in 1924; $615,000 to elect a governor of Pennsylvania who would veto a corporation stock tax; who raised $547,000 to elect Mr. Hoover in 1928. Mr. Grundy is a worsted maker and president of the Pennsylvania Manufacturers' Association. Mr. Grundy is the man who has gone down to Washington about every tariff bill since the Dingley Bill of 1897.

Last week Mr. Grundy and the tariff boosters had their shoulders to the wheel. Congress itself seemed ready to give the wheel a spin. Then Mr. Smoot was converted in Miami. Could Mr. Hoover disgruntle Mr. Grundy—who raised for the Republicans $700,000 in 1924, $615,000 in 1926, and $547,000 in 1928?

LION-TIGER-WOLF: *Manna, marmalades, and malt,*   APRIL 8
    Sarsaparilla, sand and salt;
    Mirrors, mittens and powdered milk,
    Skates, and skewers and beaded silk;
    Bismuth, bladders, rough-hewn blocks,
    Lenses, lentils and spiral locks;
    Bone dust, eggs and ebony handles,
    Skylights, matches and tallow candles;
    Madder, miso, rattan mats,
    Bricks and brooms and baseball bats;
    Bibles, borax, strips of brass;
    Garlic, gall nuts and frosted glass . . .

Behind a high semi-circular counter-like table, a dozen Republicans have sat long and heavily discussing these articles. Behind them hung a rich red curtain. Before them was a spacious oblong room with white marble columns, a high vaulted ceiling. Outside heavy double doors, securely locked, depended a small sign bearing the gilt lettering: "Executive Session." The sitters within were Republican members of the Ways & Means Committee of the House of Representatives, their heads together on the forthcoming Hawley-Smoot Tariff Bill.

Public hearings brought into this room 1,200 witnesses in 45 days who gave 11,000 printed pages of evidence on changing the 1922 Tariff Act. Now the majority members of this committee were writing an administration bill which would fulfill the Hoover campaign promises. They were inclined to give the President what he wanted (limited revision) but outside the locked door, potent U.S. manufacturers ululated demands that all duty rates be promptly and emphatically raised for their protection against foreign competition.

Complaints against the existing tariff law were: 1) Foreign producers, benefited by cheap labor, can still undersell U.S. producers; 2) Agricultural commodities are not sufficiently protected with the result that farm imports lower U.S. prices, help create surpluses; 3) Higher tariffs would mean more revenue for the U.S. Treasury, hence, possibly, a reduction of U.S. taxation.

Against raising tariff rates to new levels were massed these arguments: 1) The more domestic products are protected, the higher is the cost of living. Domestic monopoly spells domestic extortion; 2) U.S. foreign trade will be injured by reprisals of countries whose chief products come into the U.S. Canada, best U.S. customer, has already complained. If Argentine corn is more heavily taxed, that country's preference for U.S. autos, farm machinery, etc. might cease; 3) U.S. manufacturers use many imported raw materials. Raise the duty on these and U.S. prices rise accordingly.

For all its diligence, a certain futility marked the tariff labors of the House Ways & Means Committee. A quarter of a mile across the Capitol grounds waited the man who in the end would leave the largest impress of authority upon this legislation—Senator Reed Smoot of Utah. The House writes tariff bills; the Senate Finance Committee Chairman rewrites them.

Abraham Owen Smoot crossed the plains in 1846 with Brigham Young, was mayor of Salt Lake when the U.S. Army descended upon that "nest of polygamous iniquity."

To him by his wife Anne in 1862 was born a third child, named Reed. Now at 67 Reed is tall and lean and lank, but dried and greyed by the years. A widower with six children, he resides in a magnificent marble house. The family home in Provo has long since stood shuttered and vacant—supposedly a symbol of the Senator's personal sacrifice in public service. In the Senate he has become "a lion for efficiency, a tiger for economy, a wolf for detail." From his indefatigability has sprung the verb to smoot.

Only three things break into the Senator's smooting: 1) vaudeville; 2) golf; 3) the Washington Zoo. For diversion this stern man went every Friday night to Keith's Theatre to sit in the second row just behind the orchestra leader and gaze over the footlights in unsmiling delight. Great was his sorrow when the theatre closed. From 6 to 7 a.m. he plays a round on the capital's public links, shooting 110 in straight cautious jabs. At the Washington Zoo Senator Smoot liked to poke around among the birds and animals until Helen, a parrot, told him to "go to hell."

He finds his earthly happiness in absorbed service to U.S. business. The Senator agrees with Mr. Grundy that Prosperity can flourish and blossom only in the garden of Protection behind a high tariff wall. With the political zeal of a stalwart Republican he demands protection for—

Manna, marmalades and malt,
Sarsaparilla, sand and salt; etc.

BILL OUT: After four months of mulling, the Ways & Means MAY 20 Committee last week delivered to the House a ponderous Bill to revise the tariff for the benefit of the farmer—and others. Farmers, through their representatives, surveyed the measure suspiciously, began to kick dirt. Agricultural duties were raised, but not so high as the farmers had demanded and expected. The wheat rate remained pegged to 42¢ a bushel, to which point President Coolidge had raised it from 30¢. The corn duty was moved up from 15¢ to 25¢ per bushel (the farmers had demanded 30¢). Beef went up from 3¢ to 6¢ per pound (farmers wanted 8¢). Butter was left at 12¢ per lb. (they had wanted 15¢).

Tariff-making is the oldest U.S. political game next to taxation. Every U.S. producer claims special consideration, paints a terrifying picture of his ruin by cheap foreign competition. Under insistent pressure, the Ways & Means Committee as usual broke, gave ground, widened tariff revision to include many a non-agricultural product. It was these other increases which chiefly distressed the farmer. Quick came the claim that the farmer's new profits under the bill would be immediately absorbed by increased costs in building material, paint, clothing, special foods and the like (the Oregon shingle industry asked for protection against Canadian imports, got it; bricks, cement, lumber and glass tariffs also went up).

Around sugar revolved a bitter controversy. Western beet sugar producers had demanded higher rates aimed at Cuban cane sugar and a limitation on the free importation of Philippine sugar. The House bill raised the world raw sugar duty from $2.20 to $3.00 per 100 lb. New England representatives, fondly eyeing their huge candy industry, cried out in protest. Cane-growers in Cuba (75% of whom operate on U.S. capital) foresaw disaster. Estimators could show that the new rate would add $100 million to the country's retail sugar bill.

The reception of the new bill in the House was so muddled, so many grievances of special groups were so massed together, as to give the appearance of a major revolt against the Hoover-dominated Committee. The old axiom, "Tariff is a local issue," was never more clearly demonstrated.

MAY 27 **MORE COMPROMISE:** In a back-room political conference, the G.O.P. members of the Ways & Means Committee met the revolt against the Tariff Bill by holding additional secret meetings last week. Before them appeared Congressmen from farm states to state the price they would demand to support the measure on the floor. Patiently the committee heard them ask for greater duties on their pet commodities—canned tomatoes, potatoes, live cattle, hides, blackstrap molasses, dairy products *et al.* The Committee was ready to compromise to win solid party support for the bill as a whole against all Democratic amendments.

JULY 22 **COMPLAINTS FROM AFAR:** The new Tariff Bill, passed by the House and now pondered through the hot summer days by the Senate Finance Committee, became more than a domestic matter when 43 protests against its high rates were filed with the U.S. State Department by the diplomatic representatives of 25 countries. Collectively, politely, the protests told the U.S. that increased tariff schedules might prove injurious to that expansion of U.S. foreign trade so anxiously desired by President Hoover. Ambassador Claudel of France pointed out that French citizens bought an average of $6.39 worth of U.S. goods each year, whereas each U.S. citizen bought only $1.32 worth of French goods. Spain, vexed at higher rates on cork and peppers, threatened to denounce the trade arrangement between it and the U.S. Australia complained of the wool duties; Austria, of those on hats, shoes, glue; the Netherlands, on diamonds; Persia, on rugs; Switzerland, on watches, embroideries; Mexico, on fresh vegetables.

SHOW IS OVER: One morning last week Chairman Reed SEPT. 2 Smoot, distressingly fatigued after months of tariff-writing, was marched to the front portico of the Capitol by a dictatorial Movietone cameraman. He was instructed to make a speech on the Hawley-Smoot tariff bill. For an audience the cineman commandeered Senator William Edgar Borah, hastening by to the barber shop for a much-needed haircut. Senator Smoot extolled his bill. Senator Borah looked glum. When the speech ceased Senator Borah turned, walked away. Cried the cineman, no student of tariff politics: "Hey, Senator! Come back here! The show isn't over. I want you to shake hands with Senator Smoot and say loudly, *'That's fine!'*" Replied Senator Borah: "No, I won't. The show is over."

It was an epitome of the strained feelings engendered. Best Democratic comment was by Representative McClintic of Oklahoma: "The working man may worry because his shoes will cost a dollar or two more but truffles for his *paté de foie gras* are on the free list. His sugar bill goes up as does his milk bill and meat bill but he can get Gobelin tapestries for his humble home duty free."

OMEN: Before men are done to death in battle, before walled SEPT. 30 towns are razed and wide-wayed cities sacked, there is almost invariably a potent omen. In Roman days it was frequently a pair of eagles or flight of swans. Last week as the warriors of the Tariff assembled in the Senate Chamber, above their heads came a sudden whir of wings. Looking up they beheld a pigeon gliding overhead. For a moment the ominous bird alighted above the battle on the edge of the Press Gallery. An eager correspondent snatched at it. The bird soared from his grasp leaving in his hand a single tail feather. Settling above a doorway, the ominous pigeon cooed and looked down the whole day long upon the high industrial tariff army of Generalissimo Reed Smoot and the low, consumer tariff army of Field Marshal Furnifold McLendel Simmons (North Carolina).

General Borah of Idaho, leader of the Republican irregulars, opened the battle by leading a bombing attack on Manufacturing City. He dropped his major charges, one after another: "The United States Steel Company's earnings for the second quarter of 1929 were the highest in its history. The Republic Iron and Steel Company showed increased earnings of 208%. The Youngstown Sheet and Tube Company showed 145% increased earnings. Senators, this is the condition of an industry which has asked and is receiving additional protection under this bill."

The attack had barely been consummated when from the Republican side Major-General Reed of Pennsylvania leaped into a fighting plane and pursued the Borah bomber with a stream of machine-gun bullets: "I wonder whether the time may not some day come when the self-chosen advocate of the farmer's cause will himself realize the truth that we are advantaging the American farmer as we increase the prosperity of the cities of America."

Darkness came and camp fires gleamed upon the field. When dawn broke Democratic Brigadier General McKellar of Tennessee, taking a post beside the lowland dikes, cried out with lumbering Irish sarcasm: "The farmer gets his uncut diamonds free but to compensate him for this he must pay 9¢ a pound for his aluminum ware. You all know 'Uncle Andy' Mellon has a great aluminum trust, and I am sure that the farmer realizes it. He has to pay more for his ropes, jute, twine, cord and all woolen fabrics. His wife has to pay more for her towels, linens, napkins, bags, matting and linoleums." Lieutenant-General Watson shouted from the breastworks that he had advised the President to stay out of the fray. Meanwhile the low tariff troops were quietly massing for vigorous attacks on Fort Cement.

NOV. 11 **VOICE FROM OLYMPUS:** Once again across the Tariff battlefield in the Senate rumbled the Voice from the White House.

Weary Senate warriors paused in the confusion of conflict to give ear. In an Olympian third person, the Voice declared: "The President was visited by a number of Senators who presented to him the grave situation that has arisen by delays in tariff legislation. Some of the Senators considered progress hopeless. The President said that campaign promises should be carried out, that he could not believe and therefore would not admit that the U.S. Senate was unable to legislate. He urged the Republican leaders to get together and see if they could not thus send the bill to conference with the House within the next two weeks."

What had prompted this Utterance was the growing defeatist attitude of the regular Republican cohorts in the Senate. There had been talk of outright surrender to the coalition of Democrats and Progressive Republicans and leaving the Tariff Bill supine upon a deserted field.

Again stacking their arms, Senate warriors fell to loud and disputatious shouting as to the responsibilities for tariff delays. Sample war shouts: Major General Reed of Pennsylvania: "The bill's as dead as a dodo. I for one will not agree to let the bill go through without adequate debate." Democratic Field Marshal Simmons: "The President's proposal is preposterous! We can't pass a tariff bill in any two weeks!" Combat came to a farcical standstill on Saturday when brigadier generals deserted wholesale. General Edge went to New Jersey, preventing action on his earthenware schedules, whereas any action in the metals salient was checked by the absence of General Reed. Cried Democratic Gunner Harrison of Mississippi: "I come from a part of the country where people don't believe much in working Saturday afternoon. I share that view. We have had long hours here. Let's see some football, take an auto ride, play golf." Thereupon the warriors all adjourned.

THE YOUNG TURKS: Spectators of the Senate tariff war last NOV.25 week gasped with surprise at the sight of a trim new regiment marching briskly and in close order out of the Republican redoubts. These new Republican warriors were called the Young Turks, a band of about 20 who had mutinied against the feeble leadership of the Old Guard. For Senators they were young men (average age: 56). As legislative legionnaires they were mostly rookies serving their first Senate enlistment.

Old Guardsmen, weary of the eight-week fray, wanted to go home. Democrats also craved a respite; the charge, false or true, that their action on the tariff was largely responsible for the stockmarket crash and business uncertainty made them skittish about pressing their victories too far. Democratic Field Marshal Simmons wanted to get back to New Bern, N.C., where a bank failure, he explained, had cost him every cent he had. He it was who proposed the truce—adjournment of the session, putting the tariff over to December. On the vote the Young Turks marched into the breach and turned the tide to defeat (51 to 34) the adjournment motion.

Quickly to his feet leaped Democratic General Harrison, proposing, as a sort of reprisal, night sessions on the tariff. The Young Turks accepted the challenge, helped to vote three-hour sessions each night, making a ten-and-a-half hour fighting day for the Senate. The Senate worked through two night sessions. Every member was fagged by Saturday afternoon when Democratic assistant Chief-of-Staff Walsh of Montana arose to beg the Young Turks to have mercy on their older colleagues and not work them into their graves. He pleaded for a recess. Grudgingly the Young Turks permitted a breathing spell.

DEC. 2 **TRUCE:** The Senate tariff war came to a complete halt last week. Feeling fatigued and futile, the warriors voted a truce (adjournment) before beginning the long winter campaign (regular session). Only half of the salients had been fought over. Legislative forecasters declared no tariff bill would reach the President until next March—14 months after it was started.

Political Notes

JAN. 7 **"GOD'S":** On the corner of 13th and Irving Streets, Washington, D.C. stands a small meeting house of light buff brick with concrete steps and opaque glass windows. At present there is no "experienced speaker" (say the Friends: "We do not set anyone apart whose special duty it is to supply the spoken word. The experienced speaker should be watchful not to speak at undue length.") but one will be found by March 10. Beginning on Sunday, and for at least four years after, the President of the U.S. will be numbered among its congregation. A Washington official, recently passing the Church, remarked to a member: "So this is Mr. Hoover's church." "No," replied the Friend, "it is God's church."

DEMOCRATIC DEFICIT: "I am entirely dissatisfied to have the JAN. 28 Democratic party be simply a party of opposition. It must be a progressive, vigorous, militant party . . . The Democratic National Committee faces a deficit of approximately $1,500,-000. I am quite willing to bear my full share. I have decided I would forego any profit from a book containing my campaign speeches. The Democratic National Committee will present, with my compliments, a nicely bound copy to anybody contributing $2 or more."

Thus spoke Alfred Emanuel Smith over the radio to the nation. He used the same microphone that had carried his last campaign speech. Hardly had Mr. Smith turned away from the microphone when telegraphic notices of donations and congratulations began to arrive. Mrs. A. L. Love of Ottumwa, Ia. wired: "My compliments—Matthew V, 11 & 12." ("Blessed are ye when men shall revile you and persecute you, and shall say all manner of evil things against you falsely, for my sake. Rejoice and be exceeding glad, for great is your reward in Heaven; for so persecuted they the prophets which were before you.")

Alfred E. Smith: "The Democratic Party must be vigorous, militant." *Huey Long of Louisiana. "This cruel tyrant" is impeached. Page 40.*

FEB. 4   **ATROCIOUS FALSEHOODS:** "Bigotry," said New York Governor Franklin Delano Roosevelt [referring to the anti-Catholic campaign that helped defeat Alfred E. Smith in his Presidential race against Hoover], "the spread of unspeakable and un-American methods of the most atrocious falsehoods . . . cheated . . . our party out of the Presidency."

FEB. 11   **HOOVER & SMITH:** Last week a memorable meeting came at last to pass. Alfred Emanuel Smith and Herbert Clark Hoover spent 25 minutes together in the J. C. Penney sunparlor at Miami Beach, trading yarns, smoking long black cigars, laughing. Smith skipped his breakfast to make it on time. With care he picked his attire—silk-faced cutaway, striped trousers, silk-topped patent leather button shoes, semi-formal overcoat with velvet collar. One hand picked up a cane; the other put a cigar in a mouth corner. The Brown Derby, above all, was set at an undefeated angle. Away streaked the baby-blue Rolls-Royce. Mr. Hoover had not slicked up much. His coat was blue, his trousers white, his shoes blancoed. "Mr. President," Smith said, leaving, "I wish you health, success and all the good luck in the world."

APRIL 8   **LOUISIANA'S KAISER:** Louisiana is a state unto itself. Many are its traditions, fine and enviable. One of them is that in its 117-year career in the Union it has never removed a governor by impeachment. Last week it prepared to shatter this tradition.

For ten months Huey P. Long has been Louisiana's governor. To many it seemed ten months too long. He had ruled the state as a political dictator. For ten months his opponents cringed before him. Governor Long was farm-born 35 years ago in the upper part of the state. At 13 he peddled school books, developed an amazing gift of gab. He hustled through a three-year college course in seven months to jump headlong into state politics—"on the people's side." His chin is dimpled, his cheeks cherubic, his eyes small and brown—and his tongue a restless lance of dispute and invective. To win his election he promised the state's farmers paved roads, free hospitals, free school books. (He keeps the farmer's water bucket and gourd dipper displayed in his office.)

Louisiana is, among other things, an oil state. Governor Long proposed a 5 cent tax upon every barrel of refined oil and gasoline. Unsentimental businessmen rose to curse him with the charge that he would drive industry out of Louisiana. This caused the impeachment explosion. Governor Long, who was charged, among other things, with carrying concealed weapons and employing the militia to loot private property, retorted that the Standard Oil Company of Louisiana was behind the impeachment. With all newspapers against him, Louisiana's Kaiser issued a special newssheet of his own, defending himself under the head, CROSS OF GOLD: HUEY P. LONG v. THE STANDARD OIL. Lieutenant Governor Paul N. Cyr asked God to forgive him for ever supporting "this most cruel tyrant."

IMPEACHED: For three hours the Louisiana House pushed APRIL 15 and yelled. One member fainted. Then, by a vote of 58 to 40, the House impeached Governor Huey P. Long on one charge, with more to follow. The charge: Governor Long had intimidated a publisher by threatening to expose the fact that his brother was in an insane asylum. Later, in a radio speech, Governor Long made good his threat. What he did not say was that the brother in question was a shock-victim of the War. [The impeachment trial was never held.]

NO. 3 MAN: It is sometimes said that for prestige and pow- MAY 20 er, for responsibility and reward, the three "biggest" elective offices in the U.S. are 1) President of the U.S.; 2) Governor of the State of New York; 3) Mayor of the City of New York. Job No. 3 is now, and for three years has been, occupied by James John Walker (48). The City of New York pays its mayor $25,000 per annum—not much, considering the requirements of a sprightly person like "Jimmy" Walker. For three years Mayor Walker has given the people "out front" a good show. He still dresses like a vaudeville man. He has the support of the Hearst papers, and criticism of him as a flibberty "do-nothing" by other papers carries small political weight.

Arnold Rothstein, famed gambler, was murdered last autumn. Most New Yorkers have heard that the "inside story" of this crime involves so high a Tammany official that the Walker administration had to switch Police Commissioners, as a sop to divert popular attention from the subject by a great display of traffic-controlling in the mid-town district. But nobody cares deeply. The sins of an administration fail to register on the average New York voter, except as dollars and cents out of his pocketbook. Graft of $100,000 was lately uncovered in the County Clerk's Office, and no public outcry followed. Additional buses have never materialized because, with the Mayor's consent, a franchise was awarded to a worthless company. These sins of omission, New York's millions of voters are ready to forgive, owing chiefly to inertia. Thus Mayor Walker will run again on his "record," will win on his "popularity."

JULY 8 **TAMMANY TEST:** Just when Tammany Hall was bracing itself for a New York City-wide election this fall, a bloody body was last week plunked down upon its political doorstep. Frank Marlow, murdered Broadway gambler and friend of gambler Arnold Rothstein, whose murder last fall is still unsolved, had hardly been settled in his coffin before a so-called Better City Government League nominated one-time (1918-25) Tammany Mayor John Francis ("Red Mike") Hylan to run as an independent candidate against Tammany Mayor James John Walker. The Hylan war-cry: Stamp out crime, vice, corruption. Nominee Hylan hopes to gain Republican support as a fusion candidate.

Against his hopes looms the short, swart figure of Manhattan Congressman Fiorello H. LaGuardia, who expects the Republican mayoral nomination. By way of preparation, Congressman LaGuardia last week went to a U.S. Army Hospital, had his tonsils removed.

JULY 15 **TRUST-BUSTER:** Originated as a patriotic order, the Society of Tammany in Manhattan makes a great to-do over Independence Day. On that day last week the city's Democrats crowded into their hall to hear New York's Franklin Delano Roosevelt call for a new "Declaration of Independence" against "Centralized Industrial Control" in the form of corporation mergers.

Said Governor Roosevelt: "The huge mergers and consolidations are challenging in their power the very government itself." To his hearers, the Roosevelt warning sounded like a political war-cry for 1932, the posing of an economic, instead of moral, issue on which democracy might unite. Tammanyites hailed their Governor as "our next President."

BILBO, FISH: "The most inexcusable, unreasonable, contemp- JULY 22
tible, diabolical, damnable and pusillanimous falsehood ever
conceived in the twisted, corrupted, diseased, poisoned, fiend-
ish mind of a black-hearted villain and assassin" was Mississippi Governor Theodore Gilmore Bilbo's formal retort in
the State Legislature last week to the charge that he had
attempted to peddle a Mississippi bond issue contrary to law.
The same message asked each legislator to donate one goldfish
for the fish pool at the Governor's mansion.

CHICAGOLOGY: For months a Chicago University professor OCT. 7
has been investigating U.S. politics by sober scientific methods. His methods were unique. He psychoanalyzed Chicago
politics by the "word association" test. Specimen Chicago-
ans, from steer-stabbers to brokers, were told to blurt out their
immediate reactions to the examiner's key words. "Alderman," suggested the professor. "Grafter," quickly replied
one citizen. "Crook," said another. Another, "bay window."

WALKER v. LAGUARDIA: Tammany's Mayor Walker beat Re- NOV. 18
publican Congressman Fiorello LaGuardia by an eight-to-three
margin. Mourned LaGuardia: "What a shellacking! People
don't resent graft anymore. Yes, I still believe in democracy."

Corruption

*The fallout from the scandals of the Harding Administration
was still settling six years after his death in 1923. The three
chief characters in the drama were Harding's Secretary of the
Interior Albert Fall, a onetime Senator from New Mexico, and
two oil operators, Edward L. Doheny and Harry F. Sinclair,
who were said to have paid him for the opportunity of drilling
for oil on U.S. Government lands: the Elk Hills reserve in
California in Doheny's case and the Teapot Dome reserve in
Wyoming in Sinclair's. Doheny claimed that $100,000 he had
given Fall was simply a personal loan. Then it was discovered
that Fall also had in his possession some $250,000 worth of
Liberty Bonds that were traced to a Canadian firm owned
largely by Sinclair. Doheny escaped conviction. Sinclair was
sentenced to jail for tampering with a jury and refusing to*

answer a Senate committee's questions; both oil leases were ultimately declared void by the U.S. Supreme Court, and early in 1929 Fall went on trial on charges of accepting a bribe.

APRIL 15   **SINCLAIR TO JAIL:** To the large brick "common jail" on the banks of the Anacostia in Washington must go Oilman Harry Ford Sinclair for three months. The U.S. Supreme Court so ruled last week. His crime was contempt of the Senate. In March, 1924, when the oil scandals were white-hot, Sinclair was called before the Senate Public Lands Committee. Ten questions were put to him. One question was whether he had given money to Albert Bacon Fall, whilom Secretary of the Interior. Oilman Sinclair, on advice of counsel, refused to answer every question.

He was indicted, tried, sentenced two years ago. His appeal to the Supreme Court was on the ground that the Senate's questions pried illegally into his private affairs, were not pertinent.

MAY 13   **BEHIND BARS:** In 1897 another rich man, Elverton R. Chapman, went to district jail for contempt of Congress. Convict Chapman had a two-cell suite, Persian carpets, meals from outside. Declared Jailer Peake: "As for Sinclair, he'll be just one of the boys. We'll put him to work and hope he likes it." Convict Sinclair will share his 8-by-6 cell with another prison-

Harry F. Sinclair. The Teapot Dome scandal sends him to "common jail."

Albert Fall, ex-Secretary of Interior, wanted vindication. Page 45.

er, rise at 5:30 a.m., retire at 9 p.m. It will be hot in this jail during the summer. If all goes well for him, Sinclair will be free Aug. 4. But another six-month sentence hangs over him while the Supreme Court weighs a second sentence for contempt for hiring Burns' detectives to investigate the jurors during his first Teapot Dome conspiracy trial.

NO. 10,520: Clad in silk pajamas, Sinclair spent most of the MAY 20 first night in jail smoking cigarettes on the edge of cot 62. The snores of 60 roommates kept him awake. After breakfast he was fingerprinted, given No. 10,520 and assigned to the jail pharmacy. Thirty years ago in Kansas, before he shot his foot and got the insurance money that started him in the oil game, Harry Ford Sinclair was a registered pharmacist. Now he was given a white coat and set to rolling quinine pills for sick convicts.

Sinclair had a well-known stable of horses called Rancocas. In jail he met a fellow convict who knew his horses. Nick Keart is a small Syrian, a "bookie" at the racetrack. His career has been interrupted by a sentence to the Washington, D.C. jail. Last week Nick Keart had the unexpected pleasure of meeting the Master of Rancocas at breakfast. Turning to him, the bookie said: "Mr. Sinclair, I've taken a lot of bets on your horses and I've made a lot more on my own, and I've always wanted to meet you. I'm sorry it had to be in jail."

The Master of Rancocas slapped his fellow-convict on the back and said: "Don't worry about that, young fellow! We all get bad breaks. My colors will still be flying when this thing is over."

SENTENCE UPHELD: No. 10,520 heard bad news last week. The JUNE 10 Supreme Court sustained his sentence for contempt of court. He carried on in the prison pharmacy, certain in the knowledge that he would spend Christmas behind bars.

JOY RIDES: Someone in Washington with a memory for faces SEPT. 16 was startled. Soon the Capital was rife with rumors that Harry Sinclair was riding through the streets in a car. Jail officials admitted that for two months Convict Sinclair, prison pharmacist, had been detailed to accompany the jail physicians to the city wharfs to attend prisoners working there. The rides were stopped.

OCT. 7 **FALL TRIPS:** In 1898 Albert Bacon Fall went with Company H, 1st Territorial Volunteer Infantry, to fight in the Spanish War. In 1912 he made a splendid trip to Washington. He was one of New Mexico's first two Senators. In 1921 he made his greatest trip of all—to Washington to become President Harding's Secretary of the Interior. Two years later, Albert Bacon Fall made a sad trip, back to Three Rivers, N.Mex., resigned, suspect, disgraced. People were saying he had accepted presents from oil men in return for giving them rich leases and contracts on Government reserves.

While criminal and civil actions were being prepared, Fall took a trip abroad with Oilman Harry Ford Sinclair (who paid his expenses). If they had stayed abroad, as other characters in the Oil Scandals did, Fall would have been spared further sad trips. Last week began another of them. Cleared of conspiring with Oilman Edward L. Doheny to defraud the U.S., Fall has yet to be cleared of taking a $100,000 bribe from Doheny. With his 68th birthday only seven weeks off, with a physician beside him to watch over his infirmities, Fall boarded a train for Washington to undergo trial.

OCT. 21 **THE TRIAL:** Albert Fall was indeed a sick man. His right lung was congested. He showed every symptom of pneumonia. He was in an extremely susceptible condition for catching a cold, which might well terminate fatally.

Justice Hitz and the government's special counsel both seemed to feel that a mistrial ruling was in order because of Fall's illness, and the government counsel so moved. Then the door of the courtroom opened. A procession entered. It included Mr. Fall, pale, tired, bolstered by strychnine, reclining in a wheel chair. On one side walked a trained nurse. Back of the wheel chair came Mr. Fall's doctor, cousin, wife, two daughters and Witness Doheny. Dr. Safford and cousin Houston Fall lifted Mr. Fall out of the wheel chair, tucked him into a big green morris chair. Mr. Fall did not want a mistrial declared. He wanted, said Attorney Frank J. Hogan, "to be vindicated before passing into the Great Beyond."

"I deny the Government's motion [for mistrial]," said Justice Hitz. "Call the jury."

NOV. 4 **FIRST FELON:** Twelve tired-eyed jurors, taut and nervous, filed solemnly into the District of Columbia Supreme Court room one morning last week after a day and a night's deliberation. A young bank teller, as foreman, cleared his throat huskily, read from a blue paper in his shaky hand: "Guilty, with a recommendation to the mercy of the court."

That statement convicted Albert Bacon Fall of bribery. It branded him as the first felon in a President's Cabinet in U.S. history. It made him liable to a three-year prison sentence, a $300,000 fine (the fine for bribery may be three times the amount of the bribe under the U.S. Criminal Code). It changed the $100,000 in cash sent Fall in a little black bag by Oilman Edward Laurence Doheny from an innocent "loan" between old friends to a corrupt and criminal payment to influence the Secretary of the Interior to lease U.S. Naval Oil Reserve No. 1 at Elk Hills, Cal. to Doheny's Pan-American Petroleum Co. It insured the trial of Doheny.

The first conviction to be obtained by the U.S. on direct evidence of the naval oil scandals (1921-23) produced a strange courtroom scene. Defendant Fall sat wrapped in an automobile robe, his black New Mexican sombrero in his lap. His eyes were stunned. Down his white, sunken cheek rolled a teardrop, to be kissed away by his sobbing wife. Other women present moaned hysterically. Robust cow-punchers and ranchers bent their heads in sorrow for their friend.

Oilman Doheny, crimson with rage and chagrin, shook his fist at the bench and screamed: "That damned court—." Mark Thompson, Fall's attorney, slumped to the floor, lay there unconscious for ten minutes before physicians could revive him. Cried lawyer Hogan: "Tell that damned jury to come back here and smile at this, too." The wife of one of the jurors had followed the case as a Fall sympathizer. After the verdict she chased violently after her husband to a public park where he was being photographed. "You miserable *rat!*" she screamed.

The facts on which Fall was tried were agreed on both sides. Fall and Doheny, gold prospectors together in the old West, had been friends for 43 years. At the peak of negotiations for an oil lease—Nov. 30, 1921—Doheny had sent Fall $100,000 in cash by his son. Four months later Doheny's company had the Elk Hills lease from which it expected to make $100,000,000. Two years ago a jury tried Fall and Doheny on practically the same evidence for conspiracy to defraud the U.S. and acquitted them. This time the jury had to judge, independent of Doheny, Fall's intent in receiving this cash. It found his intent criminal, the cash a bribe. Only novelty: government lawyers managed to introduce the illuminating fact that Fall, in a parallel case, had received some $269,000 in Liberty bonds from Oilman Harry Ford Sinclair who in return received the Teapot Dome lease.

Defense lawyer Hogan's claims, which the jury rejected: The $100,000 cash was a friendly loan for which Doheny held a torn note; Doheny had reluctantly taken the Elk Hills lease as the result of a Japanese war scare in 1921 and as an act of patriotism for national security; the whole Government from President Harding down collaborated in approving the lease.

The defense reeked with sentimentality and patriotism. Frequent were the references to Fall's bad health. Lawyer Hogan made the women of the jury weep. He made an impassioned plea for the jury to send Fall "back to the sunshine of New Mexico." Remarked Judge Hitz to the jury: "You have nothing to do with the sunshine of New Mexico and must decide this case on its merits, without influence of sympathy or compassion."

NOV. 11 **SENTENCE:** Though still ill, Fall was able to walk into court to hear himself sentenced: "Because of the recommendation of the jury for mercy, I will impose upon Mr. Fall a fine of $100,000 and imprisonment for one year." Fall bowed his head in his hands while his wife sobbed quietly.

NOV. 25 **MRS. FALL'S STORY:** Millions of U.S. cinema-goers looked and listened as a grey-haired woman pleaded piteously on the screen for her family's good name. Mrs. Fall had posed and spoken for Fox Movietone News. She declared: "The jury stood on the second ballot nine for acquittal, two for conviction. The twelfth and last man who came over to the eleven for conviction, three days later came to me in tears begging forgiveness. He had not slept, and walked the floor since his terrible mistake."

When it became known that the basis of Fall's appeal would be alleged "forcing" of the verdict by Jury Foreman Thomas E. Norris, as exemplified by the Movietone story, newspapermen interviewed Mrs. Fall last week at El

Paso, Tex. Elaborating on her Movietone revelation, she said:

"The verdict was returned not out of the conviction of twelve, but of only three, who forced the others to accede. Daniel Weisbach told me that during the deliberation he paced the floor in agony, trying to stop his ears to the flood of arguments. Finally, he had to join in. He voted for conviction because he was worried about his wife who was an expectant mother. He told me the jury room was very cold and he was very ill and spitting blood. When the time came for the jury to report, the others bullied him into leaving the jury room."

Newsgatherers soon sought out Juror Weisbach. He accused Mrs. Fall of falsehood. He had not asked her for "forgiveness," he said. He had not said that the foreman of the jury "forced" the verdict. He would not discuss the case further.

SINCLAIR STEPS OUT: It was midnight in the District of Colum- DEC. 2 bia jail, the middle of the night for most convicts, the beginning of a new day for one. When the hour had struck, No. 10,520 stepped out to the prison yard and once more became Harry Ford Sinclair, a free oilman.

His statement was handed out—and mailed broadcast to smalltown editors throughout the land—by his Manhattan office. "Railroaded to jail. . . . Sins I have not committed. . . . A man of honor and integrity," were some of the things it said. Also: "I am a victim of political campaigns to elect honest Democrats by proving how dishonest Republicans were." Free at last on all charges, Oilman Sinclair spent the night in Washington, motored next day to seclusion on his Rancocas stock farm at Jobstown, N.J.

Heroes

LINDBERGH-MORROW: Col. Charles Augustus Lindbergh, prime FEB. 25 Hero of the U.S., is well used but by no means resigned to the idolatry of his public. When he landed in Havana last week he eyed the thronging newsgatherers more moodily than ever. He knew they were not going to ask him about the new Pan-American air mail route he had been inaugurating. They were waving slips of paper which read: "Ambassador and Mrs. Morrow announce the engagement of their daughter Anne Spencer to Colonel Charles A. Lindbergh."

Well? Col. Lindbergh compressed his lips and only opened them to say: "You know all about it. I have nothing to say. I will confine my remarks to aviation."

But it really was romantic. The country gurgled its delight. The tabloids went wild with headlines about "Lindy and Anne," " 'We' now a Trio," etc. etc. Some commentators preferred to ponder the social evolution represented in the conjunction of the Lindbergh tradition and the House of Morgan. The late Charles Augustus Lindbergh Sr. was a "radical" Congressman from Minnesota. At least "radical" is the word that J. Pierpont Morgan must have thought of when Charles Augustus Lindbergh Sr. was abusing the "Money Trust" and helping to precipitate the Congressional investigation of 1911.

An interested spectator during that crusade was Anne's father, Dwight Whitney Morrow. He was then a member of an old Manhattan law firm. In 1914 he became a partner of J.P. Morgan & Co. A subtle metamorphosis has come to pass since 1914. Not often or loudly, nowadays, is the House of Morgan called sinister or arrogant. Much of the credit for this change has gone to Dwight Whitney Morrow. The elder Lindbergh was never satisfied that any change had

Charles Augustus Lindbergh, 14, and his Congressman father: A honeymooning hero chooses to "confine my remarks to aviation."

come, however. To the end he saw large banking houses only as "accursed burdens upon the plain people."

In Mexico City [where her father was U.S. Ambassador] Miss Anne Spencer Morrow, 22, five-feet-five, brunette, blue-eyed, bashfully quiet, shrank from the glare of being her country's Hero's fiancée. Industrious press ferrets brought up Miss Morrow's poems. Her last, in *Scribner's*, concluded:

> *Still, like a singing lark, I find*
> *Rapture to leave the grass behind.*
> *And sometimes standing in a crowd*
> *My lips are cool against a cloud.*

PUTPUT: The country found its Honeymooning Hero last JUNE 17 week, lost him, found him again. He was on a boat. Five days after Charles Augustus Lindbergh, 27, married Anne Spencer Morrow, 22, a 38-ft. Elco cruiser chugged alongside a small dock in New Harbor, Block Island (R.I.). A tall young man, tastefully disguised in smoked glasses and a cap, standing alone at the wheel, shouted for aid in bringing his boat alongside. He was the Honeymooning Hero. His bride hid in the cabin below. Newsgatherers sped east.

At Woods Hole, on Cape Cod, they found him. Tricky, and famed for his practical-jokingness, he putputted sea-ward, rounded the cape and anchored at Provincetown, where the press picked him up once more. The Hero turned a spotlight on a rowboat full of reporters, picked up his anchor, and slipped away at midnight.

To conceal his identity, the Hero draped canvas over the cruiser's name, *Mouette*, on the stern. The Coast Guard announced its right to shoot at anybody who did such a thing [rum-runners often did the same to elude capture]. The *Mouette* reached York Harbor, Me. and a *Daily News* reporter who had known Lieut. Lindbergh in his pre-hero days set out for an interview. *Reporter:* "Are you going abroad this summer?" *Hero:* "Glad to see you." Defeated, the reporter left, wrote home to his paper that Mrs. Lindbergh must have been seasick because she was lying down. The honeymooners continued eastward.

HOME FROM WAR: From the far field of a war that was never DEC. 9 a war returned to the U.S. last week 75 warriors—each in a flag-draped wooden box. Twenty-nine of them were name-less. Icy cold blew the dawn wind as the S.S. *President Roosevelt* churned slowly up New York harbor, but a balmy breeze it was compared to the blasts of the North Russian winter of 1918-1919 when these U.S. soldiers died fighting the Red Army. After eleven years and by dint of diligent search by the Veterans of Foreign Wars, their bodies had been exhumed from shallow graves in the frozen tundra, brought back for homeland burial.

No declaration of war by Congress authorized U.S. participation in the sorry North Russia expedition, which began in the summer of 1918. President Wilson consented on his responsibility to the use of U.S. troops on this remote frontier. The original Allied purpose was to offer a new threat to Germany on the East, following the collapse of Russia as a fighting force, to guard supplies, keep U-boats out of the cold White Sea. But objectives became muddled. The Allied troops numbered some 27,000, of which 5,100 were U.S. soldiers. Twenty thousand "White" Russians joined them. The enemy became the Bolsheviki.

On Aug. 3, 1918, Archangel was captured by the Allies who immediately pushed south on five disconnected fronts. When the Armistice came, they found themselves frozen in for the winter.

In January, with the temperature 30° below zero, the Red Army assaulted them, drove them back. The wounded died from exposure. A bare hand touching metal was seared as by fire. Snow and continual darkness fought for the enemy. So great was the demoralization of all troops that withdrawal was ordered with the first thaw late in May.

The expedition cost the U.S. $3,000,000, with 244 men killed, 305 wounded. In November 1919, 104 of the dead were returned to the U.S. Last summer a commission searched for the rest. Russian peasants were hostile, had to be bribed to reveal each grave. The Soviet government, cooperating with the U.S., threatened to plow up one town *in toto* unless its inhabitants gave up the U.S. dead. In another case a Russian woman had nursed, fallen in love with and then buried a wounded U.S. officer. First she tried to misguide the searchers from the grave. When they found it by an ikon and paper flowers, she vainly implored them to leave its contents behind.

Labor

The South was the scene of much labor unrest in 1929. Textile manufacturers erected mills there to make use of the large supply of nonunion workers, and union organizers, some of them Communists, thereupon moved in to set up locals. Numerous clashes occurred between these militant groups and the local —often company—police; one of the worst took place at Gastonia, North Carolina.

SOUTHERN STIRRINGS: Textile mill strikes flared up last week APRIL 15 like fire in broom straw across the face of the industrial South. They were all symptomatic of larger stirrings in that rapidly developing region. A generation ago the New England textile industry began dipping from its peak to its present debilitated condition. Causes for the decline were: 1) the unionization of Labor with its new power to dictate higher wages, to call gory strikes, to obtain protective laws; 2) increased taxation; 3) increased cost of power. The mill owners cast anxiously about for a refuge from their troubles. The South seemed attractive.

Chambers of Commerce told the Northern mill operators about cheap, unorganized white labor in the South, abundant water power, lenient mill laws (a 72-hour week, night work for women and children), special tax exemptions, proximity to the industry's raw material, King Cotton. Mill after mill closed in New England to reopen in the Piedmont section of the Carolinas. The labor was new, but the proprietors were mostly the same.

In the South the union labor movement has made the smallest headway. The workers were individualists of old U.S. ancestry, long trained to stand alone. Fanatically religious, they viewed organized labor as Communism. But now they are no longer "poor white trash." They have begun to taste the power of combined action, to strike for what they want.

"DAMN UNION": Snores of textile strikers, abed in the Gas- APRIL 29 tonia headquarters of the National Textile Workers' Union, ceased abruptly early one morning last week when the snorers were nudged awake by revolvers in the hands of a band of masked men. With crowbar and sledge hammer the invaders set about wrecking the flimsy building. With the headquarters in ruins, the wreckers departed into the darkness-before-dawn, leaving this sign:

WE HAVE QUIT YOUR DAMN

UNION

Thus did the textile strike in North Carolina become rough. The *National* Textile Workers' Union is a Communist organization. The *United* Textile Workers' Union is a branch of the American Federation of Labor. A contest for control had flared up between these two. The Communist organizers had fostered the Gastonia strike, which now was not moving rapidly enough toward victory to suit the strikers. The mills had hired other workers, continued operation. Many observers were ready to believe that the raid upon the Communist headquarters was made by disgruntled strikers, weary of the Communist leadership. No excessive effort was made by the National Guard to find the raiders.

MAY 13 **WAR OF ATTRITION:** A strike, like an army, moves on its stomach. Food became the crux of the textile strikes in North Carolina last week. Supplies for the strikers were dwindling. The professional leaders were faced with a difficult psychological problem. They sought to keep some mills operating and increase union membership in these mills and thus collect dues to sustain the strikers already out. But members who glanced out of mill windows could see strikers idling in the sunshine, realized that they were in effect supporting these strikers by their labor. Many a new union member was tempted to quit the mills and join the "free grub" line in the sunshine. Professional agitators taught the strikers new words, like "sweatshop" which seemed particularly applicable to Southern mills, with their high humidity, closed windows, lint-laden air. Said one striker: "I ain't a-feared of Hell. I've spent 20 summers in the mills."

Last week strike leaders were ready to accept a 48-hour week instead of a 40 and would give up their demands for a $20 per week minimum. But Manager J.A. Baugh of the Loray Mill was "too busy" even to discuss concessions. To him the strikers were just "discharged" employees. His mill, he claimed, was running well without them.

IN GASTONIA: No shop, no office door was opened one morn- JUNE 17
ing last week in Gastonia, N.C. Grim-faced, sullen men
lounged about silent streets. They were waiting for the funeral of Chief of Police Orville F. Aderholt, murdered in a
gun fight with textile strikers. The Loray Mill strikers had
reduced their demands, hoped to be taken back to work.
Their offer was refused. Strikebreakers ran the mills. Down-
hearted, the strikers chewed over their idleness in savage disappointment.

Last week a band of them, cursing "Scabs," started for the
mill. Police intervened, turned them back [to a tent area they
had been living in since they had been evicted from their
company-owned houses]. Then a fight between two strikers
brought the police back. The strikers' guard opened fire on
the law. Chief Aderholt, three policemen and a union organizer were shot in the fracas. Chief Aderholt died the next
day. The organizer and 58 others were arrested, sixteen
charged with murder. Thus ended the twelfth week of one
of the first strikes in the "New" South.

TEXTILE TRIAL: On the bench of the Gaston County Superior AUG. 12
Court sat a tall, clean-cut, smooth-faced man of 41. He was
Judge Morris Victor Barnhill, the State's youngest judge, sent
into the county by the Governor to try an extraordinary case.
Before him were 13 men, three women. Laughing, smiling,

Judge Barnhill of the Gastonia mur-   *Prosecutor Carpenter: "There was im-*
der case is an ogre in Communist eyes.   *morality in Gastonia!" Page 58.*

they looked more like college boys and girls than the Communistic strike leaders they were. They were charged with murder and conspiracy.

For weeks through Gastonia, dominated by large cotton mill interests, had swirled passion and prejudice against the strikers. So bitter was this feeling that defense counsel asked Judge Barnhill to move the case elsewhere. They complained that they had been abused on the streets, that defense witnesses had been threatened with violence if they attempted to aid these "Godless Communists and Russian interlopers."

If ever a judge had cause to let his personal feelings influence his decision, it was Judge Barnhill, for he had just been handed a cartoon from the *Daily Worker*, Communist sheet, depicting him as a fat ogre, dripping gore. Judicious, big-minded, he smiled tolerantly at this libel on his integrity by friends of the defense—and 20 minutes later granted the request for a change of venue. Fortunate were the defendants that somebody was not punished for contempt of court. The defendants breathed easier while their lawyers joined hands, danced about, shouted: "We have won the first encounter and the enemy is ours!"

SEPT. 9 **TEXTILE TRIAL:** A dusty motor bus rumbled up the highway from Gastonia to Charlotte, N.C. Its passengers were 16 young Communists, all charged with first-degree murder. At Charlotte they were put on trial for their lives. Radical organizations throughout the land screamed that the case was "a vicious capitalistic frame-up."

At the trial's opening the defense won one large victory: Judge Barnhill limited murder evidence to the occurrences of June 7. This hampered the State's attempt to prove the inception and growth of an alleged conspiracy. It also barred out the background of the defendants.

SEPT. 23 **GASTONIA'S GASTRITIS:** Into the courtroom at Charlotte last fortnight was wheeled a ghoulish plaster-of-paris effigy clad in a blood-caked, bullet-ridden police uniform. Its face, beneath a broad-brimmed black hat, was a ghastly image of Police Chief Orville F. Aderholt, for whose murder 16 strikers and organizers were on trial.

Effective—all too effective—was this theatrical gesture of the prosecution. Juryman Joseph G. Campbell, an "eccentric" newsvendor, blanched and stared pop-eyed. That night he begged the deputy sheriff for a pistol to kill himself. Next day he confessed his sins to the sheriff, asked to be buried face downward. Then the sheriff reported: "I found him crawling under the beds." Said a doctor: "Acute emotional insanity." Said the judge: "Mistrial." New trial will begin on Sept. 30. Five other jurors, released from their oaths of secrecy, hinted that the State's case was weak, that their verdict would have been "Not Guilty."

Newspapers carried to Gastonia this inflammatory revelation. One night last week scores of grim, Communist-hating Gastonians, doubtful of justice by jury, determined on southern-style vengeance, crowded into automobiles, laid hands on three unwary strike organizers: Cliff Saylor, C.M. Lell, Ben Wells, sped away.

In one car crouched pudgy Ben Wells, recently arrived British Communist. He was shown a rope and given broad hints as to its purpose. Then he was black-jacked. When he came to, the cars had stopped in a secluded spot. His trousers were stripped off. He was thrown to the ground. While one mobster sat on his head, others took to larruping his bare withers with branches. Suddenly rose a cry, "The Law!" The mobsters vanished, leaving Wells to be picked up by his fellow captives Saylor and Lell. "The Law" proved to be a carload of 'possum hunters. Communists Saylor, Lell and smarting Ben Wells wearily trudged eight miles to Concord, told their story. Fourteen alleged flagellating kidnappers were arrested.

Then eight Communists were detained for collecting arms to "protect themselves." Headed for a mass meeting, an open truck lumbered out from Gastonia, bearing 22 Communist men and women. After it raced several automobiles. One car passed the truck, forced a collision. Men in the following cars shouldered their guns, pumped fusillade after fusillade into the unarmed herd in the truck. One woman fell dead. Others, fleeing across the cotton fields, were pursued, shot at, clubbed. Several were wounded. The overtaxed Charlotte judiciary functioned rapidly. Within 24 hours after the truck massacre, seven alleged murderers were arrested.

FRESH BLOOD: Textile mills in the Carolinas run all night. OCT. 14 After sunrise, the mill siren gives a blast to warn the day workers that it will soon be time to go to work. When the warning siren blew on the Marion Manufacturing Co.'s mill in Marion, N.C. one morning last week, Sheriff Oscar F. Adkins began to make a speech at the mill gates. Across the street was a crowd of night shift workers bent on persuading the day shift not to go to work. They had heard that the company was transferring all union workers to the night shift. Then the night shift would be discontinued and the union workers got rid of.

"Now, men," Sheriff Adkins says he said, "you will have to stand back and let anybody through that wants to come to work."

Someone in the crowd shouted: "Over our dead bodies!"

The crowd surged to hold back a would-be worker. It was then, says Sheriff Adkins, that he started discharging his tear gas gun. He got a lot of tear gas in his own face. An old man reached the Sheriff and belabored him with a stick. While grappling with this assailant, who later died, Sheriff Adkins says he heard his deputies start shooting their real guns. The crowd fled shrieking down the street. The deputies kept shooting. "For God's sake stop firing!" Sheriff Adkins says he shouted.

But already a lot more blood had been shed in the textile war of the Carolinas. Three men were dead. There were 24 wounded (mostly in the back.) One of the wounded men died before the mill whistle shrieked its next day's warning. Three more were dying. Sheriff Adkins, 13 of his deputies, two mill foremen and a mechanic were arrested, charged with murder. The Governor sent in two companies of National Guardsmen.

The funeral service was held in a scrub-oak grove. The four pine coffins, painted grey, lay on a low platform. Four girls led the hymn-singing, which included this chant:

> *We are building a strong union,*
> *We are building a strong union,*
> *We are building a strong union,*
> *Workers in the mill.*

Chief preacher was Cicero Queens, a gnarled little old man from 60 miles away in the mountains. While the men sat immovable and the women wailed amens, he cried under the bright morning sun:

"The Devil's come into the world and confused the people. Think of it—blood of our blood, bone of our bone, our own Caucasian race of God Almighty's children. And I want to say, thank God a man who believeth in Jesus Christ is not dead. We know that we are not very high in society, but God loves us. O, what would Jesus say if he passed through Marion? He's weepin' at all this scenery."

At Gastonia, the 16 defendants, mostly organizers of the National Textile Workers' Union, hired a new lawyer—an ingratiating Baptist named Frank Flowers who voted for Al Smith and has conservative social views. His standing was expected to help the "atheistic" labor radicals with the fundamentalist jury. Further help to the defendants seemed to lie in recent episodes of the textile war—unionists flogged, one woman murdered, the Marion slaughter. To meet these changed aspects, the prosecutors adopted quick new tactics. They dropped charges against nine defendants, including the three women and six natives of North Carolina. Against the seven remaining—four of them Northern Communists—the charge of first-degree was dropped and with it the shadow of the electric chair which juries shun.

GUILT AT GASTONIA: When the Aderholt trial reopened with OCT. 28 12 sane jurors, the defense counsel wanted no martyrs. Fred Erwin Beal, principal defendant, supposed Communist, weaseled when it came his turn to speak. Loudly had the Communist press hailed him as a hero. Faced with a possible sentence, Defendant Beal, 33, pale, broad, fleshy, in a low voice denied his Communist principles, did not advocate revolution, had no objection to policemen, however violent in line of duty. Myopic, though, was the testimony of Mrs. Clarence Miller. Smiling at her lawyers' horrified faces, she blithely admitted Communist beliefs, Communist teachings. The defense lawyers hurriedly changed plans, did not put her prisoner-husband on the stand.

Melodramatic was Prosecution Lawyer John G. Carpenter. He held Widow Aderholt's hand, knelt before the jury, lay down on the floor and writhed (acting out Aderholt's death.) He lost his boutonniere, got another, lost that too. He asserted that the union headquarters in Gastonia had been "not a cross-section of hell, but a whole section of hell! There was immorality there. Yes, *immorality*! Hugging and kissing in public. I'm old-fashioned. I'm a Sunday school man." He called the mill owners, his employers, a "holy gang, a God-serving gang."

After receiving a 90-page charge from Judge Barnhill the jury retired. In an hour it came back, pronounced "guilty" upon Defendant Beal and his six co-defendants. Judge Barnhill sentenced Beal and the three other northern defendants to serve from 17 to 20 years in State's Prison. The Southerners, considered less culpable, received smaller terms.

Immigration

MARCH 11 **NATIONAL ORIGINS:** A surgeon, about to make a transfusion, scientifically matches a donor's blood to his patient's to such purpose that no shock results. In like manner Congress has ordained that Immigration shall be scientifically matched to the U.S. racial bloodstream.

In attempting to execute the orders, a large corps of census experts, statisticians and genealogists have wrestled for four years with the problem of tracing back for 140 years the ancestry of 120,000,000 people. The chief results so far have been expert disagreements and rancorous race disputes. In 1921 the quota system was first applied to restrict European immigration. A method of admission was set up, its size crudely fixed at 3% of the number of foreign-born U.S. residents enumerated in the Census of 1910. Because this seemed too large, in 1924 it was closed to 2% of the foreign-born population of the 1890 census.

This was not a *scientific* way to filter aliens into the U.S. if the original native stock of the country was to be preserved. The 1924 law therefore carried a provision for the establishment of quotas based on National Origins. Scientists were to determine the racial composition of the present day U.S. starting from the first U.S. census (1790), analyzing the growth of population to date with reference to national ancestries, and thus, in effect, fixing the proportion each foreign country contributed to U.S. "native stock" and the development of that stock since. To the U.S. were then to be admitted 150,000 immigrants annually, in direct proportion to the contribution their native countries have made to the whole U.S. population, past and present, Negroes excluded.

This policy was to go into effect by Presidential proclamation July 1, 1927.

But the British burned most early U.S. census details in the sack of Washington in 1814. Native stock, clear in the early days, was blurred by intermarriage. Racial names have become meaningless through social change. So the 20th Century scientists bogged down in confusion and Congress postponed the effective date of National Origins to July 1, 1928; later to July 1, 1929, where it now stands.

As a Presidential Candidate, Herbert Hoover said: "The basis now in effect [2% quota] carries out the essential principle of the law and I favor repeal of that part of the law calling for a new [National Origins] basis of quotas." Last week President Coolidge sent to Congress the final "scientific" figures, showing what would happen under National Origins.

No great *numerical* difference would mark the change. At present the 2% quota system admits about 164,000 immigrants per year. There would, however, be a marked change in the *composition* of U.S. immigration. For example, the 2% quota system now admits 51,227 Germans each year. Just prior to the census of 1890, there was a heavy tide of German immigration, far above Germany's average in earlier and subsequent periods. Under National Origins, the German quota would be cut down to 25,957. On the other hand, the majority of U.S. people are of British ancestry. British immigration had dwindled when the 1890 census was taken and the present British quota allows only 34,007 newcomers. Under the National Origins systems Great Britain's quota would be 65,721. National Origins would reduce Irish immigration from 28,500 to 17,500; Norwegian from 6,400 to 2,300; Swedish from 9,500 to 3,300. It would increase Italian immigration from 3,800 to 5,800, Dutch from 1,600 to 3,153, Spanish from 131 to 252.

GIRL FROM COBH: From Cobh, Ireland, Mary Callaghan, 22, APRIL 15 sailed up New York harbor aboard the S.S. *Baltic*. Ahead was the Statue of Liberty—as grand a sight as Mary ever saw. She felt like cheering. She waved her arms. Down into the sludgy water fell her purse with $60, and her precious passport to the U.S. To Ellis Island she was taken to await identification. In Pittsburgh, Secretary of Labor James John

Davis read a news story of Mary's predicament. Once an immigrant himself (from Wales at the age of eight) he commanded that Mary Callaghan's cheers and waves could be her passport. She was admitted, and went to work in Chicago.

Crime

One of the most gruesome crimes of the '20s was the St. Valentine's Day Massacre in Chicago, described in this section. The seven murdered gangsters were archenemies of the notorious Al Capone, then in the declining years of his reign as the nation's top racketeer. The motive for the murder was a gangland battle over the distribution of illegal liquor. In 1929, the 10th year of Prohibition, it was becoming increasingly evident that the antiliquor laws were unenforceable. Millions of people kept right on drinking, and the demand for contraband alcohol was so great (see Prohibition) that an underground system of speakeasies and wholesale suppliers was set up. The corruption and brutal warfare exemplified by the Chicago massacre was one result.

FEB. 25 **CHICAGO'S RECORD:** It was 10:20 o'clock on St. Valentine's morning. Chicago brimmed with sentiment and sunshine. Peaceful was even the George ("Bugs") Moran booze-peddling depot on North Clark Street, masked as a garage of the S.M.C. Cartage Co., where lolled six underworldlings, waiting for their breakfast coffee to cook. A seventh, in overalls, tinkered with a beer vat on a truck. Two of the gang drifted aimlessly into the front office where ink wells stood dusty dry.

Ten minutes later they glanced at each other, startled. Was that a police gong? Into the curb eased a car, blue and fast, like the Detective Bureau's. Through the office door strode four men. Two, in police uniforms, swung sub-machine guns. Two, in plain clothes, carried stubby shotguns. The gangsters in the office raised their hands. Their visitors marched them back into the garage, prodding their spines with gun muzzles. Tin coffee cups clattered to the stone floor. Snarled orders lined the six gangsters up along the north wall, their eyes close to the white-washed brick. The visitors "frisked" away hidden guns. One of the men at the wall said: "What is this . . ."

"Give it to 'em!" was the answer. The garage became a thunder-box of explosions. From the four guns streamed a hundred bullets. Only eight of them ever reached the brick wall behind the seven targets. One man, all blood, tried to crawl away. A volley at six inches ripped away his head. The others toppled over into the careless postures of death.

A Mrs. Alphonsine Morin, across the street, saw two men, hands over head, walk out of the garage, followed by two uniformed policemen with leveled guns. Obviously a raid and an arrest. She watched captors and captives enter the blue car, which flashed down the street, passed a trolley on the wrong side, melted away in traffic. Real police came jostling through the gabbling crowd that quickly collected. They counted the neat row of bodies by the wall—six dead, one dying. It was a record even for Chicago.

"Bugs" Moran, the proprietor of the garage, was not among the dead. He was spending St. Valentine's Day in Detroit. The perforated bodies were those of Moran's brother-in-law and co-leader, James Clark; No. 1 Gunman Peter Gusenberg, Con-Man John Snyder, Gorilla Al Weinshank, John May, the man in overalls, and Reinhart Schwimmer. Frank Gusenberg, Pete's "Kid" brother, carrying 20 bullets, lived for three hours after the shooting, but gangland's curious code of honor sealed his lips. Besides him, the only living thing in the garage when the slaughterers left was the Gusenbergs' police dog, a fierce animal raging on its chain.

There was only one motive—jungle justice. Chief Gangster Alphonse ("Scarface Al") Capone's West Side mob was under suspicion. Tony Lombardo, Capone's good friend, wilted last summer under a spray of bullets. And a shipment of Canadian whiskey from Detroit's "Purple Gang" to Capone was hijacked last fortnight, presumably by Moran men. Capone was reported to be lolling innocently in Florida.

IN SPOONER'S NOOK: Southward out of Chicago early one MAY 20 morning last week slipped three automobiles. They crossed the Indiana line and parked at Spooner's Nook in the desolate outskirts of Hammond. Something heavy was flung into the brush. One of the cars was driven into a ditch. The other two cars drove away.

Just before daylight two Hammond policemen came upon the bloody contents of Spooner's Nook. The object in the bushes, the two objects in the ditched car, were dead men's bodies, ragged with bullet holes. Chicago detectives readily identified the three corpses as what remained of John Scalise, Albert Anselmi and Joseph Guinta, gangsters all. Scalise and Anselmi were professional assassins, members of the modest remainder of "Scarface" Capone's once-invincible "mob." They had wriggled through three murder trials to freedom. For the mowing down of seven members of the "Bugs" Moran gang on St. Valentine's Day, Scalise had been indicted, had obtained temporary freedom the fortnight prior on $50,000 bail.

Chicago's police adopted the handiest explanation: the Moran gang had avenged the massacre. The Spooner's Nook find brought the number of Chicago underworldlings who have met violent death this year to 20, an all-time high for the first five months of any year.

MAY 27 **CAPONE COUP:** Jails keep prisoners in and prisoners' enemies out. Last week Alphonse Capone, once Chicago's No. 1 underworldling, now a hunted exile "on the spot," went behind bars in Philadelphia for a year's "stretch." Philadelphia and Chicago officials were sure that Capone had deliberately taken refuge in prison, where the only bullets he would have to worry about would come from the guards' rifles.

For a week Capone, with his ever-present bodyguard, Frank ("Slippery") Cline, had been teasing Atlantic City police with his presence in that resort. He motored to Philadelphia, missed the Broadway Limited for Chicago, made a reservation on the Manhattan Limited. With two hours to kill, he went to a cinema. Detectives picked him up as he came out, took from him a .38 calibre revolver, courteously escorted him to police headquarters. Bail was set at $35,000. At midnight he was questioned and made these statements: "I went into the racket in Chicago four and a half years ago. During the last two years I've been trying to get out. I want peace. I'm willing to live and let live. I'm tired of murders and shooting. I'm retired and living on my money."

The next morning Capone faced the detective line-up at 9:30 A.M., was indicted by the Grand Jury at 10:25 for carrying concealed weapons, went on trial at 11:30, pleaded guilty at 12:15 P.M., started a year's sentence at 12:50. Exactly 16 hrs. 35 min. elapsed between his arrest and the beginning of his sentence. Remarked Capone: "They work fast here."

AT LEAVENWORTH: From New York [where riots had oc- AUG. 12 curred at Auburn and Dannemora prisons] the contagion of revolt last week spread to the Federal penitentiary at Leavenworth, Kan. The prison temperature was 100°. Spanish rice was repeated at the noon mess. Nine hundred inmates rebelled, threw their food about, seized knives and forks. Ordered back to their cells, they bolted for the prison yard. When a fire hose failed to break them, guards opened fire with riot guns. One convict was killed, three fell wounded.

Reasons given for the Leavenworth uprising: overcrowding; lack of sufficient work; effect of heat on drug addicts. Reasons given for the New York revolts: heat; lack of food (no eggs, milk, fresh meat), bedbugs, lice, plumbing; overcrowding; petty graft by guards.

THE ALIEN CORN: Tall and green is the corn grown by the SEPT. 2 Farmers Hoffman on their Blue Ribbon Farm near Somerville, N.J. Tall and grim are the factories that have grown up there. Broad and white is the twelve-room house where live the stocky Teutonic Farmers Hoffman. Narrow and dingy, made of lath and tarpaper, are the shacks where some of the unskilled immigrant factory workers, mostly Poles, live.

In one of the shacks lives the Widow Kolesar, a dumpy little Slav who chars for her living and fills her four children's bellies with vegetables from their scrawny "garden." Her "old man" was killed while working on the railroad. Nearby lives the Klementovich family. Mother Klementovich is virtually a widow; her "old man" is serving a two-year term for beating her. She works in a factory, tends chickens. There are four little Klementoviches.

One afternoon last week Johnny Kolesar, 12, suggested to his sister Anna, 10, that they make an expedition to the Hoffman brothers' cornfield. Anna had been there before and told of its glories. Barefoot along the path they rolled their hoops. Passing the Klementovich shanty, they invited Helen and Joe to come too. As Anna told the story later, this is what happened:

"We all spread out in the cornstalks. I heard a gun go off and a bullet whiz. I saw Johnny fall. He didn't cry; he just lay there. I heard Helen cry out: 'Johnny, I'm shot! . . . I went through the corn and looked out. There was a man with a gun. He had on a hat and brown pants. . . . Then I started running toward home. On the way I met Helen's mother. I told her 'Hurry up, Helen's shot.' Then I went and told my mother."

Johnny Kolesar died instantly. Joe Klementovich was taken to a hospital, apparently dying. Helen's wounds were less dangerous.

Police, fearing a lynching, dispersed muttering crowds, locked up Farmer Craig Hoffman, charged him with murder, assault with intent to kill. Farmers of the region viewed the shooting elementally. They said that in defense of his crops, especially prize corn like the Hoffmans', a man is justified in killing, especially when the thieves are "little Polacks" from shanty-town. Bernarr Macfadden's horror-loving New York *Evening Graphic* sent a man out to pose and photograph the Widow Kolesar lamenting in a cornfield. The caption: *She stood in tears amid the alien corn.*

Prohibition

JAN. 7 **"CONSPIRACY TO TRANSPORT":** Such U.S. citizens as may habitually order their liquor by telephone discovered last week that they may be prosecuted under that section of the Volstead Act which prohibits the transportation of liquor. A decision with that effect was handed down in Philadelphia by Federal Judge William H. Kirkpatrick. It was rendered in the case of Alfred E. Norris, Manhattan broker, and Joel D. Kerper, Philadelphia bootlegger (now in Atlanta Penitentiary). It was admitted that on at least 12 occasions Mr. Norris had ordered 'Legger Kerper to ship whiskey from Philadelphia to New York, that these shipments were disguised as ink, paint, olive oil and other commodities, and had been consumed (but not sold) by Broker Norris and his friends. Norris maintained that the Volstead Act forbids the *sale*, not the *purchase* of liquor, that as a *buyer* he had committed no crime.

Judge Kirkpatrick agreed that the purchase of liquor is

not an offense. But, he continued, "it does not follow that where transportation is required by the agreement, there may not be an indictment of the buyer and the seller for conspiracy to transport." Broker Norris was found guilty, was fined $200.

"FROM AND AFTER": In a Lansing, Mich. courtroom last JAN. 14 week Judge Charles B. Collingwood was sentencing Mrs. Etta Mae Miller. It had taken a jury only 13 minutes to find her guilty. She was charged with having sold two pints of liquor and also with being a "habitual criminal" inasmuch as this was her fourth such offense. So to her said Judge Collingwood: "It is the sentence of this court that from and after this day you shall be confined in the Detroit House of Correction for the remainder of your life." Mrs. Miller has ten children. Her husband is serving his first liquor-conviction sentence. Lest any feel that Mrs. Miller had been too severely punished, Dr. Clarence True Wilson, General Secretary of the Board of Temperance, Prohibition and Public Morals, spoke up for Methodism: "Our only regret is that the woman was not sentenced to life imprisonment before her ten children were born. When one has violated the Constitution four times, he or she should be segregated from society to prevent the production of subnormal offsprings."

THE COST: How much does the U.S. Government spend on JAN. 21 Prohibition? From $13,000,000 to $15,000,000 yearly has been the usual direct appropriation. Prohibition Commissioner James Doran once estimated that $300,000,000 a year would be needed to enforce Prohibition properly.

THE TUSHES OF THE LAW: By a vote of 65 to 18, the Senate last MARCH 4 week passed and sent to the House a bill to furnish the Volstead Act with larger tushes. The present penalties for illegal manufacture or sale of liquor are: for a first offense, up to $1,000 fine or up to six months' imprisonment; for subsequent offenses, $200 to $2,000 fine and one month imprisonment. The proposed penalty for first *and* subsequent offenses is a fine up to $10,000 or imprisonment up to five years, or both.

The debate did not take place without magnificent fireworks. Missouri's ruddy-faced Senator Reed cracked once more the stinging lash of his invective over the heads of dry-voting, wet-

C. T. Wilson, a Dry, applauds a life term for selling two pints of liquor.   *Mrs. F. D. Roosevelt, a Wet, thinks Hoover may get folks to stop drinking.*

drinking Senators. The biting tongue of Senator Caraway retorted: "I marvel at the motive that makes him seek to lead the people to think that this is a body of sots." Connecticut's Senator Bingham, objecting to the bill because its penalties were greater than for more serious crimes, offered a list of other punishments for comparison:

¶ Shanghaiing Sailors: Not more than $1,000 fine, a year's imprisonment or both.

¶ Hovering on the Coast with Slaves for Sale: Not more than $10,000 fine nor more than four years' imprisonment.

MARCH 11   **DRY HOPE:** Herbert Hoover went into the White House last week as the Dry Hope of all U.S. Prohibitors. They recalled Harding and the well-filled whiskey flask (for medicinal purposes) in his White House desk, and Coolidge, dry as a Vermont tinder box, but deficient in the hot crusading flame of the true prohibitor. Now—bless the day—had come a President in whom for years has been seen a steady, scientific glow of enthusiasm for social uplift.

MARCH 18   **MRS. FDR SPEAKS:** The potency of Mr. Hoover's Dry leadership was shown by the wife of the Wet Governor of New York, Mrs. Franklin D. Roosevelt, who went so far last week as to say to a Y.W.C.A. meeting in Manhattan: "A woman of my acquaintance remarked that while she never had lived up to the Prohibition law, she almost believed Mr. Hoover could get her to do it."

In Peoria, Ill., on the first two days of Mr. Hoover's administration, 20 persons, including two women, died from drinking poison gin.

THE FIVE & TEN: Because of its provisions (five years and MARCH 25 $10,000) the new enforcement law had been nicknamed the Five & Ten. The movement of diplomatic liquor from the Port of Baltimore to Washington's embassies and legations was badly snarled by the Five & Ten. The State Department ruled that non-diplomatic truck drivers were liable to be arrested, advised foreign representatives to drive their own trucks.

THE AUTHOR: Andrew J. Volstead, once an inconspicuous APRIL 1 Minnesota lawyer, has never deeply regretted the fame that came to him when he tagged his name upon the National Prohibition Act. It was a nuisance, of course, when intoxicated traveling salesmen called Mr. Volstead up in the middle of the night to curse him. But he has surmounted this drawback by 1) concealing his telephone number; and 2) remembering all the good people who admire his Act.

INTERNATIONALE: Temporary seizure of diplomatic liquor enroute to the Siamese legation in Washington created an Incident. The State Department obtained a Treasury Department ruling that embassy liquor could be transported by private U.S. trucks and drivers, provided an accredited diplomat was actually aboard the vehicle. Then, the U.S. Coast Guard sank the British auxiliary schooner, *I'm Alone* and killed one of her crew. The British Ambassador called at the State Department. The Coast Guard Commandant called the *I'm Alone* a "notorious rum-runner" and explained that the U.S. cutter *Walcott* had ordered the two-master to halt for inspection. Instead of stopping, the *I'm Alone* turned and fled. Cornered by other U.S. craft 24 hours later on the high seas, the *I'm Alone* was sent down by gunfire. One man was lost. The rest of the crew, in irons, were carried to New Orleans.

The *I'm Alone's* skipper said his schooner was "anchored 14½ to 15 miles offshore" and did not heave to because he did not think the U.S. had jurisdiction. His ship, he figured, went down 225 miles offshore in a heavy sea under 120 U.S. shots.

APRIL 8 **FATAL ZEAL:** In January one Boyd Fairchild, Dry snooper, reported to the Illinois State's Attorney a purchase of liquor at the home of one Joseph De King, 38, in Aurora. For this information he was paid $5. A "John Doe" Warrant was sworn out. Last week Deputy Sheriff Roy Smith, fat, officious, went to the De King home with the warrant. De King refused to let him in. Smith returned with three more deputies. They surrounded the house, threw mustard bombs, rushed the door. De King was clubbed into unconsciousness. Lillian De King, his wife, was at a telephone, screaming "Help! Help!" to their lawyer. Smith fired a shotgun loaded with slugs point-blank into her abdomen. She wilted to the floor, dead. Gerald De King, 12-year-old son, flipped up a revolver, sent a bullet plowing into the fleshy leg of Deputy Sheriff Smith. Later a gallon of weak wine was found.

Said Sheriff Smith from his hospital bed: "I wish there was no such thing as prohibition. I'm through with it. Try to enforce the law and see what happens."

APRIL 29 **THE CHASE:** Pursuing a mysterious craft up the Miami River, a Coast Guard picket boat opened fire with a machine gun. Some 200 bullets whined through the dark. They did not stop the runaway but they: 1) startled Mrs. Robert V. Latham, sitting up in bed aboard her husband's houseboat, one shot missing her by six inches; 2) "fanned" George D. Broughman, night watchman along the river; 3) penetrated the "parlors" of Undertaker John Gautier; 4) lodged in two houses on Miami's Flagler Street; 5) aroused hundreds of Miami sleepers; 6) stirred Miami's City Commission to consider a formal protest to Washington.

Fortunately for the Coast Guard, the pursued craft turned out to be a real rum-runner. Even so, the reckless rattle of bullets stirred afresh the anxiety of many a law-abiding yachtsman who had experienced the service's quick gunfire, its brusque raids, its salty backtalk. They cite many other cases.

JUNE 10 **ON THE SIDELINES:** One more state—Wisconsin—withdrew last week from the field of Prohibition enforcement, handed the drying-up job back to the U.S., joined New York, Maryland, Montana, Nevada on the Wet sidelines.

LINE OF DUTY: Henry Virkula lived in Big Falls, Minn., ran JUNE 24 a candy store. He had a wife, two children, a car. One day last fortnight he drove them all to the Canadian border, started back for home along the highway after dark. Mrs. Virkula was in the front seat with him, the children asleep in the back. He stopped to light a cigaret, then drove on along the lonely wooded road. Suddenly two figures leaped up before him. One held a sign: STOP! U.S. CUSTOMS OFFICERS. Virkula braked his car but had not stopped before a volley of shot tore through the rear windows. The car plunged into a ditch. Virkula was dead, a slug in his neck. U.S. Border Patrolman Emmet J. White, 24, came up to the car. Shrieked Mrs. Virkula: "You've killed him." Replied White: "I'm sorry, lady, but I done my duty." No liquor was found. The Virkula children woke up, began to cry.

Patrolman White had fired five rounds from a sawed-off shotgun into the Virkula car. His defense: the machine did not stop when Patrolman Emil Servine held up the stop sign. White was lodged in jail, charged with murder. The little town's citizenry seethed with indignation against White and "the system" he represented. Banding together they wrote a public protest to President Hoover which concluded: "In our utter helplessness, terror and distraction, we are at last resorting to you. For God's sake, help us!"

"FULL OF HOLES": The President answered the plea from Big JULY 1 Falls: "I deeply deplore the killing of any person. The Treasury is making every effort to prevent the misuse of firearms. I hope the communities along the border will do their best to help end the systematic war that is being carried on by international criminals against the laws of the United States."

This reply was too general to please the friends of Citizen Virkula, who was not regarded as "an international criminal." Editorial writers wrote: "It is not enough for the President to 'deplore'"; "the President's answer is as full of holes as Henry Virkula's car."

BUCK-PASSING: There are, by police count, some 32,000 speak- SEPT. 9 easies in New York City, all of them profitably patronized.

There is in the Penal Code of the State of New York a section (No. 1530) providing for the closure of a public nuisance. Also in New York are Grover Whalen, the Police Commissioner; Maurice Campbell, the local U.S. Prohibition Administrator; and a tidal sentiment against Prohibition.

Last week Administrator Campbell rolled up a batch of several hundred uninvestigated complaints against speakeasies, despatched them to Commissioner Whalen, told him, in effect, to get busy and dry up New York City. Commissioner Whalen exclaimed "Buck-passer!" Wrote Commissioner Whalen to Administrator Campbell: "If you are unwilling to discharge your sworn obligations or wish to make a confession of your inability to direct the activities of your department, the admission should be made to your superiors in Washington, instead of 'passing the buck' to State law-enforcement officers. Your plan would necessitate increasing the police by 5,000 men, costing the taxpayers of New York City a minimum of $15,000,000 per annum."

The national significance of this incident seemed to be that it was first concrete test—and failure—of the Hoover policy of Federal and local cooperation on Prohibition enforcement. If other cities follow New York's lead, the Hoover policy will resolve itself into a one-sided thing tantamount to urban non-enforcement.

SEPT. 23 **INTOXICANTS:** In Des Moines a jury retired, returned to the court room with the verdict that bay rum sold in three-ounce bottles at Woolworth's 5 & 10 Cent Stores was an intoxicating beverage within the meaning of the law.

In Detroit prohibition agents discovered an underwater cable along which liquor cargoes from Canada were towed on a sledge while Customs boats patroled overhead.

OCT. 14 **BOOTLEGGING:** The decision in Philadelphia by Judge Kirkpatrick that New York Broker Alfred Norris was guilty of aiding and abetting in the transportation of liquor by a bootlegger was over-ruled in the U.S. Circuit Court of Appeals and Broker Norris was exonerated. The Treasury Department declared it would carry the case to the Supreme Court.

NOV. 11 **"GREEN HAT":** Casually up the marble steps which lead to the Senate Office Building walked George Lyons Cassidy one day last week. Under his coat something was hidden. Police stopped him, found a pint of whiskey on him, other bottles in his car.

Quickly followed the identification of Cassidy as the "Man in the Green Hat"—a 'legger who long has specialized in trade around the Capitol. Three years ago he was going his rounds in the House Office Building when his liquor-laden brief case fell to the stone floor. Amid fumes of alcohol, he fled to the street. His only identification then was his bright green hat. When arrested last week he wore a hat of sober grey. Always ready to believe the best, Senator Wesley Livsey Jones of Washington, author of the Five & Ten Law, remarked: "There was nothing to *show* that he was delivering liquor to a Senator!"

MILESTONES

MARRIED: Richard Harold Saxon Tudor Bold, songster of Earl Carroll's *Vanities*, great-grandson of Ralph Waldo Emerson, descendant of English Kings (Harold the Saxon, Richard the Bold); and Rae Gardner, Colonial scioness, of Albany, N.Y.; in Greenwich, Conn.

ENGAGED: Helen Wills, 22, holder of U.S., English and French tennis championships, fair-to-middling painter; to Frederick Shander Moody, Jr., stock broker of San Francisco, fair-to-middling tennis player.

DIED: Lillie Langtry, 76, of Monte Carlo, onetime actress and "toast of two continents"; of influenza. In her 20s she neglected Husband Langtry for social acclaim climaxed by the openly effusive attentions of Albert Edward, Prince of Wales (later Edward VII). Langtry hats, shoes, gowns were standards of fashion. She once said: "I got on famously with Prince Edward until I put that piece of ice down his neck."

VANISHED: Chinook, 12, famed brown husky lead-dog, from the Byrd expedition headquarters at Bay of Whales, Antarctica. His team,

consisting of eight sons and grandsons, remained intact. Chinook apparently crept away to die alone.

MISCELLANY

In New York City, Frank ("Daredevil Jack") Latkowski did a jackknife dive from Brooklyn Bridge into the East River (138 ft.). He sprained his thumb.

In Santa Cruz, Calif., one Amandus J. Paulsen, paralysed in legs and hands, cut his throat, lay in a tub full of water, turned on the gas. He was found and taken to a hospital, awoke to find he had recovered from his paralysis.

In Waxahachie, Tex., a golfer drove a high ball that landed in a rising airplane, was carried 158,400 yd.

In Chapel Hill, N.C., one Harry Meacham, college student, played bridge, had bad luck. Annoyed, he laid a gun on the table, declared: "I'm going to shoot the next person who deals me a sorry hand." When his turn came he dealt himself a Yarborough (a bridge-hand with no face cards), picked up his pistol, killed himself.

FOREIGN NEWS

International

One of the most vexing problems facing Europe and the U.S. in 1929 was what to do about the reparations that Germany still owed the Allies as an aftermath of World War I. In 1924 a plan had been accepted whereby Germany was allowed to mortgage her railroads and industries in order to stabilize her economy and facilitate payment. This was known as the Dawes Plan after Charles G. Dawes, the financier and later Vice President of the U.S., who was chairman of the committee that prepared it. But the problem remained of determining the ultimate amount that Germany owed and the terms of payment. France, Britain and Italy insisted that they would not accept cuts in German reparations payments unless they could also reduce their own substantial war debts to the U.S. The U.S. refused to link the two items and in 1929 sent Industrialist Owen D. Young and Banker J. P. Morgan to Paris for another round of negotiations on the problem.

JAN. 14 **"GERMANY CAN PAY!"**: Since the whole fiscal structure of Europe is based today upon the Dawes Plan for German reparations, it is clear that the mightiest event which looms for 1929 is revision of the Dawes Plan by the new Reparations Committee of Experts. A report has already been prepared for the Committee on Germany's capacity to continue her huge Reparations payments. It bluntly declares: "No question can fairly rise as to the ability of the German budget to provide the full amount of its standard contributions under the Dawes Plan. Germany has been re-established as a going concern on a relatively high level of economic activity." That means, and jubilant Paris dailies whooped the news last week, that "GERMANY CAN PAY!"

Contrasting with French joy was the raging fury of the German press. As German anger mounted, imaginative correspondents cabled the suggestion that if Mr. Seymour Parker Gilbert, the American expert who wrote the report, had

Owen D. Young and Seymour Parker Gilbert, U.S. experts on reparations:
"Germany has been re-established as a going concern." Page 73.

remained in Berlin last week, he would have been mobbed.
He had left Germany before issuing his report, however,
and last week the *Berengaria* brought him safely to Manhattan.

CASH TALK: Last week a news leak from the secret Repara- MARCH 25
tions Committee sessions revealed that of all the Allied delegates only M. Emile Francqui, Belgium's picturesque, chol-
eric ex-Finance Minister, has roughly baited and tried out
cross-examination methods on Germany's correct and stiff-
necked "Iron Man," famed Dr. Horace Greeley Hjalmar
Schacht, Chief German Delegate and Governor of the Reichs-
bank. When Dr. Schacht proceeded to dwell again, last week,
on the palpable iniquity of expecting Germany to pay Reparations for 62 years, the five fingers of Croesus Francqui's
right hand were observed to tap impatiently on the Committee table. As the Governor paused for breath the Belgian
leaped up, fire in eyes.

"But why not 62 years, Dr. Schacht?" he challenged. "Don't
you know that Belgium has been paying such a debt for 99
years?"

"*Nein!*" snapped Berlin's Schacht. "What debt?"

"My country," cried Belgium's Francqui, "is still paying
£3,000 a year to the descendants of the English Duke of Wel-
lington. That is part of the price of our freedom after Waterloo.

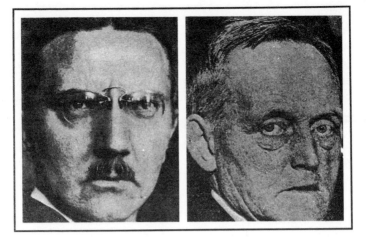

Dr. Schacht, Germany's "Iron Man," opposes 62 years of reparations.

Chancellor of the Exchequer Snowden: "I cannot compromise." Page 78.

The agreement was made in 1830. We have paid £297,000 ($1,443,420) in 99 years and we still pay, without grumbling!"

After dashing over to Berlin "so as to attend my daughter's wedding"—and also to confer long and earnestly with President Paul von Hindenburg and Chancellor Hermann Müller—Dr. Schacht returned to Paris to mention for the first time a definite annual Reparations sum which Germany *offers* to pay. Although shrouded in official secrecy this offer was soon known to be 1,500,000,000 gold marks per year ($356,850,000). Promptly the Allied delegates repeated their demand for $625,000,000; and Messrs. J. Pierpont Morgan and Owen D. Young, U.S. representatives on the committee, were understood to be suggesting $500,000,000.

Thus after a month of cautious trafficking in generalities, the Second Dawes Committee got down to coldest cash. Europeans grew increasingly fearful, last week, lest what they persisted in calling the "Morgan-Young Bank" should turn out to be a glittering U.S. strait jacket for Europe. The dread lest a controlling interest in the new Bank would be vested in Wall Street would not down.

APRIL 29 **CRISIS OF REPARATIONS:** Less than eleven weeks ago, Lord Revelstoke, the John Pierpont Morgan of the British Empire, joined with Morgan, Owen D. Young and other financiers of unsurpassed prestige in a supreme effort to place the reparations debt of Germany on a *business* not a *political* basis. No irony can be more keen than the fact that the death of Baron Revelstoke last week, with its consequent effect of quelling passions, alone preserved the fiscal conclave from immediate and ignominious adjournment. The crisis came when the 28-billion-dollar bill for reparations which the Allies presented last fortnight was countered by a German offer to pay 15 billions. Creditors and debtor were absolutely nowhere near each other. A distinct impression was received that the German offer was made in a deliberate attempt to break up the conference.

A breakdown of the negotiations came suddenly chiefly because of personal animosity stirred up by the "Iron Man," Dr. Schacht. In Prussia, heads come square and hard—so much the worse for Germany. At about 9 p.m. a correspondent reached Baron Revelstoke by telephone. His voice suggested weariness, resignation, resentment. [He had been warned not to sit on the committee by physicians who had for years been tending his weak heart.] "I can't understand Dr. Schacht," he said. "In fact he astonished me. . . . It was quite a shock." Soon after 11 p.m. England's mightiest Man of Property knocked out his pipe and began to undress. His valet switched off the light and left him. He died of heart failure in the early morning hours.

A DYING HOPE: J. P. Morgan returned to Paris and the Second MAY 6 Dawes Committee last week, having shaken off a cold by cruising the Adriatic in his black yacht *Corsair* with the Archbishop of Canterbury. There seemed little enough for the greatest financier to go back to. "If our committee is not already dead," croaked a Japanese delegate, "it is certainly dying with despatch."

YOUNG PLAN: The problem of how much Germany shall MAY 13 pay in reparations—incomparably the greatest fiscal issue of the age—seemed in a fair way to be solved last week by a one-time plowboy from Van Hornesville, N.Y., General Electric's Owen D. Young, chief negotiant for the U.S. in Paris. A fortnight ago all negotiations were abruptly broken off. The Allies were particularly incensed by the fact that Germany's "Iron Man"—Hjalmar Schacht—made a portion of his offer conditional upon the return to the Fatherland of certain territory and colonies which she gave up by ratifying the Treaty of Versailles.

During that black interlude Chairman Young, working far into every night, consulting frequently with the senior U.S. delegate, J. P. Morgan, drafted an entire new plan. Key points: 1) Germany to pay 18 billion dollars over 37 years; 2) The annual payments to average $487,600,000, and of this $165,900,000 to be paid *unconditionally*, with payment of the rest *conditioned* on German capacity to pay; 3) Bonds to be issued against the unconditional portion of Germany's pledge to pay; 4) The bonds to be sold to the world public through an international bank of settlement (already agreed upon); 5) Profits from this operation to be so huge that after the 37th year they would pay off in 21 more years the full total of the German debt.

ENTER, POLITICIANS: Britain's General Election was too near for Chancellor of the Exchequer Winston Churchill to keep silent longer. He arose from the Conservative bench in the House of Commons and said: "[The Young Plan] will in the opinion of the government be unacceptable." For home consumption the Churchill speech was most effective. By the Young Plan, Great Britain's percentage of the total of German reparations would be reduced from $20\frac{1}{2}$ percent to $19\frac{1}{2}$ percent, would cut 670 millions from Britain's total receipts. Mr. Churchill felt that even a one percent reduction was more than the country could stand. The electoral stock of Winston Churchill, previously depressed, rose perceptibly, and, as usual, the blame for everything was passed on to the U.S.

MAY 27 **U.S. "SACRIFICE":** President Hoover was quick to sense the necessity of assistance for the reparations conference. Therefore, last Sunday, he held an extraordinary conference at which a reduction of German payments to the U.S. was agreed upon. This would, if accepted, put the U.S. in a position where its representatives in Paris could argue that their government was ready to make a "sacrifice" to secure a new agreement. U.S. claims against Germany totaled, last September, 350 million dollars—207 millions for the cost of the U.S. Army of Occupation, 143 millions in mixed claims. It was learned that the "sacrifice offer" amounted to about a 10% reduction in Germany's *annual* payments to the U.S. Though *total* payments were not to be cut, the U.S. was ready to allow Germany a longer time to meet them.

LEAVING PARIS: There was a great folding of silk pajamas and JUNE 10 brushing of well cut suits in Paris last week. J. P. Morgan was leaving town. The nations which fought the World War had agreed at last how the staggering costs and damages were to be paid by the loser. By the Young Plan the total was fixed at $8,806,000,000 cash. On the instalment plan, over an agreed stretch of 58 years, this sum will become, with cumulative 5% interest, 27 billions. This sum, huge though it sounds, is 116 billions less than the creditor nations demanded at Versailles ten years ago.

SNOWDEN v. EUROPE: A thin-lipped little Yorkshireman with AUG. 19 the cold, drawn face of a stone gargoyle—that was Right Honorable Philip Snowden, Chancellor [since the Labor Party victory in June] of His Britannic Majesty's Exchequer. What he wanted was for twelve nations to reopen the question of how German reparations are to be divided among the creditor powers. In homely Yorkshire fashion he referred to the Young Plan as "a sponge cake" in need of being re-carved. For Britain a bigger piece of cake! Stumping about painfully on his two rubber-tipped canes, and cornered from the start, Chancellor Snowden said with a twisted smile: "If the Young Plan could be adopted by majority vote, I suppose it would be carried today, but fortunately adoption must be unanimous." Clutching the heads of his canes until his knuckles showed white, he hurled his ultimatum: "I have behind me the unanimous support of my government, the support of the House of Commons, irrespective of the party in power. I cannot compromise."

"All is consternation at The Hague!" headlined *La Liberte* in Paris. "Snowden is torpedoing everything—the conference, the Young Plan, the peace of Europe!"

THE HAGUE HAGGLE: Pale, flabby-fleshed, glisteningly bald AUG. 26 Dr. Gustav Stresemann played last week an astute, unobtrusive dickering game for Germany. The quarrel over whether Great Britain should get a larger share of the Reparations "sponge cake" was the German Foreign Minister's

big chance. Speaking with vigor and emotion Dr. Stresemann urged that the Allied troops be withdrawn from the
Rhineland by Christmas. *"Mais, mon ami!"* responded
M. Aristide Briand, French Foreign Minister, "I fear it
would be a great hardship to move our troops in the cold
winter months. Why not wait till Spring?" "Permit me to
suggest," replied Dr. Stresemann smilingly, "that your troops
could be spared the inhuman experience of a winter evacua-
tion by leaving now."

The French joined with Belgium, Italy and Japan in pre-
senting to Shylock Snowden a highly complex "final offer"
which they claimed met 80% of his demands for more
"sponge cake." He denounced it. "It is not the money in-
volved that counts with us," he rapped. "The prestige of
England is at stake." Furious delegates of France, Belgium and
Italy told correspondents that they would rather let the conference crack.

SEPT. 2   **A DUTCH PARTY:** The Conference did not get back on the high-
road of common sense until a jolly royal banquet had been
tendered to all concerned by sensible, buxom, motherly Queen
Wilhelmina of the Netherlands. The house was full of crisp,
sweet-scented Dutch flowers. There was drink to match the national taste of every guest: French champagne, German
hock, British whisky, Japanese sake, also long black cigars
from Dutch Sumatra. Somehow or other the party became a
marked success.

To avoid protocol problems the delegates were seated not
at one straight table but at ten round ones. Each statesman
might fancy that where he sat was the head. Not many hours
after the royal banquet, Mr. Snowden lunched informally
for the first time with his chief foe, French Foreign Minister
Briand and with Dr. Stresemann. As every U.S. businessman knows, the bigger the deal, the more vital is lunch.

As ultimately presented, the Latins' written offer gave
Great Britain an increase of $6,500,000 annually in her share
of reparations. Surprisingly enough the major part of this
concession was made by Italy, whose chief delegate has not
had a free hand but has been forced to keep in hourly telegraphic touch with Prime Minister Benito Mussolini, no
softie. But Patient-as-a-Job Snowden pondered the offer,
then rejected it. Worn to a frazzle, sleepless and mad clear

through, the French and Italian delegates were undoubtedly in a mood to let the conference crack up then and there. But a few more days for dickering were left.

SNOWDEN'S SLICE: From midnight on the Continental powers steadily though stubbornly yielded. Soon it was known that Mr. Snowden had accepted an offer satisfying 82% of his demands. SEPT. 9

"Without the help of my wife," he said later, after twitching himself painfully into his limousine, "I could never have achieved it." A deft nurse, an adoring confidante, a staunch political helpmate is Mrs. Philip Snowden. From the first she told correspondents that her husband would get his way. When they doubted she said simply, "I guess you just don't know how stubborn a Yorkshireman can be."

The fiscal side of the agreement means that Germans now know how much it cost them to lose the war. The political side pledges France, Britain and Belgium to withdraw the last of their troops from the occupied German Rhineland not later than June 30, 1930.

Great Britain

THE CROWN: After lying in the same bed and room since Nov. 21, 1928 [gravely ill with blood poisoning] His Majesty the King-Emperor was removed to an adjoining chamber, last week, enjoyed the change. The Roman Catholic Archbishop of Liverpool returned from Rome and was quoted as quoting four words which came from the Pope: "The King will live." JAN. 14

Lumps rose in many honest English throats when it was popularly rumored that during the crucial stage of His Majesty's illness Queen Mary broke down and wept hysterically, until soothed by the Duchess of York. Broth, whipped eggs and juices (fruit and beef) were mentioned last week as constituting the royal bill of fare, and the patient was said to have "lost considerably in weight." Last week Dr. Edward Charles Dodds, barely 29 and one of the king's eleven doctors, determined that the blood royal contained less than the normal .298 per cent calcium, drew his hypodermic, injected a minute mite more calcium into George V.

Queen Mary and King George V.
"The King will live."

Prince of Wales in the coal fields: "I
never thought things were so bad."

"The public is fully aware," said the London Feature Service, "that the King has by his bedside the finest physicians and specialists in the country, but a certain number of them are apparently dissatisfied. Every day sees new additions to the pile of bottles, and phials and philtres which are being stored away unopened in special rooms. One old lady arrived at Buckingham Palace with two ring doves in a wooden cage. 'These,' she told officials, 'must be placed in His Majesty's sleeping room for their breathing purifies the air.' The birds were retained and, so rumor has it, were released afterwards in the Palace gardens. If faith and loyalty could cure King George, he would rise from his bed today."

FEB. 11 **"THIS IS GHASTLY!":** Jauntily, impishly, Edward of Wales appeared in evening dress with a *red* carnation one night last week, thus setting London's impeccable chappies terribly agog. "How adorably *ghastly!*" thrilled smart Mayfair women. Meanwhile, Jester Wales, having had his joke, was speeding nocturnally toward the north of England, to visit in grim earnest the stricken coal fields where a half-million miners are workless and nigh to starving. On the outskirts of each village the royal motor halted. Resolutely the rubbers waded, and the bowler advanced toward drab little rows of tiny cottages. The village of Winlaton was the first major halt, for there Edward of Wales expected to find an old man who had challenged him—Frank McKay, a miner of 74. "I'll show you misery, Your Royal Highness," he had written. "I challenge you to come!"

"Where's Mr. McKay's cottage?" cried Challengee Wales. The white-faced, starveling villagers pointed. He climbed the muddy stoop, rapped on the sleasy door. "Come in!" cried a child's voice, and H.R.H. entered to find two weeping little girls beside the bed of a grey-haired woman who lay stark and motionless. "Dead!" croaked a villager, "Starved—an' Old Frank 'as gone for 'er coffin!"

Meanwhile a white-faced, scant-clad crowd had gathered —men who had had no steady work for three years past, men who eat meat never more than once a week, but Britishers, for they gave the well-fed young man in two overcoats a thin but loyal cheer. Cried a quavering old man: "Ay, ay, the dear lad's a champion."

Seemingly it was not until the second or third day of such royal slumming that Edward of Wales fully and deeply sensed the misery around him. He reacted by demanding to see the books and pay sheets of several employers, and appeared scandalized when one such sheet showed that a gang of four men, working five shifts, received at the end of the week only 29 shillings ($7.10).

"For each man, surely!" exclaimed H.R.H. incredulously.

"No, for all four."

Said the Prince, "What causes all this?"

"Management."

"Bad management?"

"No, just hard management."

As the third day wore on, as he slopped down street after street and peered into hovel after hovel, the Prince's face hardened. "This is ghastly!" he ejaculated frequently. "I never thought things were so bad. A ghastly mess!" With duty done, H.R.H. hopped a local train for his favorite hunting centre. After a sound night's sleep he sprang to horse, and galloped off with many another after a frightened little red fox. [The Prince of Wales later sold his string of hunting horses and renounced the royal sport of fox hunting, as a gesture of responsibility.]

WALES "GAGGED?": An indignant young man and a genial, FEB. 18 flabby-handed oldster conferred last week in the Prime

Minister's Room of the House of Commons. Edward of Wales told Stanley Baldwin about his recent tour of the North English coal fields, described scenes of bitter misery and awful squalor. Oldster Baldwin did nothing overt, but presently the press was informed that youngster Wales would not make his announced trip to South Wales, where the poverty and near famine of unemployed miners is even more notorious. Correspondents thought that the Prime Minister's large, flabby hand had stayed the Prince. Copies of the official report of H.R.H.'s tour by his private secretary were confidentially passed out to Cabinet Ministers during the week, but not published. It gave the Laborites a chance to cry: "Baldwin has gagged the Prince."

MARCH 4 **WISE WALES:** Trooping in, last week, to dine off the City's plate of gold, went not only H.R.H. but Prime Minister Stanley Baldwin and the Empire's choicest assortment of Industrial Tycoons. The guests were met—or thought they were—merely to toss off a few champagne toasts to the British Industries Fair, which would open next day. But no sooner had Edward of Wales risen and begun to speak, than the Tycoons realized with an unpleasant shock that they were in for one of the most thorough-going rebukes ever administered to rich old men by a young heir apparent.

"Even on such an occasion as this," said the Prince, "no good can come of patting ourselves on the back. We can congratulate ourselves on our successes only when we have seen and rectified our faults." The great lords of trade and peers of the realm are not accustomed to being told that they have faults. Several sat up palpably bristling as Edward of Wales laid down two premises which, if valid, lead straight to the conclusion that even Tycoons may be slothful, obtuse, incompetent.

Premise One was the unchallengeable statement by H.R.H. that 1,400,000 Britons are out of work. Premise Two consisted of the speaker's royal testimony that on his recent travels to every part of the Globe he has personally seen that British salesmanship and merchandising methods overseas are still far behind the standard set by competition. From Premises One and Two arose the inescapable conclusion that work could be found for Britain's unemployed if only Britain's employers would pep up their salesmen.

ROYALTY: Among the bulletins that were issued last week MARCH 18
from Craigwell House, Bognor, where the King-Emperor
rests after his illness, was one over the signatures of His
Majesty's Chief Physicians. Innocent-sounding enough, it
was secretly carried to London, and submitted to Prime Minister Stanley Baldwin and the Prince of Wales before being
published. "The King," said the bulletin, "is now able to
read and apply his mind *for short periods of time.* Complete
recovery is still some months distant."

Thus for the first time official cognizance was taken of the
King's mental state. He eats and sleeps well. He walks, leaning heavily on two nurses, from one room to another, and
sits by an open window for hours, watching the horses exercise on the sands. But he does not seem able to concentrate
on anything for more than a few minutes. All his most personal belongings have been taken to Craigwell House to help
him recover: his famed stamp albums, his collection of gram-
ophone records, most of them jazz tunes, his terrier, and
Charlotte, the parrot.

THE CROWN: Without counting "extras and incidentals," the APRIL 8
King-Emperor's illness will likely cost his people almost a
quarter of a million dollars. Sir Hugh Rigby who made an
incision between two Royal ribs and drained a poison pus
pocket, was slated last week to receive £5,000 ($24,300).
About £3,000 ($14,580) was spent to install the special anti-
fog machinery which purified the air in George V's bedroom,
and was considered indispensable in saving his life. To set
up a special pharmacy in the Palace cost £3,000 ($14,580),
and £9,500 ($46,170) more went for X-ray pictures. The four
royal nurses (English, Scotch, Irish and Welsh) were paid
weekly from five to eight pounds apiece ($24-$38) and will
receive from His Majesty personally "a substantial gift."

P'INCESS IS THREE: If Death should come soon and sudden- APRIL 29
ly to three men—George V, Edward of Wales, the Duke of
York—England would have another Virgin Queen Elizabeth.
Last week, romping in a yellow frock, the Princess Elizabeth
passed her third birthday. It is barely a fortnight ago that
she knocked with chubby fist upon a door, and when her
mother called "Who's there?" answered in an important little
voice, "Lilybet, the P'incess." "Lilybet's" mother, Her Royal

Princess Elizabeth, 3, is still three re-moves from being Queen.

Prime Minister MacDonald wants the U.S. ". . . to narrow the Atlantic."

Highness the Duchess of York, is herself only *two* removes from becoming "Queen Elizabeth"—which title is constantly and teasingly applied to her by Edward of Wales. She would be less than human if she did not sometimes wonder how much truth there is in the story that he once said he would renounce his rights upon the death of George V—which would make her nickname come true. With a Throne in the balance it must be a trifle nerve-wracking to be called "Queen Elizabeth" by a man who can make you that. [Both the Duchess of York and her daughter "Lilybet" did, in turn, become Queen Elizabeth as a result of Edward's abdication in 1936.]

OCT. 7 **VOYAGE EXPLORATORY:** It was the first visit in history of a British Prime Minister to the U.S. Everyone felt the moment keenly. The U.S. Ambassador, Charles Gates Dawes, arrived to make friendly suggestions. Also came (impossible in a less civilized country) the leader of the Opposition, Stanley Baldwin, the ousted [in June] Conservative chief saying "good-bye-good-luck" to the installed Labor Chief, Ramsay MacDonald. Ishbel MacDonald, roseate daughter and hostess of the Prime Minister, was discovered buying wearing apparel for the trip. Laborite feelings were reassured by news that she and her father intended to live from three suitcases apiece—he trusting to luck for golf clubs.

As his penultimate word to the *Daily Herald*, Labor's organ, Prime Minister MacDonald said: "I go on a voyage of exploration. The greatest contribution which this generation can make to history is to establish peace among nations and induce them to feel a sense of security by political agreements carried out by political means. The United States and ourselves, having the same objects, should proclaim them with a united voice." His final word as the boat-train pulled out of crowded Waterloo Station was: "I hope to be able to do something to narrow the Atlantic."

BLAZING TO PEACE: The home of Secretary of State Henry OCT. 21
Stimson was the last place where Prime Minister clasped hands with President. Two hours previously they had formally farewelled at the White House, but Mr. Hoover slipped over to his Secretary's stag dinner for Mr. Mac-Donald. Most of the stags were potent Congressmen and Senators of both parties. Sound meat for conversation was a joint declaration issued earlier in the day by Stags Hoover and MacDonald, momentously summing the results of their conversations:

"Both our governments resolve to accept the [Kellogg-Briand] Peace Pact as . . . a positive obligation. . . . The two governments not only declare that war between them is unthinkable, but that distrusts and suspicions arising from doubts and fears must now cease to influence national policy. The exchange of views on naval reduction has brought the two Nations so close to agreement that the obstacles in previous conferences seem now substantially removed." One result of the meeting was Britain's invitation to major naval powers to attend, in January 1930, a conference to discuss the limitations of all types of surface war vessels and the abolition of the submarine.

WORK FOR WALES: Eight hours, plus four hours overtime NOV. 4
every day last week was the stint of brawny fellows toiling with haste and mighty thwacking in the wing of St. James's Palace called "York House," famed bachelor quarters of Edward of Wales. Definitely His Royal Highness is preparing for indefinite bachelorhood. He has refused to move into huge, regal Marlborough House, especially renovated at large public expense for no other purpose than to accommo-

date a Prince & Princess of Wales. Last week at his own expense the occupant of York House started extensive alterations which would be silly if he intended soon to wed.

NOV. 18 **"COME ALONG, GANPA!":** "They say the King looks *younger!*"—breathlessly loyal Britons passed the word. Beloved George V was coming home at last to Buckingham Palace after his long convalescence at the rustic royal estate of Sandringham, and thousands stood huddled along London curbstones to see for themselves.

Almost before Their Majesties' salon pullman stopped, the door flew open. Out popped a deep-dimpled little girl in blue, her chubby legs cased in white gaiters. She gave a joyous hop-skip-and-jump along the platform. It was "Baby Betty," Her Royal Highness Princess Elizabeth, only granddaughter and unspoiled darling of George V. When His Majesty followed the babe it was seen at once that he did look younger. Firm of step and with a new vitality of movement, the King-Emperor escorted Queen Mary to the waiting royal Daimler. Already Baby Betty had plumped into the back seat. "Come along, Ganpa!" piped she.

NOV. 25 **NOTABLE KNITTERS:** Her Majesty the Queen officially opened the annual exhibition of Queen Mary's London Needlework Guild last week. She beamed with pride at the principal exhibit: three soft woolen scarves knit by the busy fingers of Edward of Wales, her eldest, and three other scarves knit by her youngest son, Prince George.

DEC. 30 **MEMORY OF A COUSIN:** Grigorie J. Sokolnikov, newly appointed Soviet Ambassador to Britain, arrived in London fortnight ago, bought a new dress suit in which to present his credentials to King George, and waited. Eight days passed. The delay was the fault of His Majesty the King-Emperor. Stubbornly, and to the huge embarrassment of his Labor Government, George V refused to shake the hand of any representative of Soviet Russia, for it was the Soviet Government which decreed the assassination in 1918 of a brown-bearded nervous little man known to the world as His Imperial Majesty Nicholas II, Tsar of All the Russias, known still to George V of Britain as "Dear Cousin

Nicky." Though Britain began full diplomatic relations with the Soviet in 1924, the necessity of shaking hands with the Tsar's murderers did not arise. At that time Russia had only a chargé d'affaires in London and mere chargés need not meet the Crown. Ambassadors are different, but all last week Cousin George V remained adamant. "I have not forgotten," said he.

Finally it was Edward of Wales who saved an embarrassing situation. He was still officially a member of the Regency Council appointed to deputize for King George, and for duty's sake he would shake hands with *anyone*. Relieved palace officials announced that His Majesty was "too ill" to receive the new Ambassador. Edward of Wales dressed himself in the scarlet and blue of the Welsh Guards, strewed medals on his chest, clapped a monumental fur busby on his head and walked round the corner to St. James's Palace.

H.R.H. may have taken comfort in the fact that it would be hard to find a less murderous Communist than Ambassador Sokolnikov. Indeed Soviet leaders are none too sure of Ambassador Sokolnikov's loyalty. So accompanying him to St. James's Palace was Dmitri Bogomoloff, Councilor of the Embassy, whose real job in London would be to follow every move of Ambassador Sokolnikov, to report directly to Stalin himself.

France

A GRAND VITALITY: Below stairs in the dignified stone man- MARCH 25 sion, where Marshal Ferdinand Foch, 77, lay dying, a group of Paris reporters completed their second month of fidgeting and fuming. The first month was the hardest. It climaxed in a duel between two star reporters, M. Georges Chapreau and M. le Marquis Henri de Sombrieul, who had rasped each other's nerves. However, since le Marquis fired into the ground and M. Chapreau into the air—as Frenchmen will—the shots served happily to steady the nerves of all concerned. Last week the corps of reporters five was informed by the corps of physicians nine that quite possibly they would have to wait another two months, although of course they might not.

Above stairs lay the Generalissimo—the man who won the War if any one man did—dying by inches. Pathos was not in the room but instead a grand vitality, a dauntless courage. They had called a priest, weeks ago, and the Generalissimo lived on. Sometimes he would call for his baton— the baton of a Marshal of France—and with the tips of his old fingers would caress along the shaft the hard and prickly stars.

Perfectly alert and mobile, the brain followed each move of the Mexican revolution as Mme. Foch read rapidly from the latest editions of *Le Temps*. And the Generalissimo continued, even last week, to eat with a precision which his doctors declared absolutely astounding in a patient thus far gone. He had long since lost all appetite, but he ordered his jaws to chew, his gullet to swallow, and so far as in him lay, his stomach to digest.

APRIL 1 **GLORY TO FOCH:** It is known in France how to honor even the greatest of heroes, not by many words, but with a few deeds less cheap. During the two days and nights that Marshal Ferdinand Foch lay in state, last week—beneath the Emperor Napoleon's tremendous Arch of Triumph—the government suppressed and darkened every electric sign which might have profaned the scene. As thousands and tens of thousands filed past the bier, all night long, the only light was that from funeral torches and the blue "Sacred Flame" which burns eternally for the Unknown Soldier.

Excepting only the Unknown Soldier, the last hero to lie beneath the *Arc de Triomphe* up to last week was Victor Hugo, 43 years ago.

Italy

FEB. 4 **BLACK FARINACCI:** With a solemn flourish and a little very black ink His Majesty Vittorio Emanuele III last week signed away the Constitutional rights of Italians to democratic government. This was the last act in a drama which began three years ago—a great drama for which Signor Mussolini supplied the livid theme: fascism has already stepped, and, if need be, will step once more, over the more or less putrid body of the goddess liberty!

King Vittorio Emanuele signs away democracy with a flourish.

Benito Mussolini—98 $^{28}/_{100}$ per cent of the voters endorse his rule.

The royal signature was first affixed to a decree dissolving the Chamber of Deputies of United Italy. The second decree established the new supreme organ of state, the Fascist Grand Council, by appointing 44 *Fascisti* to sit as "the first two categories" of the Council. Keenest interest focused on the First Category, since its 16 members will constitute a sort of extraordinary upper house. One name eclipsed the other 15 in significance—Roberto Farinacci. His rôle has been the most sinister in Fascist Italy. Originally swart, nervous, cynical Roberto Farinacci was famed as the Castor Oil Man of *Fascismo*. Politicians who rashly opposed *Il Duce* were ambushed and forced to swallow a pint, a quart, even a sickening gallon of what Farinacci called his "golden nectar of nausea." As Secretary General of the Party he wielded Ku-Klux powers of life and death. His emergence last week on the very pinnacle of power, at the right hand of *Il Duce*, seemed a black omen for Italy.

98 28/100% PURE: Leaning forward in a carved armchair at APRIL 8 the Palazzo Chigi, Signor Benito Mussolini sat with his hard chin cupped between contented palms, last week, watching newsreel flashes of Cardinals and Monsignors marching to the ballot box, attended by blaring brass bands and wildly cheering throngs.

Never before have Princes of the Church shepherded their

clergy and people to vote in a Parliamentary Election of the present Italian Kingdom. Always before the priesthood has abstained, urging their flocks to do likewise, in protest against the Government's suppression of the Pope's temporal power in 1870. Recently, however, *Il Duce* has restored a mite of earthly authority to *Il Papa* and last week purring cinema machines proved how mountainous is the Pontiff's gratitude to the Dictator. Especially vivid were the footages showing Cardinal La Fontaine, Patriarch of Venice; Cardinal Gamba, Archbishop of Turin; and Cardinal Maffi, Archbishop of Pisa, all of whom proceeded directly from the celebration of High Mass to vote at the head of their clergy.

Dopesters estimated that His Holiness' influence had flung into the scale of *Fascismo* at least 1,000,000 extra votes. Last week's election statistics prove that those Italians who went to the polls are $98\,^{28}/_{100}$ per cent pure endorsers of the *Duce*—a record eclipsed in the U.S. only by Ivory Soap.

MAY 13 **ALL BUT FIVE:** Shrill, fussy Minister of Public Works Giovanni Battista Giuriati was last week elected President of the new 100% Fascist Chamber of Deputies. Casting about for some one to fill the vacant Ministry of Public Works, the powers-that-are came upon Signor Benito Mussolini. Since he already held seven of the 13 Cabinet portfolios he might as well hold eight. Soon he did. Cabinet posts *not* held by *Il Duce* are: Justice, Finance, Public Instruction, Communications, National Economy. Since *Fascismo* has always vaunted itself the "Party of Youth" and the foe of paunchy middle age, watchful observers thought it remarkable that the new deputies, all hand-picked by *Il Duce,* are nearly all men of elder-middle age.

JUNE 3 **SKIRTS DOWN:** Acting in his capacity as Minister of the Interior, *Il Duce* notified all prefects of Italian provinces that "beauty contests, with their consequent naming of 'queens' and 'princesses,' lower the moral standard of communities and tend to dangerous exaltation of feminine vanity as well as constituting a parody on very serious matters." Therefore, let there be no more beauty contests.

Correspondents in Rome learned other more practical reasons for the new prohibition. After two years of competing in these strange, international competitions, it has been noticed that Italy invariably loses. Any competition in which Italy loses is not one to be encouraged by the Fascist State. "Foreigners might get the impression," explained a Blackshirt chieftain gravely, "that there are no pretty girls in Italy!"

Immediately following Prime Minister Mussolini's circular came an order from the Secretary General of the Fascist party, Signor Augusto Turati. Last month he had ordered all "young and even little" Italian girls to have their skirts at least *two fingers' lengths* below their knees. Last week he altered his order to apply to all females, regardless of age.

BIRTHDAY: "I order that there be no public observance of my birthday." So read a memorandum boldly scrawled by Benito Mussolini last week, shortly before he achieved age 46. Next morning, spruce and whistling, he stepped from his Roman residence, slipped behind the wheel of a low-slung Alpha Romeo roadster. Venturesome, a correspondent asked why there would be no public birthday observance, received for his pains a blasting, withering glance. AUG. 12

"Rest assured it is not because I dislike being a year older!" flashed *Il Duce* as he engaged the gears. "No—my reason is that nothing must interrupt the ordered rhythm of Fascist work. There are enough holidays on our Italian calendar already—in fact too many!" and letting in his clutch the Dictator vanished, inconsistently, for a birthday holiday.

In the 47th year of Signor Mussolini's age, in the seventh year of Dictator Mussolini's régime, how do his achievements stack up against his failures? Last week it seemed especially pertinent to examine both in ordered sequence:

¶ Trade Success. Prior to the War, imports to Italy exceeded her exports by 51%, and as late as the period 1921-25 the average "adverse balance" was still more discouraging, 57%. In 1927 the adverse balance of trade had been pared down to 33%. Credit for what has been accomplished rests with the Fascist régime exclusively.

¶ Water Power. Since Italy has no coal mines it is an impressive achievement that in recent years her constantly increasing demands for power have been met by installing half a billion dollars worth of hydro-electric machinery, not by importing more coal from abroad. Today Italy leads every other European country in the amount of energy she filches from "white coal"—water power.

¶ Employment Success. Starting with 500,000 unemployed, the Dictator has steadily cut down this figure—by no matter what methods—until today 250,000 Italians are idle. He is now pushing forward a huge, perhaps top-heavy, Land Reclamation Program, asserts that it will wipe out the unemployment bogey utterly.

¶ Wheat Failure. Despite Farmer Mussolini's energetic example in growing wheat by the most advanced methods on his own estate, it is a fact that Italy still buys abroad a third of her wheat, as she has done for decades. The "improved farming methods" constantly mooted by Fascismo have absolutely not increased the average yield per acre. As yet there is no victory in the "Battle of the Grain."

¶ Birth Failure. Taxes on bachelors, subsidies to prolific parents, even the inspiring gift of the Dictator's signed photograph to mothers of twins and over, have not produced the desired result. The birth rate in Italy continues to decline.

¶ Revalorization? Mussolini took a coin quoted at 3.27¢, jacked it up to 5.26¢ and stabilized it there on a gold basis. This coup dazzled the Italian populace, favorably impressed financiers abroad, and stiffened the country's fiscal backbone. But since then the road of readjustment has been hard. Prices have not fallen to anything like equibalance with falling wages. Paralyzing strikes have been avoided only by Fascismo's abrogation of the right to strike. It is still a question whether the Italian test tube will stand the strain of the experiment.

Papal State

JAN. 14 **CONCORDAT?:** At Rome the swashbuckling soldiers of Pope Pius IV were savagely attacked and soundly defeated by troops of King Vittorio Emanuele I. Momentous, this defeat was suffered in 1870. Ever since the Papacy has been without temporal power, the Pope has remained "The Prisoner of the Vatican."

Last week there were signs that the old feud between Church and State is soon to be composed. Today the numeral of Pope Pius is not IX but XI, and that of King Vittorio Emanuele is not I but III. The case has become plainly and simply one of "two other fellows," and last week a report was made that they are moving toward *rapprochement*. A confirmative despatch, succinct and unequivocal, declared: "A prelate generally known as the spokesman for Cardinal Gasparri (famed, beetling-browed Papal Secretary of State) frankly said today that basic points have been substantially agreed upon" between representatives of Dictator Benito Mussolini and Pope Pius XI. The points:

That the State cede to the Holy See a plot of territory west of the Vatican; that absolute sovereignty over this territory be vested in the Pope, inhabitants of this new Papal State being deemed subjects not of the King of Italy but of the Supreme Pontiff; that the Italian Treasury pay to the Papal Treasury 1,000,000 *lire* in reparation for the numerous seizures of Papal property in 1870; that the Papal State and the Italian State formally recognize one another and exchange ambassadors.

"CHRISTUS VINCIT!": The project for a compromise between JAN. 28 Church and State was said, last week, to await only the election of a new Italian Parliament in March. Especially significant, in view of all that the Papacy is about to gain, seemed the well-worn inscription on an obelisk erected by Sixtus V, which faces St. Peter's:

Christus Vincit (Christ is Conqueror!)
Christus Regnat (Christ is King!)
Christus Imperat (Christ is Emperor!)

"THE DAY OF GOD": The son of a sheep herder and the son FEB. 18 of a blacksmith entered the palace of a Roman emperor, last week, and there signed a concordat reconciling the State and the King of Italy with the Papal State and the Pope. The son of a sheep herder is Pietro Cardinal Gasparri, for 14 years Papal Secretary of State. The son of a blacksmith is Prime Minister Benito Mussolini, a personage well able to return with interest the lightning of Cardinal Gasparri's paralyzing glance. Unquestionably these two sons of peasants are the greatest Italian statesmen of their century. They met face to face, last week, in the Lateran Palace, an austere and gloomy pile, presented to the papacy 16 centuries ago by the Roman Emperor Constantine the Great. It contains the *Santum Sanctorum* Chapel, reached by a flight of steps which no Catholic, not even the Pope, may ascend otherwise than on his or her knees.

Fortunately, there are other staircases in the Lateran. Cardinal Gasparri, Signor Mussolini and their suites entered militarily erect, sat across a massive table, 16 feet long and 4 feet wide, the top hewn from a single log of deep red *narra* wood from the Philippines. The door was locked and Papal Attorney Pacelli [brother of Eugenio Pacelli, later Pope Pius XII] read solemnly the text of the agreement. The Vatican supplied a gold pen with which the document was signed in deathly secrecy. Not until after the signatures had actually been affixed did the Vatican's news organ, *Osservatore Romano*, print the only authorized announcement, an editorial entitled "The Day of God":

"The Holy See declares definitely and irrevocably that it recognizes the Italian Government under the rule of the House of Savoy . . . and that Italy recognizes the state of the City of the Vatican under the sovereignty of the Holy Fathers."

FEB. 25 **"IL PAPA! IL PAPA!":** Sixty thousand Italians fired with religious zeal knelt in the Basilica of St. Peter's last week and 100,000 bared and bowed their heads under a driving rain outside. Signor Benito Mussolini was not present, but his daughter Edda was on her knees in a part of the Basilica usually reserved for princes of the blood. For the first time since 1870 several cabinet ministers had officially entered St. Peter's. And now a papist host had met for joyful and pious celebration. "*Il Papa! Il Papa!*," shouted the throng.

He came, entering St. Peter's from the Vatican for the first time since his coronation (exactly seven years ago). He was borne aloft on the *Sedia Gestatoria* by attendants in flame-colored livery. He was fanned by other minions majestically agitating great clusters of ostrich plumes. His garment was white of a creamy richness, but his robe was all blood-red. On his breast blazed a great cross of diamonds. And above the shapely, bespectacled head of Pope Pius XI towered the holy apostolic tiara of pure, massy gold.

He came as the lord spiritual, and for the first time since 1870 as the lord temporal. Commenting afterward upon the new treaty, His Holiness exclaimed in vibrant tones of pious emotion: "It gives God back to Italy, and Italy to God!"

Denmark

ICED IN: Denmark's elongated King, Christian X, dislikes MARCH 18 hitches. Things can never run too smoothly to suit the precise mind of the six-foot-five-inch ruler, and yet recently a number of annoying little accidents have happened to His Majesty. A fat Frenchman fell over his feet in the theatre at Cannes. He paid a State Visit to Madrid, only to have the Queen-Mother of Spain die suddenly. So it has gone. Last week King Christian returned to Denmark from the Riviera, determined that if possible, *this* voyage would be uneventful.

The train rolled smoothly across France to Paris, from Paris to Berlin, Berlin to the Baltic and slid on the ferry that was to carry the train across an arm of the sea to Denmark. Six hours more, and they would be in Copenhagen. Practically nothing more could happen, unless the royal car should slip off the ferry into the sea. This very nearly had occurred on a previous occasion, and worried trainmen roped and chained the train securely to the track. The ferry left the pier, King Christian sighed with relief, inserted himself in the royal berth, went to sleep.

Three hours passed, when the King awoke and realized that he was not in motion. "What seems to be the trouble?" cried His Majesty, thrusting himself for some distance out of the window.

"A little accident, *Majestaet*," quavered an unfortunate railway official. "We are iced in!"

It was true. So heavy were the ice jams in the Baltic that train and ferry were caught fast in the midst of the frozen sea. King Christian and his consort and their son were forced to spend the night marooned on a motionless ferryboat until released by icebreakers in the morning.

"OUGHT TO PLAY BOULE!": In the *baccarat* room of the APRIL 8 Cannes Casino—smartest on the French Riviera—elegant males and svelte women leaned breathlessly over the tables, betting thousands of dollars as card after card came out of the "shoe." Through the rococo gilt doors of the gaming room stalked King Christian X of Denmark, six and a half feet of majesty in faultless evening clothes. Leaning on his arm was the blonde pride of Broadway, the world's most expensive playmate, Peggy Hopkins Joyce, ablaze with diamonds.

King Christian approached a bearded cashier, who sat in complete indifference behind square lavender piles of thousand franc notes. "Please change this," said His Majesty disengaging his right arm from the left of Miss Joyce, and laying down a five-franc note—worth at the current rate just under 20¢.

"People who want change for five francs," purred the cashier, nastily, "ought to be playing *boule* at Ostend" (a deadly insult, except in August, when some very nice people go to Ostend, and give their children francs with which to play *boule*, an infantile sort of roulette).

"My good person," said the shocked Miss Joyce. "This is for the King of Denmark—Le Roi Christian Danemark!"

Magically five small brass coins appeared and amid profusest, most voluble French apologies, His Majesty strolled away, to do whatever one does with Peggy Hopkins Joyce and 20¢.

Russia

JAN. 14 **ANTI-RELIGION:** A major feature of last week's new anti-religious campaign was a series of articles by the most famed and heeded woman in Soviet Russia, a woman known simply as *Krupskaya*. She, a widow, would be called in other lands, "Mrs. Lenin." Last week Relict Krupskaya wrote: "The need is imperative that the State resume systematic anti-religious work among children. We must make our school boys and girls not merely non-religious but actively and passionately anti-religious. . . . The home influence of religious parents must be vigorously combated. Skill and persuasion must be used. I do not approve of the over-zealous methods of some school teachers who make a practice of tearing off every crucifix which they espy on a child's neck. Such methods are not efficacious. We must be more subtle."

FEB. 11 **BACK TO THE WORLD:** From remote, barbaric Alma-Ata, on the distant rim of Russian Turkestan, Leon Trotsky returned, last week, toward the civilized world. With him traveled his wife and son, glad to end a bitter exile. But in European Communist centres it was feared that Trotsky's release from banishment was a trick, and prophets croaked that he would be "accidentally" killed *en route*. The trickster, if any, was Soviet Dictator Josef Stalin, who banished Trotsky a year ago for the crime of organizing a political opposition. Stalin brooks *no* opposition. Last week he muzzled correspondents in Moscow with a censorship so drastic that the only thing really known about Trotsky was that he had left Alma-Ata.

EXILE TROTSKY: "Trotsky is hooked up with Capitalism and MARCH 11 writing from Constantinople for the New York *Times!*"

This bizarre half-truth was shrieked in Manhattan, last week, from the platform of a hall into which had jammed 5,000 men, women and children, all members or hangers-on of the Workers' [Communist] Party. This group of U.S. Reds looks for leadership to silent, ruthless Josef Stalin; and consequently hates and fears famed Leon Trotsky, despite the fact that Trotsky was one of the first and greatest leaders of the Soviet Revolution, the friend of Lenin and the creator of the Soviet Army. Of all the leaders of Communism, Leon Trotsky is the one least "hooked up with Capitalism." But last week Comrade Trotsky *did* write exclusively for the *Times* the story of his exile from Russia and the history of how, according to Trotsky, Stalin seized illegally the powers of Lenin, the late mighty founder of the Soviet state.

Leon Trotsky (real name Lev Davidovich Bronstein) declared that agents of Dictator Stalin appeared suddenly at Trotsky's place of exile, Alma-Ata, on the borders of Russian Turkestan, and informed him that he, his son and Mme. Trotsky must pack up their possessions and prepare to leave Russia. Soon all were bundled into a motor bus, and since the snow was all but impassable a tractor was attached to pull the bus. Presently bus, tractor and Trotskys sank into a snowdrift. Seven hours were spent in extricating the exiles and conveying them by sledge to the nearest railway station, Pechweke Peke.

A special train had been provided, and so potent is the name of TROTSKY still, in Russia, that at his mere request another special train chuffed down from Moscow to meet the first, bearing two of his relatives for a family reunion. All along Comrade Trotsky had told the dictator's agents that he "refused" to leave Russia at Stalin's "illegal" order, and seemingly the agents were so perturbed by this that they stopped the special train for 12 days amid open fields to query Moscow for further orders.

Every day the engine would chuff to a neighboring village and return with food, mostly canned. While the empty tin cans were piling up on either side of the track, Trotsky amused himself by re-reading several works by Anatole France, famed and precious French scoffer. When, in obedience to fresh orders from Moscow, the Trotskys were booted into Turkey, Comrade Trotsky sent the following note to Turkish President Mustafa Kemal Pasha: "I was brought here against my will."

In describing how Stalin was able to seize supreme power, Trotsky declares that, during Lenin's last and protracted illnesses, the present dictator organized a veritable camarilla of self-seekers who conspired secretly against Trotsky (Lenin's logical successor) and took advantage of the fact that Trotsky himself was often ill to foment against him an opposition so strong that when Lenin died Oppositionist Stalin was able gradually to oust Trotskyists from their posts and finally to seize the government.

Suggesting that he might have been able to stop Stalin had he tried hard enough, Trotsky admits that he did not try his hardest. "I don't regret it," he concludes with a peculiar fatalism. "Some victories lead to an impasse and some defeats open up new avenues."

JULY 1 **CALICO IN FIVE YEARS:** Soviet reports of drought and dry winds following a late spring sowing have again come out of the Volga grain belt. The peasants are said to be worrying not only for their grain but for their potatoes. During the War and the subsequent Revolution, when all else failed there were still potatoes to dull hunger. Under the present rationing system, [installed not so much to conserve bread as to force the population to conform to the Soviet policy of control and socialization], inhabitants of Russia's larger cities are allowed but one pound of bread per person per day. The decision was made last week to retain bread ration cards for at least another year. The Soviet Government and "Boss" Stalin have committed themselves to transforming the Soviet Union into an industrial giant, nourished during the next four years by a 24-billion-dollar investment in factory equipment. Therefore Soviet stores have little goods on their shelves. Calico is as expensive as silk.

In retaliation the peasant farmer is growing less grain than he can because 1) he cannot buy anything with the money he gets from his grain, and 2) the Government is levying heavy grain taxes upon him by forcing him to sell most of his crop at a low fixed price. The fact that there is more grain planted this year is not due to peasant efforts but to State farms and cooperatives inaugurated to combat the negative attitude of the peasant.

Of late, also, the Russian peasant, ingenious in his discontent, has discovered yet another way of annoying the Government. Of 9,000 peasant houses destroyed by fire in one province (Samara) last year, 3,000 were due to arson. Fire insurance paid out totaled four million rubles ($2,000,000). The peasant explains with a wink: "The cottage soon grows sick and draughty. Then comes a fire—is it an accident? The peasant gets a fine new home from the Government." A cogent scratch of the nose and then a conclusion: "They take taxes and fix a low price for grain, but little Uncle Fire is free from their control." Even here the peasant is being trammeled, for recently the Government has clamped the death penalty, rare in Soviet Russia, on arson crimes.

Despite famine fears and fire, Stalin and the Kremlin pursue their plan. Last year they inspired such confidence that International General Electric Co. contracted to the extent of 25 million dollars to electrify the Soviet Union. More recently contracts have been let to other U.S. corporations for a 100-million-dollar hydro-electric plant in the Ukraine (to be the world's largest), and also for steel mills, coal mines, apartment houses in Moscow, tractor factories at Stalingrad, etc. After 1933, Industrializer Stalin promises, if necessary, to turn to lesser tasks—such as keeping the population supplied with food and clothing.

FIRST OF FIVE: Last week Dictator Stalin published figures SEPT. 9 which, if honest, showed astounding progress made during the first year of his Five Year Plan. Russian industrial production and factory wages have been increased, he declared, almost exactly according to schedule. Only by failing to achieve notably reduced prices for manufactured goods of sustained quality did Soviet Russia fall behind her schedule.

Proud of his success thus far, Dictator Stalin announced that he would add another billion dollars to Russia's budget for 1930, thus raising the total expenditure to five billion dollars per annum (13% more than is spent by the U.S. Government). Most startling of all, Russian industrial production is to be raised 35%.

Wrote famed Walter Duranty, doughty dean of U.S. correspondents in Moscow, last week, commenting on Dictator Stalin's titanic project:

"Every economist knows what it means to increase an annual industrial production of a great country by even 10%. To try to increase it by one-third sounds like madness. But Josef Stalin does not think so. He knows that Russia is a land of unlimited possibilities, almost unscratched resources and largely unused manpower. Moreover M. Stalin has behind him young Russia, that never knew Tsarist slavery and is free from the faults and vices of servile psychology. He and they have a faith which one greater than Danton said could move mountains."

To help shove some of the mountains which must be moved if Russia is to increase her industrial production by one-third, the Union Council of People's Commissars debated last week a decree which would abolish Sunday, institute a seven-day working week in all factories and other institutions. Said Moscow's daily *Pravda*; "All-week work will be a mighty factor in the country's cultural revolution and will deal a smashing blow to religion."

NOV. 18 **STALIN'S LOVE SONG:** "Is Stalin really dying?" "No, but I've heard his liver's going bad." "I've heard it was his lungs." "Some say it's his heart." "Anyhow he's back from that sanitarium."

Thus all Russia has gossiped for a month or more. Stalin's signed articles in Soviet news organs had ceased to appear. Comrades were fearful. Suddenly one night last week, the enigmatic Dictator, who dresses like a common workman, holds no office in the government and rules in all-potent obscurity as Secretary General of the Communist Party, rent the clouds of fear and rumor by a dramatic appearance.

It was the eve of Revolution Day—twelfth anniversary of the proletarian conquest. In the once Imperial Theatre the Soviet of Moscow had met to jubilate. On the platform

Widow Lenin: "Boys and girls must be anti-religious." Page 97.

Dictator Stalin. The people ask: "Is he really dying?" Page 101.

stood a nervous peasant, Comrade Michael Kalinin, the puppet President of Russia. He started uneasily when someone shouted, "Is Stalin sick or well?" He looked as though he would like to run when the whole hall began to clamor, "Tell us! Sick or well? We demand to know!"

Pounding for silence, and securing instantly a dead hush, the President said: "I hope there will soon be a favorable answer to these questions." Then, amid discontented grumbling, he proceeded with a stodgy though important speech, announcing that Soviet grain collectors have succeeded in forcing the peasants to sell at the Government's price some eleven million tons of grain. This is 10% more than last year, will amply suffice to feed the Red Army and the proletarian population of Russia's cities throughout the winter. "Let us rejoice and sing!" cried the Peasant-President, motioning to the orchestra leader. "Once more the good Russian Land has given us plenty of bread!"

Stirred as Russians easily are by music, the docile audience sang revolutionary songs with gusto for a half-hour, broke off in confusion when suddenly the Committee on the stage began to clap. Sharp-eyed, they had seen a swarthy man of medium build enter the once Imperial Box and sink into a back seat where he sat stroking his long, dark moustache.

"STALIN!" shouted someone and Comrade jostled Comrade as the audience roared frenzied cheers, then burst spontaneously into the Red anthem, *The Internationale.* Delirious minutes passed before STALIN would step to the front of the box. Smiling but silent, he took the cheers. He looked thin but well.

Still refusing to speak, the Dictator returned to his seat, affably shook hands with President Kalinin who had rushed to pay respects. Meanwhile a troop of "Revolutionary Entertainers" had skipped cavorting onto the stage. Only one number seemed to please Stalin, who is an Asiatic from the Republic of Georgia, adjoining Armenia. When a singer named Zagorskaya sang a Georgian love song, The Man of Steel applauded vigorously, unbent, began to chat animatedly with Kalinin.

Next day all Soviet news organs signalized Stalin's reemergence by printing over his signature a slashing three-column article entitled *The Year of Mighty Change!* Exultant over what he considers the successful launching of his famed Five-Year Economic Program, Comrade Stalin wrote: "With giant strides we move toward Lenin's aims—industrialization, electrification and mechanization. We are attacking capitalism all along the line and defeating it."

Rumania

JAN. 7 **SPEECH FROM THE THRONE:** With splendrous pomp and a majesty almost Byzantine, the common peasants who have recently arisen to dominate the Rumanian Government convoked a newly elected Parliament last week, and proceeded briskly to the business of the Realm. Splendrous was the singing of a grand *Te Deum* in the National Cathedral at Bucharest, with the bearded Patriarch Miron Cristea presiding in his twinkling medieval mitre. Lustily sang the new peasant Deputies and Senators, clad in immaculate white homespun blouses and white legging trousers. For them the *Te Deum* was a stately song of triumph. Good honest fellows—some could not forbear to skip a bit for joy as the procession moved from Cathedral to Parliament.

There it was quickly seen how complete had been the triumph of Peasant Prime Minister Juliu Maniu at the elections last week. Of the 376 seats in the Chamber of Deputies

361 are now held by Maniu peasants, whereas last year the now ousted Dictator Vintila Bratianu had 318. Today the fallen House of Bratianu, which had dominated Rumania since the creation of the Kingdom (1881) controls but 14 Chamber seats. Similarly in the new Senate, Prime Minister Maniu holds an overwhelming majority of 168 over the 36 followers of Dictator-Reject Bratianu.

Last week, tall, aristocratic, big-boned M. Bratianu sat as a mere Deputy, disconsolate, while a broad, confident peasant grin spread under the small, black moustache of M. Maniu. Just prior to the opening of Parliament, the black moustache brushed ever so lightly and reverently the hand of Her Majesty the Dowager Queen Marie. Though she had no part in the ceremony, her motherly and grandmotherly heart could not be otherwise than aglow. The Throne was occupied by her seven-year-old grandson Mihai (Michael) and the Speech from the Throne was now about to be read by her son, Prince Nicholas, thus opening the first freely-elected Parliament in the history of the Kingdom.

On the whole Prince Nicholas acquitted himself well. He spoke in his official capacity as one of the three Regents of Rumania, the other two being Patriarch Miron Cristea and Chief Justice G. Buzdugan, both aged gaffers. Reading in a loud, penetrating voice His Royal Highness declared Peasant Prime Minister Juliu Maniu's policy: to convert Ru-

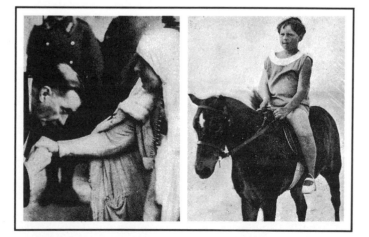

Rumania's Premier Maniu greets Marie, the Dowager Queen Mother.

King Mihai. On his eighth birthday he wants a tugboat. Page 106.

mania into a democracy, retaining constitutional monarchy; to decentralize the Government, granting more authority to provinces and municipalities; to accord to Rumania's minorities—hitherto exploited and oppressed—a just and lawful share in government; to reform the notoriously corrupt and unscrupulous Police and Secret Service; to reverse the Bratianu policy of shutting out foreign capital.

While these promises will take at least a decade to perform, they are the most hopeful words officially spoken in Rumania since the War. They show, moreover, that the whole nation is solid in support of Boy King Mihai—or as Queen Marie calls him "Our Tender and Lovely Hope."

JULY 22 **FANTASTIC COLONEL:** Early last week the streets of Bucharest were still as a Puritan Sabbath. Shop fronts were steel-shuttered. As the day advanced, groups of soldiers in steel helmets and khaki appeared on the street corners, leaning against lamp posts, smoking cigarets when their officers were not looking.

Correspondents soon learned the basic facts: the popular peasant government of Prime Minister Maniu had successfully suppressed an attempted coup d'état.

It was easy to guess the responsible group. For months the Bratianus and the remains of their "Liberal" party have chafed, muttered, plotted, as one by one the holders of Bratianu sinecures were dismissed, Bratianu pensions were cancelled.

No one in the Maniu government dared blame the Bratianu "Liberals" openly. Elected scapegoat was a little-known artillery colonel. "A certain August Stojka, a former Colonel of fantastic personality, has been attempting for two months to create a Fascist organization."

A disquieting feature of the plot had been the discovery in Bucharest of papers signed, "In the name of His Majesty, King Carol." Peasant-Prime Minister Maniu feared that exiled, slack-chinned Carol, for all his promises, had been misbehaving again. He was reported last week at Bled, Jugoslavia, only 250 miles from the Rumanian border.

NOV. 4 **KING GLEAMLET:** To a bright young boy, one of the great advantages of being brought up in the Greek Orthodox Church is that you have two birthdays—your own real birthday and your name day, the day in the Church calendar assigned to your patron saint. Last week cannons booming at dawn woke Bucharest to help celebrate little King Mihai's *real* birthday, his eighth. In the ornate National Cathedral, His Majesty, proud of his first long trousers, marched up the aisle with green-&-gold Generals to hear a *Te Deum,* marched down again to review two squadrons of the royal bodyguard.

"Where are the presents?" he demanded as soon as he was back in the palace. "Where is my tug-boat?" Most successful of last year's presents was a minutely perfect scale model of a locomotive and train which cost $1,100, the gift of the Rasitza Locomotive Works. This year King Mihai has been asking for an equally elaborate tug boat, complete with miniature barges. But there was no such gift last week. No barge company had felt the urge. Tactfully His Majesty's mother, frugal Princess Helen, explained that he would receive presents from the Royal Family not on his real birthday but on his name day, the custom in Rumania. However, there was a nice gentleman waiting in the antechamber with quite a lot of presents.

Baldish, sharp-nosed and Polish was the nice gentleman, Foreign Minister August Zaleski. He was in Bucharest, last week, to keep warm negotiations toward a Rumanian-Polish treaty of friendship and arbitration. From Dictator-Marshal Pilsudski of Poland he brought to King Mihai some brightly painted wooden toys; a railway train (considerably inferior to last year's); a big book of Polish fairy tales, *The Story of the Dwarfs and the Little Orphans*, translated into English— the language Mihai most easily reads, usually speaks.

According to a Court functionary, His Majesty ignored everything but the fairy tales, pounced on the big book, buried his nose. Soon, perhaps, Boy-King Mihai was reading the story of Dwarf-King Gleamlet, getting ideas about Kingship from the tale of how Royal Gleamlet dealt with Whisk, the field rat who had stolen his grain:

"What have you to say?" asks King Gleamlet.

"Nothing . . . but hunger . . . terrible hunger," replies Whisk. "My children were dying of hunger."

"But hunger does not give us the right to take what does not belong to us. You surely know that?"

"I feared the Winter, gracious King . . . The Winter so terribly long and hard."

Tender-hearted, King Mihai doubtless approved the end of the story, when King Gleamlet breaks down, sobs aloud in Polish pity and orders: "Release that unhappy creature and feed his family."

Palestine

SEPT. 9 **ISLAM v. ISRAEL:** The fighting that began between Jews and Arabs at Jerusalem's Wailing Wall spread last week throughout Palestine, then inflamed fierce tribesmen of the Moslem countries which face the Holy Land. Sacked and burned by fleet-riding Arabs was the ancient town of Safed, for centuries a seat of mystical Jewish learning. The Moslem version of the affray could not be learned, but Jews told of fleeing headlong through the streets, dodging into houses, making what resistance they could while the Arabs battered down doors, put bullets indiscriminately among the Jews and ended by igniting the town. Reports from Safed stressed such accusations as "pillage," "butchery," "rape."

Sporadic clashes continuing at Haifa, Hebron and in Jerusalem itself, rolled up an estimated total of 196 dead for all Palestine. A known total of 305 wounded lay in hospitals. Speeding from England in a battleship, the British High Commissioner to Palestine, handsome, brusque Sir John Chancellor, landed at Haifa, hurried to Jerusalem and sought to calm the general alarm by announcing that His Majesty's Government were rushing more troops by sea from Malta and by land from Egypt, would soon control the situation.

Moslems outnumber Jews 13 to 1. That is, there are more than 209 million Mohammedans on earth and slightly less than 16 million Children of Israel. In Palestine there are 591,000 Moslems and only 150,000 Jews, of whom some 2,000 are from the U.S. Last week Jews all over the world rallied to aid their outnumbered brethren in the Holy Land. Most potent of Jewish demonstrations last week was a meeting of 25,000 (including many a Gentile) who jammed Manhattan's Madison Square Garden and roared approval of a tactful telegram read on behalf of President Herbert Hoover (". . . My profound sympathy . . . good citizens deplore . . . Our Government is deeply concerned . . .").

Slouching forward to keynote from the platform came

High Commissioner Chancellor rushes troops to Palestine. Page 107.

Senator William Borah: "The Arabs are virile and resourceful."

famed Friend-of-Oppressed-Peoples William Edgar Borah, Chairman of the U.S. Senate's Foreign Relations Committee. Said he: The establishment of a national home for the Jewish people in Palestine is a task calling not only for the highest of statesmanship, but calling also for eternal vigilance and vast sacrifices.

"The Arabs are a virile people, resourceful in character, indefatigable in purpose and imbued with a national spirit which, at times, partakes of fanaticism. To deal with such a situation, there must be an understanding, there must be some definite arrangement, some definite program."

Without dreaming of saying so, Senator Borah seemed to imply that Zionists may have proceeded too rapidly in colonizing Palestine without first achieving a sufficiently "definite arrangement" with the British for adequate protection.

Moslems mass-met and demonstrated violently against Jews last week in Syria, Transjordania, Irak and Arabia. They shouted "Palestine for the Arabs!," jabbered of Holy War and of the booty to be got by plundering expeditions into Palestine. Syria is a protectorate of France, but her civilized soldiers have never been able to quell the wild, rebellious Sultan El Atrash, who lives in a mud palace high in the remote mountains and sallies forth on sporadic raids at the head of his hard-riding, fanatical Druse tribesmen. Last week the dread Atrash was reputed to be rampaging toward Palestine with 800 of his own horsemen and 2,000 Bedouins who recently joined his plundering banner.

Utterly different from bold Sultan El Atrash is the mild spoken little Amir Abdullah of Transjordania, a contented British puppet whose chief delight is in breeding priceless Arab steeds. Last week the Amir dutifully hastened across the River Jordan, successfully dissuaded some 300 of his subjects who had set out minded to wage plunder in Palestine.

London editors thought last week that Arabia was the only really likely kindling place for a Holy War. There tall, sagacious, tortoise-spectacled Ibn Saud is Sultan, and King of the Hejaz to boot. He alone has sufficient prestige to galvanize and weld Moslem tribesmen of the Near East into mass enthusiasm for an Islamic pogrom.

SEPT. 16   **VENGEANCE INTO MURDER:** When an ugly fact bobbed up to bother Queen Victoria she knew how to tuck the thing away comfortably out of mind. There are still Britons with that talent. Last week His Majesty's government decided to tuck away the fact of racial conflict between Jews and Arabs in Palestine. The thing was attempted by Prime Minister James Ramsay MacDonald in the course of his speech outlining policy. Said he:

"There was no racial conflict in what happened in Palestine the other day. This is no conflict between Moslem and Jew; this is simply an uprising of lawlessness and disorder, whatever its motive may be. So far as we are concerned it is not a question of Moslem or Jew, Christian or non-Christian. It isn't a question like that at all."

Intellectually such words are nonsense. Emotionally, they may prove to be the acme of British commonsense. The situation in Palestine had become quiet last week, with 5,000 British troops policing the land, disarming both Jews and Arabs, recovering loot seized in the riots, massacres and town-burnings of last fortnight.

Lurid were the tales told by U.S. citizens who escaped the massacre at Hebron where eight U.S. Jews were killed by Arabs. Typical was the account given by David E. Winchester of Chicago, who reached Palestine only eleven weeks ago for post-graduate work at the Talmudic school in Hebron. "When the trouble started a friendly Arab hid me in the building where he was living," said Student Winchester. "When a marauding party entered, he said there were no Jews there. But they searched the building and found me. An Arab with a knife advanced toward me as the door was flung open. I prayed for mercy. We struggled and I grabbed the knife and wrested it from the Arab. Only the Almighty could have given me the strength. Another Arab, however, felled me with a long piece of iron. I did not lose consciousness and could feel the cold blades of knives cut into my flesh as I lay there stunned and defenseless. They left me for dead."

Jewish campaigners for the Palestine emergency relief fund staged rallies throughout the U.S., last week, whooped up Arab atrocity stories, collected cash which reached a total of $607,718. Among non-Jewish orators who warmed up such gatherings, Manhattan's obliging Roman Catholic Mayor James ("Jimmy") Walker was well nigh without a peer. Clapping on a Hebrew skullcap he cried to 2,000 Jews in Brooklyn: "Lead on! Whether to Palestine or elsewhere, we will follow and see that never again shall the hand of the persecutor be laid on you in any other land!"

SHEIKS & STRIKES: In Jerusalem last week the British Crown OCT. 28 tried to prosecute an Arab, potent Sheik Taleb Maraka, for instigating the "Hebron Massacre" of Jews. August upon the Bench in beehive wigs and flowing gowns sat Mr. Justice Corrie and Mr. Justice Defreitas. This was going to be an exemplary trial. The Arab prisoner would be grilled by an Arab prosecutor. There were plenty of prosecution witnesses, already lamenting and smiting their breasts in the corridor. With a smile of contempt for the witnesses Prisoner Sheik Taleb Maraka entered, was escorted to the dock by an armed policeman.

Sixty-six Jews were butchered at Hebron. The Arab prosecutor did not seem to want to probe into that. Even so the witnesses managed to testify that they had seen the Sheik publicly inciting Arabs to massacre, shouting that the faithful could settle any debts they might owe to Jews by slaughtering their creditors.

[The Justices finally became incensed with the Arab prosecutor and ordered another Arab to take over.]

"Tell me, Sheik Taleb Maraka," began the second Arab prosecutor, "are you an enemy of the Jews?"

"As a matter of fact," smiled the prisoner blandly, "I am their friend."

"Did you incite the massacre of any Jews?"

"Never!" shouted the Sheik, smacking his fist on the dock. "Never in all my life have I led or addressed a crowd. I did not even learn of what happened until I read the police reports."

Exploded Mr. Justice Defreitas: "I refuse to believe that you, as a member of the Arab Executive Committee, did not know what was going on!"

"*I* refuse to believe," coolly observed the Sheik, "that the respectable Moslems of Hebron are capable of committing atrocities."

Since the Crown seemed unable to get an Arab to prosecute and dared not incense Moslems by calling in a Jew, the trial dragged on in farcical doldrums. Meanwhile the most potent Moslem in Palestine, the young and vigorous Grand Mufti Haj Amin El-Husseini, President of the Supreme Moslem Council, ordered a general strike of Arabs, in protest against the British Government's determination to bring to justice the suspected authors of the Palestine massacres.

Among the first and most enthusiastic strikers were Arab schoolboys at Nablus, several of whom were nabbed by Assistant Director of Education Farrel and soundly spanked. Screaming they rushed home to tell their parents. Within an hour the previously ineffective "General Strike" halted every Arab activity in the community. An ugly situation loomed. [British troops quickly suppressed the rioting, though the political controversy involving Zionists, Arabs, and the British continued.]

India

JAN. 7 **MAHATMA, PANDIT & KHAN:** The myriad eyes of teeming, docile Indians turned in mild approval and amazement, last week, upon Mother India's three greatest and most potent sons: Mahatma Gandhi, the Aga Khan, Pandit Motilal Nehru.

The famed, ascetic Mahatma is the Saint of India's Hindus; and the Pandit [father of the future Prime Minister of India, Jawaharlal Nehru] is now their sword. The great Aga

Khan is neither Saint nor Sword, but a very rich, fat and astute descendant of Prophet Mohammed, and therefore the most influential of Indian Mohammedans. Last week the Aga Khan traveled from his sumptuous home in Bombay to Delhi and there prepared to sit as chairman of the all-India Mohammedan Congress. Meanwhile at Calcutta the predominantly Hindu so-called Indian National Congress met under the chairmanship of Pandit Nehru and under the aegis of sainted Mahatma Gandhi. These two gatherings—neither of them Parliamentary or authoritative —speak for Mother India, insofar as she is articulate. The pity is that too often her Moslems and Hindus speak at absolute cross purposes. Last week, however, each assemblage met with fervent protestations that at last Hindu-Moslem unity against the British *Raj* was about to be attained.

Pandit Motilal Nehru, the sword of India's Hindus.

Moslem Aga Khan, neither saint nor sword, but influential.

Anxious talk buzzed all up and down the English clubs and offices in Calcutta. It was surely no good sign when the 6,000 delegates to the Hindu Congress and their more than 11,000 sympathizers proceeded to burn huge piles of Made-in-England goods before sitting to business.

Mahatma Gandhi, squatting as usual on his little dais, naked except for a loincloth, proposed in unusually keen-cut terms that the Congress deliver to the British Government an ultimatum in the following sense: Either grant to India full and free Dominion status before Dec. 31, 1929; or from that day forward the Congress will declare a non-violent but absolute boycott on British goods, British officials, British schools and British taxes.

JAN. 14 **WATER, WORDS & GOLD:** Whenever a bath is taken by His Highness the Aga Khan, the bathwater is carefully preserved, bottled and shipped to Mohammedan communities throughout the world. Thus the faithful are provided with a priceless boon, Holy Water in which a descendant of Prophet Mohammed has laved himself. No niggard, the Aga Khan charges for the really enormous quantity of water in which he bathes each year, only his weight in gold. The ceremony of weighing His Highness takes place each twelvemonth at Aga Hall, Bombay. No fool, the Aga Khan keeps fat. Also he is at pleasure to stand in with the British Government which pays him privily a fat subsidy for his good offices among the Mohammedan subjects of George V.

Last week at Delhi, it was His Highness who presided as Chairman of the All Indian Mohammedan Conference. On the agenda was a momentous question. Should the assembled Mohammedans endorse the demand that India be given "Dominion Status" within a year, which was voiced last fortnight in Calcutta by the Indian National Congress of Hindus.

When the matter had been thoroughly thrashed out, the Aga Khan deftly guided the Mohammedan conference into adopting a resolution which absolutely ignored the Hindu demand upon Great Britain for "Dominion Status," voicing instead merely the desire that Mohammedans should be accorded greater representation in the present native Assembly of the Government of India. Since it is the virile Mohammedans and not the lackadaisical, jabbering Hindus who might be expected to strike a blow for "Dominion Status," the service of His Highness the Aga Khan to Britain, last week, was worth incalculably more than even the fat Khan's great weight in gold.

FEB. 25 **MENACE OF INDEPENDENCE:** Highly agitated was His Britannic Majesty's lean and dramatically tall Viceroy of India, Baron Irwin, when representatives of India's "farm bloc" met recently in Calcutta and adopted a resolution demanding a new Constitution. Interpreting this as a veiled intimation that what the "farm bloc" really demands is Indian independence, Lord Irwin rushed to Calcutta and delivered what was, for an Englishman, a remarkably passionate pronouncement: "Loyalty to the British Crown is the only thing that forms a bond between Hindu and Moslem, Brahmin and non-Brahmin, British India and Indian States. Destroy that and you have erected an enduring and inseparable barrier to a free Indian nationhood!"

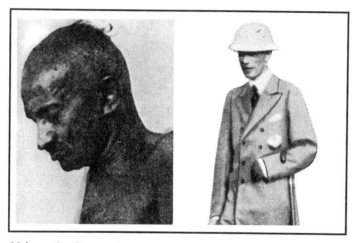

Mahatma Gandhi weaves his own rags, burns good British cloth.

Baron Irwin, India's Viceroy: "Loyalty to the Crown is the only thing."

Having spoken, the tall cadaverous Viceroy stepped into his sumptuous private car and sped back to New Delhi. There Lord Irwin busied himself in arranging a counter demonstration against Independence. Naturally it was to the Maharajas, the princes of India, many of whom are supported on their petty thrones by British might, that the Viceroy turned. Presently no less than 40 of these resplendent potentates addressed, to the Chamber of Princes in New Delhi, most powerful pronouncements against "the menace of independence." Each little Raja or big Maharaja read his speech from a typewritten copy, and the perfect unanimity of the proceeding was an impressive tribute to what is called "the genius of Great Britain for governing Backward Peoples."

APRIL 8   **SAINT FINED:** When a Most Holy Mahatma or Hindu Saint is caught red-handed staging a bonfire of British cloth for propaganda purposes, how stiffly should the Saint be fined? Emaciated, bandy-legged Mahatma Gandhi is Most Holy. He lives on cold water and Indian leeks. Skinny, always nine-tenths naked, and to occidentals often ridiculous in appearance, he yet evokes from myriads of Hindus the purest devotion, the blindest obedience. Just now Gandhi is crusading afresh for a boycott of British goods. He has ultimatumed that by 1930 India must be as free as Canada, and time is getting short.

Therefore, bonfires! Rip and burn the British cloth! Scream that no Hindu needs more clothes than a breech clout! Let each patriot weave his own rags, as the Mahatma does! Boycott the British! Freedom for India!

Last week in Calcutta, where Saint Gandhi had sat in jail 22 days charged with holding one of his bonfires, he was finally brought to trial. As the "Biggest Little Man in India" stepped sprily into Court, everyone rose, even the Crown Prosecutor, in deference to the Prisoner-Saint. "I did not desire to break your law!" piped the high-pitched, treble voice of the Mahatma. "The cloth was ours to burn. Always I advocate non-violence."

On the second day of the trial, Saint Gandhi was allowed to remain away from court. Absent, he was fined one rupee (36¢) which his lawyer refused to pay. As always happens when the Mahatma is fined—and invariably refuses to pay —an unidentified "friend" stepped briskly up and laid down the requisite rupee.

China

FEB. 11   **NATIONALIST NOTES:** Ever since the Nationalist Armies drove from China proper that rapacious, blood-thirsty War Lord Chang Tsung-chang, many an occidental has asked "What's become of Chang?" As the notorious Dictator of Shantung province Chang squeezed the wretched people by outrageous taxes, precipitated the present famine by seizing produce when they could not pay, and unquestionably took for harem any women or children who kindled his desire. Last week he was found to be living at Dairen, Manchuria, under Japanese protection, with a "household" of 35 women and allegedly with $10,000,000 salted in foreign securities.

BAD NEWS: The conquest of all China by Marshal (now MARCH 4 President) Chiang Kai-shek was completed almost a year ago, but last week a piece of bad news made it seem that Mr. Chiang must lay down his presidential fountain pen, gird on his old sword and Mauser pistol, and sally forth from Nanking to conquer all over again two great provinces, Shantung and Hunan.

Each became last week the theatre of a miniature civil war. Troops loyal to President Chiang battled with disaffected soldiery left over from the old regimes of the detested war lords who held sway over China like robber barons before the Nationalist conquest. To picture the situation in terms of U.S. geography, imagine President Chiang in New Orleans (Nanking) hearing that civil war has broken out on the North Atlantic seaboard (Shantung) and also far inland on a tributary of the Mississippi (Hunan).

The bad news was that detested and notorious Chang Tsung-chang, onetime rapacious war lord of Shantung, was back in his old province and battling for possession of it with 26,000 ragged, nondescript troops. Chinese devoutly hoped they had seen the last of Chang and his fat, well-chewed cigars when the Nationalist armies chased him into Manchuria. Last week Chang chartered a tramp steamer and boarded her at Dairen, with 250 hired soldiers of fortune including the "White Russian" General Ataman Seminov. Without the slightest hindrance from the Japanese authorities, the tramp steamer wallowed out into the Gulf of Chili and steamed the short 100 miles to the port of Teng-chowfu in Shantung. There Chang landed amidst a rabble army of soldiers who had served him as war lord. All night long they labored, unloading from the tramp steamer rifles, machine guns, light artillery.

CHIANG MARCHES: Chefoo—where hair nets come from—was APRIL 8 the scene of lively doings last week. In marched dread Marshal Chang Tsung-chang. Within an hour Chefoo's terrified Chamber of Commerce had presented him with $100,000 spot cash gold, in return for his promise not to issue his favorite order, "Loot!" The man is a double-dyed dastard, and his return at the head of a band of military adventurers bode untold evil to the wretched, famine-stricken people of Shantung. Cowed by the scowling marshal, who particularly likes to spit tobacco juice in people's faces, they could only groan, "How do the wicked flourish!"

One evening it was creditably reported that the General Staff had mutinied in Nanking and deposed President Chiang Kai-shek; but the very next morning China's bantam-weight President—who as Marshal Chiang conquered all China—marched forth against the rebels. He left behind him in jail the governor of Canton, General Li, who had earlier been reported executed, and denounced Li as "a traitor to the sacred cause of Nationalism!" Seemingly Li was in league with the rebels, a clique of military leaders with their base of operations up-river on the Yangtze-kiang in what are called the Wuhan cities. As Marshal Chiang and his army bore down upon the rebel areas, the Cantonese colleagues of General Li made a neat right-about, in the famed manner of Chinese generals, loudly proclaiming allegiance to President Chiang.

War Lord Chang Tsung-chang spits in people's faces.

President Chiang Kai-shek takes the field against traitors.

SCUM!: Often called "the foremost Chinese thinker of today" is Hu Shih, for nine years Professor of Philosophy at Peking University, later Dean of the English Department and the first Chinese to write poetry in the spoken vernacular. From the forthright pen of Professor Hu leaped, last week, a scorching indictment of China 1929: "We must confess that our political life is corrupt to the core. . . . We must see with open eyes that we are ruled by militarists who arose from banditry and from the scum of society, and whose education and training never qualified them to rule. Dr. Sun Yat-sen's philosophy aims at instructing the people to obey leaders who have intelligence to guide them. But this philosophy will fail in a situation where the blind are leading the blind and know not where they are going. . . . For all this we have ourselves to blame!"

REBELS ABSCOND: Like a house of cards, like a set-up of APRIL 15 nine-pins, the revolution in Central China collapsed suddenly and utterly last week. Miles of trenches and barbed wire entanglements, which the rebels had constructed to defend Hankow, were simply abandoned, as a half-dozen rebel "Generals" absconded from their commands and fled for their lives across the sluggish Yangtze-kiang.

There was absolutely no resistance at Hankow when spruce Marshal Chiang Kai-shek stepped ashore from a Nationalist gunboat. The moral victory which rendered battle needless should be credited almost entirely to Chiang, victorious marshal and astute President. A fortnight ago he was advancing with 150,000 Nationalist troops against a rebel army of 100,000 strongly entrenched. Quite possibly huge bribes turned the trick, as they often do in China, for it is known that the Treasury was abruptly tapped by the President for $5,000,000 cash.

DESPAIR IN DAIREN: The hugest, most lavishly gorgeous MAY 6 mansion in Dairen—near Port Arthur on the Yellow Sea—contains 35 pleasingly proportioned young women of assorted races. Last week they peered out over the Yellow Sea, tried to see a low, rakish ship. Aboard would be, they hoped, the "Sweetest Sugar Daddy in the World," as Marshal Chang Tsung-chang is called by one of his English-speaking women, Miss Anabelle ("Trixie") Cronan.

Two years ago, after wringing more than ten million dollars from Shantung's hapless people, Chang tried to settle down with his 35 females at Dairen. It was no use—too much of a good thing—and the grizzled Marshal sailed off conquistadoring. He captured Chefoo and laid siege to Ninghaichow. Suddenly, last week, at blackest midnight, the wily Nationalist General Liu Chen-nien made an unexpected sortie, fell upon and routed Chang's army. He fled. The Imperial Japanese Government, hitherto friendly to Sugar Daddy Chang, announced that he would not be allowed to re-enter Dairen. When this news reached the hugeous mansion, "Trixie" Cronan succumbed to hysterics. Chang's 34 other women had all the blinds of the house drawn, waited.

JUNE 3 **TEAKWOOD FUNERAL COACH:** The body of sainted Dr. Sun Yat-sen, preacher of democracy, left last week Peiping's Temple of the Azure Cloud, where it has been for the past four years. Six hundred miles away on a hillside overlooking Nanking, a monumental mausoleum was ready to receive it. Bearing it thither for the second funeral of China's first president was an elaborate railway funeral coach, built of hand carved teakwood, fitted with solid silver doors, its floors muffled with a blue silk run of double thickness.

Most important of all, there was in final readiness the last bit of pavement on the *Chung Shan Chi Nien*—great straight memorial road, eight miles long, 140 feet wide, leading from Nanking to the new mausoleum. Therefore, China's most exalted morticians and highway contractors rested last week from their labors. Everything was in readiness.

To build this impressive approach, eight contractors were allotted mile sections each. They ruthlessly tore down peasants' houses, appropriated land. Intent on honoring simple democratic Dr. Sun, they paid little attention to each other. When the eight single miles of road were finished they failed to connect, some sections by as much as ten feet. Despite the fact that 108 peasants had committed suicide when their homes were confiscated, the eight contractors tore down more houses to straighten the roadway.

JULY 22 **C.E.R. SEIZED:** With a suddenness that jolted the world from its hopes for peace in war-torn China, pygmy President Chiang Kai-shek seized Manchuria's 250-million-dollar Chinese Eastern Railway, 1,179 miles long, which belies its name by belonging to Soviet Russia. The 174 Soviet railway officials and employees were sent scuttling north into Siberia, minus their belongings. In Peking Foreign Minister C. T. Wang announced the end of all diplomatic relations between China and Soviet Russia. He eased off the threat of war thus: "We are not inimical to Russia. Positively we are not unfriendly. But we will not tolerate Soviet propaganda." While troops were reported massing on both sides of the Sino-Russo boundary, the Soviet Government signified it would do its utmost to prevent their clashing.

Foreign Minister Wang: "We will not tolerate Soviet propaganda."

T. V. Soong. He is sick of raising money for bootless wars. Page 122.

IMPOSING PEACE: Severally and collectively, the U.S., Brit- AUG.5 ain, France and Japan all admonished China with especial sternness and advised Nanking that the Chinese seizure of the Russian-staffed Chinese Eastern Railway in Manchuria was indefensible. In the eyes of the Great Powers the Soviet Government has a vested right in the C.E.R. under the Sino-Russian Treaty of 1924. If the treaty rights of any nation—even Bolshevik Russia—are not sacred in China, then the treaty prerogatives of other nations are clearly menaced. The Powers in order to uphold their own rights (such as Japan's hold on the South Manchurian Railway) were obliged last week to uphold Moscow's rights.

The most drastic action taken by Moscow against Nanking, last week, was to put an absolute embargo on China tea —of which $7,500,000 worth was stewed in Soviet samovars last year. The few U.S. correspondents "on the spot" at Harbin and Mukden heard that Soviet planes were dropping occasional bombs along the Siberian-Manchurian frontier, and also that six armored Russian trains were drawn up athwart the frontier city of Manchuli. When Chinese riflemen sniped at the Russian planes, a few pieces of Soviet field artillery were unlimbered and warning shots whined across the border.

But presently the Chinese Foreign Office announced that the Nationalist Government did not actually "seize" the C.E.R. but merely "took it under temporary control" and that the Nationalist Government reaffirms that "all foreign interests in China for legitimate purposes will continue to be respected." Moscow despatches soon told that Russia's enigmatic Josef Stalin, most secretive of dictators, was believed ready to keep the peace, but demanded that all Soviet citizens detained in China be instantly released. Atrocity stories reaching Moscow told of 40 Red Comrades chained and beaten by Chinese and White Russians at Pogranichnaya, Manchuria.

AUG. 12 **UGLY CUSTOMER:** Shooting the Emperor of China's cousin is not the dangerous feat that once it was. For one thing the "rightful" Boy Emperor is a deposed nobody. The shooting occurred last week at Beppu, a Japanese summer resort. There Prince Hsien Kai, the emperor's handsome, 21-year-old cousin, was strolling in the garden when he felt the stab of a bullet in his back. The shot came from a window of the hotel's grand suite, occupied by its most prosperous and ugly customer—the rapacious former war lord Chang Tsung-chang—who had moved in some time ago with his harem.

The shot caused Prince Hsien Kai to sink groaning into a bed of Japanese chrysanthemums. Eventually, several wiry little Japanese policemen went up to tackle Ugly Customer Chang. He appeared affable, passed around his famous fat cigars. The accident was regrettable, he said, but easily explained. He had been "handling" a new pistol to get its hang and feel. He had not noticed anybody in the garden. Somehow or other the pistol had gone off.

Prince Hsien Kai expired quietly after coughing up much blood. It was then explained by Chang Tsung-chang that not he but his secretary had been handling the pistol. The secretary swore that this was true. A dozen of Chang's concubines confirmed the fine new story. Policemen scratched their heads. Finally, officials indicted Chang for murder, suspecting him of having suspected the Prince of fiddling about in his harem.

SOONG'S SONG: A brilliant young Chinese banker of barely AUG. 19
38 swiveled round from his desk in Shanghai last week, read in flawless English a crisp, resolute announcement. He was sick and tired, he said, of raising the scores of millions of dollars which Nationalist China has been squandering annually on bootless wars. He, T. V. Soong, scion of the great "Soong Dynasty" of Shanghai bankers, would no more be a party to China's orgy of military waste and announced his resignation as Finance Minister of the Nationalist Government.

In 1922 the Nationalists, who have since conquered all China, were an insignificant group of zealots dominating only the region of Canton. On an income from local taxes of only one million dollars per month they could not finance a China-conquering expedition.

Two years later young T. V. Soong, who had learned sound banking and business principles at Harvard, was called to the Finance Ministry. Without increasing taxes Banker Soong magically increased the tax yield to ten million dollars per month. He has said that he did it by cutting down graft, by rigid Harvard budgeting.

For five years Finance Minister T. V. Soong has found the money for the bigger-and-better conquests of his brother-in-law Marshal (now President) Chiang Kai-shek. Last week President Chiang was so distressed that he dropped all official business, rushed to Shanghai and day after day argued and pleaded with Soong.

The banker's principal grievance had to do with the conqueror's reluctance to cut down Nanking's stupendous military forces. Today Nationalist China has the largest standing army in the world, though by no means the most effective. A rabble nearly 1,500,000 strong are ill-drilled, often ragged. Some of their commanders are hired bandit chieftains, others are feudal War Lords left over from previous régimes. The whole motley gang have costly appetites.

Optimists professed to believe that the Soong resignation was a potent bluff. Object: to scare President Chiang Kai-shek and the more recalcitrant militarists into adopting a sound Harvard budget.

NOV. 11 **"GEOGRAPHICAL REASONS":** In a long awaited proclamation the Nationalist Government clarioned last week: "The nation's hopes accompany President Chiang Kai-shek as he goes northward to do battle!" Chiang has put off his going from day to day for over a month. So chaotic is the state of civil war throughout China—with disaffected "generals" constantly forming new combinations for and against the government—that the president has often not known from whence to expect attack.

Last week, however, the presidential gunboat sailed with definite purpose up the broad Yangtze to the great inland city of Hankow. Far into the night he studied maps, despatches, tried to gauge the strategy and numbers of the so-called "People's Army" which for several months has been advancing slowly southward from the region of Peiping (once Peking). Next day the president set off by armored train for the battle area. Subsequent despatches reported quaintly that "the Nationalist forces are holding their own but are not advancing at present for geographical reasons." Startling was a Japanese despatch from Hankow reporting a great "People's Army" victory in Honan Province, and streams of wounded Nationalists pouring into the city of Tengchow "the majority suffering from sword and bayonet wounds, indicating that the People's Army were engaging in hand to hand combat to conserve ammunition."

DEC. 9 **"NOT ONE SQUARE INCH!":** Soviet troops had advanced more than 200 miles into China's great Northern Province of Manchuria on two fronts. Then, obeying orders from Moscow, the long grey Soviet armored trains which plunged their fangs into Manchuria last fortnight withdrew last week to their own frontiers. In Moscow the Prime Minister of the Soviet Union, Comrade Alexis Rykov, strode across the Red Square in his old leather overcoat and shiny workman's cap to tell correspondents: "Gentlemen, conquest is not our purpose. We will not keep one single square inch of Chinese territory."

In the areas the Russians had raked and ravaged Chinese fright and confusion grew from panic to anarchy. Soldiers deserted their colors, looted indiscriminately. A good many Chinese fingers had been cut off by Chinese soldiers impatient to snatch rings from old refugees.

The Russian raids were saying: "We mean business. China must yield to our demands respecting the Chinese Eastern Railway. Our rights date back to Tsarist times. We are ready to strike again." Moscow's smart move of withdrawing her armored trains stilled nearly all talk of intervention at Washington, London, Paris. But Japan has huge commercial interests in Manchuria and wants above everything to prevent the great powers from intervening in her bailiwick.

400 MILLION HUMILIATIONS: Four hundred million Chinamen DEC. 16 seemed to be wrong last week, or at least totally incapable of setting right the affairs of their country. On the north they suffered a supreme humiliation. Governor General Chang Hsueh-Liang of Manchuria capitulated to the Russians. Cowed by the Red Army's raid three weeks ago, Chang humbly agreed that the Chinese Eastern Railway shall again be placed under the management of Soviet citizens. In return the Soviet Government agreed to cease propagandizing in Manchuria. No Chinaman believed that this promise will be more than technically kept. It is not the Soviet Government but the Third International—consisting of almost exactly the same group of men—which spreads Communist doctrines abroad.

At Peiping ("Northern Peace") a total of 39 generals signed a telegram to field commanders, last week, denouncing as incompetent their commander-in-chief, President Chiang Kai-shek. In Nanking, the new capital, martial law was in effect. Several mutinous army divisions were menacing the city. China was another name for Anarchy.

REPRIEVE FOR CHIANG: Attacked on three fronts, the National- DEC. 23 ist Government of slender President Chiang Kai-shek teetered perilously on catastrophe's brink last week, then swung back to safety. Chief stabilizer was a high and bloody victory over the rebellious "Ironsides" divisions of General Chang Fa-K'uei in his attempt to capture Canton. Despatches announced the complete destruction of an entire "Ironsides" brigade, 2,000 rebel casualties, 7,000 rebels captured and disarmed, and the flight northward of Chang Fa-K'uei himself. Swollen bodies floating like logwood down to Canton bore mute corroboration. Last week's victory left President Chiang as firmly established as he had been at any time in the past year. Rebel generals, severely practical, talked of suspending hostilities until March and warmer weather.

DEC. 30 **HAPPY DAYS:** Wasp-waisted little President Chiang Kai-shek made a proclamation last week which resembled nothing so much as a long shrill "Whew!" Whewed he: "The recent upheaval against our Government was the greatest yet experienced. Our fate hung by a single hair. What was this hair? The loyalty and bravery of our officers and men, whose courage never faltered! Again they met the flood and carried us to firm ground."

Mexico

FEB. 18 **"IN LUCK":** One hundred thousand persons at the lowest count turned out last week, in Mexico City, to follow the hearse of a young man whose sole distinction is that he assassinated Mexico's President-Elect General Alvaro Obregon July 17, 1928. The assassin, José de Leon Toral, had been executed by a firing squad earlier in the week. The officer in charge, with a pistol which once belonged to General Obregon, had stepped up to the prostrate, bullet-riddled body of Toral, pressed the pistol to the temple and delivered the classic Mexican *coup de grace*.

As the hearse slowly proceeded along a three-mile route to the cemetery, thousands of blossoms were showered upon it, and the crowds roared: "Long live Toral! Long live Christ the King!" Within 24 hours after the execution, a dynamite bomb was exploded under the locomotive of the special train of Mexico's provisional president, Señor Emilio Portes Gil. The engine was derailed, one fireman was killed, and two coaches left the track. President Portes Gil descended unhurt from his salon car, walked forward to the locomotive, shrugged his broad shoulders and remarked: "The revolution star is in luck!" (The ruling party in Mexico is called "Revolutionary Party.")

MARCH 18 **AGAIN, MEXITL:** To the great and furious war god, Mexitl, after whom their land is named, Mexicans again paid costly homage last week—by flying at each other's throats. Eighteen thousand warriors—the greatest single army in recent Mexican history—were rumbling out of Mexico City in freight cars, led by ex-President General Plutarco Elias Calles, to do battle with the rebels in Durango, Chihuahua and Sonora. As bombing planes roared into the zenith, as President Herbert Clark Hoover hastened the despatch of 10,000 Enfield rifles and multitudinous rounds of ammunition to the Mexican government, as despatches announced that poison gas would be used, God Mexitl must have ruefully reflected that his own symbolic arms are a shield made of reeds tufted with eagle's down and a handful of spears, each with an eagle's tuft.

There is, of course, an important religious element in the present Mexican situation. The government consists of the anti-Catholic, broadly Socialist and efficiently militant forces of President Emilio Portes Gil and General Plutarco Elias Calles—a burly, bull-necked fighter who would certainly have the sympathy of Mexitl. Arrayed against the government are the avowedly pro-Catholic, Conservative and less efficiently militant forces of Presidential Candidate Gilberto Valenzuela. The great social and religious forces now interacting were first generated in the 16th Century when Spain overthrew the pagan empire in Mexico, imported the Catholic Church, and set up in Mexico City an inquisition to extirpate such beliefs as that in Mexitl.

As opposing forces were waging a battle in Juarez, just across the Rio Grande from El Paso, Tex., a stray bullet traversed the river and broke a window pane on the 13th floor of El Paso's First National Bank. Also in El Paso, a two-year-old U.S. child, Miss Lydia Roberts, was killed by a second stray bullet.

Throughout the northern states controlled by the rebels, Catholic priests were permitted to resume the public celebration of the mass for the first time since 1926 when General Calles (then President) commenced to enforce the anti-Catholic laws. In Nogales, Sonora, Father José Pablos grimly said: "Either this present movement must triumph or we [Catholics] must once more give up our liberty."

From all this it must not be supposed that the causes of the present civil war are *purely* religious. There is also the very strong element of personal rivalry among Mexico's many men of the sword.

MAY 13   **THE END:** Two months ago the *insurrectos* held the northern half of Mexico. Then they were forced back into their base of operations, the State of Sonora where U.S. citizens go to get hard drinks and easy divorces. Weeping bitterly, last week, Governor Fausto Topete of Sonora ordered the *insurrecto* flag hauled down, then fled across the invisible line which divides Nogales, Sonora, from Nogales, Ariz. The rebel Commander-in-chief, General José Gonzalo Escobar, was deserted by the last 1,000 of his original army of 20,000 men and vanished as a hunted fugitive into the mountains along the U.S. border.

Mexico's President Portes Gil. A bomb was under his train. Page 125.

Rebel General Escobar. He vanishes after his troops desert.

In Mexico City, President Portes Gil said: "The Catholic clergy can resume services when they desire, the only obligation being that they obey the laws. The official attitude toward the Church will continue the same as now." The "laws" which the Church is not able to accept, and on which the State continues to insist, chiefly require that members of any clergy before officiating must present themselves at a registry office and subscribe their names and addresses. They also state that churches and religious institutions must belong to the Government of Mexico, that all priests must be native born, that parochial schools must be suppressed. The Protestant clergy complied with these laws from the first, are officiating unmolested. The Catholics, deeming any obeisance to the existing civil power, however slight, incompatible with conscience, continue to regard themselves as persecuted.

PEACE: The President resumed his more prosaic task of governing Mexico. His first move was to demote and dishonorably discharge from the Mexican Army 55 generals, "unworthy to belong to the nation's military forces because of their active participation in the recent rebellion." Despite this catharsis, Mexico's army will not lack for generals. There were 350 of them at the beginning of the revolution, and only four got killed. So 291 are left to command an army of 76,000 men. (The 1929 U.S. Army, 134,505 strong, contains 81 generals.) MAY 27

Afghanistan

Mountainous Afghanistan, situated between Russia and India, was in the throes of a bloody revolt that started in 1928 after its King had returned from a trip to Europe, full of ideas for new reforms. The Soviet Union, which in 1919 had moved to dominate Afghanistan when British rule ended, sent combat planes in a futile effort to defeat the rebels and accused the British of fomenting the revolt to regain their influence.

"BACK TO BARBARISM!": Bitterly did King Amanullah regret, last week, that he had ever sought to sow "reforms" among his people, for it began to seem that he had reaped a revolution quite capable of toppling down his throne. Spurred by reform-hating, fanatically religious Mullahs, the rebels again surrounded Kabul on three sides. A symposium of rumors confirmed reports that His Majesty had proclaimed the termination of all "reforms"—such as the edict requiring men to wear pants—and was making desperate efforts to rally his troops and recover the loyalty of his people. Joyous Afghans prepared for a new order, "Back to Barbarism!" JAN. 21

COUP D'ESCAPE: Headlines blared: Afghanistan has three kings in one week! First off, the doughty brigand Bacha Sakao, called "The Water Carrier," stormed Kabul and JAN. 28

forced King Amanullah to abdicate in favor of his brother Inayatullah. Secondly, the bandits continued their storming until Second-King-of-the-Week Inayatullah abdicated, hefted his 280 pounds into an airplane, flew away. Thirdly, "The Water Carrier" occupied the *arg* or citadel of Kabul and proclaimed himself "Padishah Habibullah." Padishah means "emperor."

Some of the bandits were described as "swathed in cartridge belts up to the eyes" and "jingling with as many as three rifles, six pistols and two swords." The new Water Carrier-Emperor was said to have ridden into Kabul on a saddleless horse, guiding the beast by knee pressure.

SEPT. 2 **FRENCH-FRIED GENERAL:** Bearded Afghans moved mum as ghosts about Kabul last week, afraid of losing their ears, anxious not to be blown into bloody fragments from a cannon mouth. Their bandit-king, fierce Habibullah Khan, was in one of his wild rages. For weeks he has been stubbornly defending Kabul against the potent Nadir Khan, another ruthless seeker of the crown lost last winter by deposed King Amanullah, who is now in bitter exile in Italy. Last week Habibullah heard that one of his favorite generals had just been captured by the Nadir Khan. Cringing, the messenger gibbered to the flashing-eyed king that his general had been boiled alive by the Nadir Khan in a huge, sizzling cauldron of vegetable oil.

French-frying one's generals is an insult no potent bandit king can tolerate. Fierce King Habibullah therefore decreed that any of his own subjects who should publicly utter the name of execrable "Nadir Khan" should be: 1) nailed by the ears to the city wall; 2) torn from the wall next day and blown from the mouth of a cannon. Indian editors noted that while boiling in oil is a venerable Asiatic custom, blowing prisoners to bloody fragments from a cannon is a British invention instituted as official punishment for mutinous Indians.

OCT. 21 **FALL OF KABUL:** Kabul grew too hot last week for gleaming-eyed King Habibullah. Last week the ruthless, white-chinned Nadir Khan converged three armies of overwhelming might upon Kabul. Prudent Habibullah fled in an airplane to escape being French-fried. Without resistance the city fell.

CANNONS AFTER PRAYER: Pretty, resourceful Mme. Andrée OCT. 28
Viollis was last week the first journalist to enter freshly captured Kabul. Her paper in Paris had staked her to an airplane. With quick, appraising eyes she took the measure of the Conqueror, Nadir Khan, told how he rode through the streets on a prancing charger preceded by musicians, how his warriors danced and sang, how the people hailed him with shouts of "Liberator! Liberator!"

After fervent prayer cannon boomed a 21 gun salute. First and only country to recognize Conqueror Nadir last week was his northern neighbor, Russia.

Hardly had the smoke from Kabul's ancient brass saluting cannon died away than Afghans were telling each other hot news. Servants searching the hastily deserted palace of "Usurper" Habibullah came upon a locked closet holding six smouldering corpses. Three were recognizable: the brother and half-brother of exiled Amanullah and Mohammed Osman, onetime governor of Kandahar, whose great Afghan influence once won him the title, "King-maker." All three, held as hostages, had been murdered as the armies of Nadir approached Kabul.

MILESTONES

MARRIED: Mr. Tifft, paper box manufacturer of Brooklyn, N.Y., and one Ruth Esther Petersonn of Fryburg, Me. A parental tiff over first names left Mr. Tifft first nameless; he remains so, is listed in the telephone book as TIFFT.

DIED: Laddie Boy, 9, Airedale beloved of the late Warren Gamaliel Harding; of old age and an abscess in the ear; at the home of Secret Service Man Harry L. Barker, who had been his master since the death of President Harding. Laddie Boy preferred sugar and cream in his coffee. He was a halfbrother of President Coolidge's dog, Laddie Buck.

SUED FOR SEPARATE MAINTENANCE: Michael Franz Bohnen, Metropolitan Opera basso; by Mary Lewis, blonde and sometimes beautiful soprano; married in 1927 by Mayor Walker. Miss Lewis charged that: In Manhattan Mr. Bohnen tried to make her leap from a window; in Paris he dragged her around by the hair; in Berlin he banged her head against a door until the hinges broke; in Los Angeles he slammed her against a wall. After a settlement had been made outside court, Miss Lewis said: "He is a fine man and I love him. It seems that we cannot live together."

MISCELLANY

In Pawtucket, R.I., Dr. William Rothwell, 63, is known as a good physician, a generous host. For 30 years he has always reached for his wallet, always stood treat. Recently he ordered his tombstone. A great boulder, it now stands, ready, in a local cemetery. His inscription: "This is on me."

PEOPLE

"Names make news." In 1929 the following names made the following news:

JAMES JOSEPH ("GENE") TUNNEY, "retired" world's heavyweight champion, entered the lobby of a hotel in Cannes, France, with his wife, bade a group of press photographers begone. They stayed. He lost his temper, hurled their cameras about the lobby. When one French photographer set his camera up again, Tunney knocked him out.

HERBERT HOOVER, GEORGE-OF-ENGLAND-AND-EDWARD-OF-WALES, COL. CHARLES AUGUSTUS LINDBERGH, CALVIN COOLIDGE, BENITO MUSSOLINI, HENRY FORD, THOMAS ALVA EDISON, CHARLES CHAPLIN, DAVID LLOYD GEORGE, PAUL VON HINDENBURG–are the "ten most important news personalities in the world today," said President Karl August Bickel of United Press. Bickel afterthoughts: Pershing, Clemenceau, Stalin.

JOHN DAVISON ROCKEFELLER III, Princeton senior, was given two titles by vote of his class: "Most likely to succeed," "Third most pious."

CHARLES AUGUSTUS LINDBERGH flew his fiancée, Anne Spencer Morrow, and her sisters Elizabeth and Constance, and Mrs. Morrow from Manhattan to the Morrow summer home in Maine. It was no mere pleasure jaunt. Constance, 15, a sophomore at Milton Academy, Milton, Mass., had received letters threatening her with kidnapping, maltreatment, possible death unless she left $50,000 at a stipulated spot.

Col. Lindbergh whisked her quietly away. She was impersonated at school by a girl who left a bundle according to the kidnapper's behest. This trap failed to function. The letters were similar to those sent to several persons prominent in the news.

MAE WEST, fat actress, was told to close *Diamond Lil* in Detroit because it was "silly and stupid, holding no moral and teaching no lesson." Later Mayor John Christian Lodge relented.

JOHN GILBERT, cinemactor, honeymooning with **INA CLAIRE,** actress, besieged by reporters, said: "Really, I'm not the world's greatest lover."

REV. WILLIAM ("BILLY") SUNDAY, silent these many months, screamed at a Pitman, N.J., camp meeting: "The Church has got its back to the wall! They're building nine theatres to one Church. All people think of is entertainment. They offered me $1,000,000 to go into the movies, but I turned it down. I can do more good speaking to the people face to face."

SIR ARTHUR CONAN DOYLE was sitting in his garden near Southampton, England, when flames suddenly burst from the roof of his house. For an hour, local firemen, 100 villagers and the Doyles (wife, two sons, a daughter) labored to save books and manuscripts. An old part of the house was consumed, a new addition saved. No Sherlock Holmes was needed to detect the cause: a spark on the old dry roof.

SAMUEL INSULL of Chicago, potent public utilitarian, in an address before several hundred U.S. reserve officers, said: "One of the great troubles with our young people today is their lack of respect for authority and law. They want to kiss their way through life." [In 1934 Insull went on trial on charges of embezzlement and using the mails to defraud. He was acquitted.]

AIMEE SEMPLE McPHERSON, marcelled evangelist, asked the members of a Denver audience who were willing to give $1.00 to combat Satan to stand up. Only a few rose. "Play *The Star-Spangled Banner*," she told her bandsmen. All rose.

EDSEL FORD'S new $400,000 yacht *Sialia* went aground in a gale off Buzzard's Bay, Mass. After the crew of 18 was saved, a man was drowned trying to land an insurance agent on the wreck.

THE THEATRE

JAN. 14 **"CAPRICE"**—There are those plays so delicately, so truly funny that one forgets to laugh until a perhaps clumsy joke, inserted for no other purpose, ignites the fuse of amusement that a superlative dialog has laid. *Caprice* is such a play. "You are the most abandoned woman I have ever known," says Albert to Ilsa, and she replies, "Abandoned? No one has ever abandoned me!" It is a college quip which serves less as a cause than an excuse for laughter.

The Theatre Guild has made mistakes in selecting plays, but as long as Lynn Fontanne and Alfred Lunt, the busiest and perhaps the best Manhattan mimes, have anything to do with it, it will possess an element of perfection. They stroke the velvet and stir the smooth cream of *Caprice*.

JAN. 21 **"STREET SCENE"**—The Manhattan house is divided against itself. There are apartments on both sides of the hall, on every floor. The June day has been a scorcher. Mrs. Maurrant pokes her head out of a second-story window. There is talk of the heat and Mrs. Jones, on the porch, asks Mrs. Maurrant to come down and have a chat. While Mrs. Maurrant is coming downstairs Mrs. Jones asks Mrs. Fiorentino if it isn't awful, the way Mrs. Maurrant is carrying on with that Sankey, who collects money for the Borden milk people. There is banal chatter. Mr. (Third Floor) Buchanan, whose wife is in laboring pains, says a few words. Mrs. Jones admonishes him to give Mrs. Buchanan plenty of food. "Remember, she's got two to feed."

It is quiet except for the rumble of the subway, the bell of a fire engine, the bark of a dog. Maurrant appears, drunk. Instinctively he looks upstairs, becomes insanely enraged. He rushes to the second floor where his wife and Sankey have gone. There are screams and bellowing curses. There are shots. Sankey is dead. Mrs. Maurrant opens her eyes only once. In the afternoon two child's nurses push perambulators upon the scene. "This heah's the place." Fascinated they stand gibbering, comparing the scene with a tabloid's composograph of the murder. Life goes on as usual. The murderer is caught.

This is one of the best plays of the season. Best of all the characterizations is Beulah Bondi's Emma Jones. Erin O'Brien-Moore is beautiful and restrained as Rose Maurrant. Able Elmer Rice wrote the play and directed it. The single setting of the Manhattan home—once drearily respectable, now only dreary—is by Jo Mielziner.

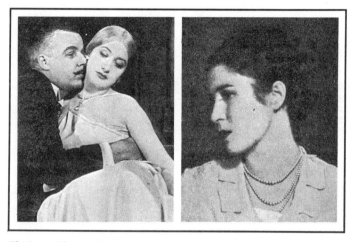

The Lunts. They stir the smooth cream of "Caprice." Page 133.

Erin O'Brien-Moore. She is beautiful, restrained in "Street Scene."

DEAN HAMPDEN: When John Drew died in July 1927, MARCH 4 Walter Hampden really had no rival as "Uncle John" Drew's successor to the deanship of the U.S. stage. The Barrymores, though actually of Hampden's age (John is now 47; Lionel, 50; Hampden, 48) seemed too young. There are, of course, a great many people who feel that Actor Hampden has been Dean for a number of years. He is the only actor-manager, in the sense of the term as it was applied to such as Edwin Booth and Richard Mansfield, in the U.S. today. Last week found him proceeding comfortably into the third month of his second triumphal revival of *Cyrano de Bergerac*, with his own company, under his own direction, in his own theatre—the Walter Hampden Theatre on upper Broadway.

Hampden is the Dean's middle name. His family name is Dougherty, the "Dockerties" of Brooklyn. The first boards he trod were in the Brooklyn Polytechnic Institute, where he was a gangling "Shylock" in itchy whiskers at the age of 16. His father, a judge, had stipulated that if actor he must be, he must be a Shakespearean actor. He went to England and trouped for three years, playing in that time 70 parts. In London he found an engagement with Harry Brodribb Irving, son of the late great Sir Henry. He was playing Laertes when his big chance came: Mr. Irving fell ill. The next day London's critics hailed a new Hamlet, only 25 years old, a prodigy.

Art is art, but one cannot give Shakespeare all the time. Finally, in 1923, he hit upon Poet Brian Hooker's translation of *Cyrano*. Perhaps it is ironic that a high tragedian should have to fall back upon Cyrano's buffoonery for the bed and board of his art. But, even as Cyrano cries after the duel with Valvert: "As I end the refrain, thrust home," so perhaps there never was a neater thrust than when Walter Hampden offered Rostand's sentimental hero to the sentimental U.S. public.

Walter Hampden as "Cyrano." He is the dean of the U.S. stage.

Le Gallienne: "Sea Gull" Mondays, "Peter Pan" Saturdays. Page 139.

APRIL 1 **"JOURNEY'S END"**—The theatre's ways are sometimes stranger than its plots. Some months ago the Kingston Rowing Club, near London, found the Thames too cold for paddling and decided to put on a play by way of diversion. The members turned to R. C. Sherriff, one of their number, who had had "experience" in amateur dramatics. Sherriff, 32, dark, taciturn, was an insurance broker. He said he would try. The only drama he knew was the War. He sat down and wrote the story of a dugout in which he had lived. The plot is a simple war story of ten men during 36 hours that precede a German attack. They snarl, they laugh, they fight, they cower, they die. Standing out among them is one who hopes for death. In the end it is the youngster, eager for life, who dies. The other goes out to face the attack.

The play was produced. But London managers turned it down. Finally the script fell into the hands of a semi-professional group which put it on one Sunday evening. A producer saw it, moved the play to London's West End. That was in late January. Today *Journey's End* is London's outstanding success.

Shortly after its opening, U.S. Producer Gilbert Miller attended a performance. He negotiated for the U.S. rights, sailed for the U.S. with an English company that rehearsed all the way over on the boat. Thus the story of *Journey's End.* It deals with elemental emotions, with a simplicity that is devastating. Its British cast leaves nothing to be asked. It is a perfect interpretation.

"THE LITTLE SHOW"—Like an animated issue of such smart   MAY 13
charts as *Vanity Fair* and *The New Yorker* is this review. Merry, squint-eyed Fred Allen, whose voice sounds as though it ran over a ratchet, is chief wisecracker. Elongated Clifton Webb does a variety of turns, including elegant ballroom maneuvers. Libby Holman, that singing girl who improves so tremendously on Helen Morgan, has a full-throated Harlem sonata, "Moanin' Low."

"SHOW GIRL"—Part of Producer Florenz Ziegfeld Jr.'s policy   JULY 15
has always been to stimulate with hints of fine talent rather than satiate with too much. But with happy frequency there does reappear a property man, impersonated by Jimmy Durante (pronounce the final *e*) who is one of the funniest things that ever happened in Manhattan. He is a tousled, electric fellow whose frothing utterances combine lunacy with bad grammar. He sings his old night-club songs for his new public, including "So I Ups to Him," "Shades, Yellow Shades for the Window," and "Who Will Be With You When I'm Far Away (Far Out in Far Rockaway)?" The Durante part-

ners are Lou Clayton, lean-jawed dancer, and Eddie Jackson, moon-faced strutter. The three are as inseparable off-stage as on. Like most baroque structures, *Show Girl* inclines at intervals to be burdensome. Clayton, Jackson & Durante are chiefly responsible for getting it often and uproariously agog.

The inseparable Lou Clayton, Jimmy Durante and Eddie Jackson keep "Show Girl" often and uproariously agog.

OCT. 7 **KEITH CLEANSING:** Last week, as it must from time to time, the Keith vaudeville circuit cleaned its houses. From orchestras and balconies were swept gum wrappers, cigaret butts, hairpins. From stages were swept all manner of objectionable "gags" and "business."

Sample "gags" prohibited: "Hell." Word "rabbis" in the line, "The dog had rabbis." Remark about girl as a "broad." "Damn." "She thinks 'lettuce' is a proposition." Remarks about Boston being a lighted cemetery.

Sample "business" prohibited: Kicking man in seat of trousers. All maneuverings of lady's skirt. Throwing vest into audience, as damage could easily be done by buttons.

NOV. 18 **"BERKELEY SQUARE"** is a dignified and cerebral romance on the Bergsonian-Einsteinian notion of Time, which hints that past, present and future are illusory, that the impression of fleeting moments, hours and years is not to be trusted. The story is of Peter Standish, young U.S. citizen living in his ancestral London town-house, who likes the 18th Century so well that he suddenly finds himself back in it in the person of his great-great-grandfather. But he retains his own 20th Century consciousness, which makes for much disappointment. The periwigged gallants, for instance, had crude methods of bathing.

On the other hand, Peter creates a reputation for brilliance by using, as though they were his own, remarks from Lincoln's "Gettysburg Address" and "some cheap epigrams by a fellow named Oscar Wilde." His companions, astonished by his strange fore-knowledge of events, come to regard him as a sort of unholy ghost. The girl whom he knows his ancestor did marry turns away from him in fear and he finds himself falling in love with her sister. The lovely Helen knows of his long journey through the years. She is unwilling to see him suffer in an age ill-adapted to his experience, so back he goes to his own century to fondle Helen's memento, still preserved in the old house.

Punctilious, sensitive Leslie Howard strikes a proper balance between the comic and serious aspects of Peter's career. Margalo Gillmore is his wide-eyed partner in super-temporal romance. These two extract fine philosophical nuance as well as fantasy from their curious rôles. Heywood Broun in the New York *Telegram*: "I can think of nothing in several seasons which has moved me so much. If you plan to see only one play this year go to *Berkeley Square*. If your budget provides two evenings in the theatre see it twice."

"BITTER SWEET"—Sated with brassy music, near-nudes and NOV. 18 ribaldry, Manhattan theatregoers were ready for this so-called "operette" composed and directed by London's smart, versatile Noel Coward, and containing his catchiest songs—"Zigeuner" and "I'll See You Again."

CIVIC VIRTUE: Monday night: *The Sea Gull* (Tchekov); Tues- NOV. 25 day night: *The Would-Be Gentleman* (Molière); Wednesday night: *Mlle. Bourrat* (Anet); Thursday night: *The Cradle Song* (the Sierras); Friday night: *Inheritors* (Susan Glaspell); Saturday morning: *Peter Pan* (Barrie); Saturday matinee: *Peter Pan*; Saturday night: *The Sea Gull*.

Above is last week's schedule of Manhattan's Civic Repertory Theatre. It is a sample week in the current career of that theatre's galvanic founder-directrix, Actress Eva Le

Gallienne. Monday and Saturday nights she was the dour daughter of a Russian steward. Tuesday she was a sleek and satined marquise. Saturday she was Peter Pan both morning and afternoon, zooming on concealed wires out over the heads of gasping, wonder-struck children.

Typical also were the capacity crowds which last week, while a sinking stockmarket thinned most audiences, filled the dilapidated Civic Repertory Theatre. Last week, and every week this season, it was jammed. It was Mrs. Hoover's first choice of a theatre to go to when she visited Manhattan last month. Top price at the Civic Repertory is only $1.50. Though her associates would merit headlines anywhere, major credit for a serious venture which is one of Manhattan's greatest civic virtues must inevitably be Eva Le Gallienne's.

Far from being the hyper-sensitive and woeful person she often appears on the stage, Actress Le Gallienne has always been busy and capable as a dynamo. When she was 14 she copied out the entire memoirs of Sarah Bernhardt in longhand. She still has her copybooks, inscribed by Bernhardt, to prove it.

The essence of the Civic Repertory idea is that a new play shall be introduced every five or six weeks, that those already in repertory shall be constantly repeated. The theory is that, as actors become increasingly familiar with a part, their performances improve, and that, with several parts in mind, they will not stagnate. Directrix Le Gallienne would like to install a Civic Repertory Theatre in every principal U.S. city.

But at present her life is fairly full. Each morning at 9:30 she fences. At 10:30 she writes letters, attends to odds & ends. From 11:30 to 3:30 she rehearses a new play—for lunch she eats raw eggs and coffee on the go. From 3:30 to 5:30 she rehearses an old play which is being put back in repertory. After dinner she naps for a half-hour before going to her dressing room. For efficiency's sake she lives on the roof of her theatre with her four dogs and several canaries. The predominant color of the menage and all that is Le Gallienne—suits, stationery, draperies, her Studebaker—is a rich blue.

SPORT

RICKARD'S HEIRS: When the will of Tex Rickard, famed fight JAN. 21 promoter, dead of an operation for appendicitis, was read last week, it was discovered that he had left his estate, amounting to between one million and three million dollars, to his wife Maxine and to his daughter, Maxine Texas Rickard. The body of Tex Rickard was laid in the exact centre of Madison Square Garden, the arena which he built, enclosed in a $15,000 glass-topped coffin, through which 35,000 members of the migratory public peered.

Two nights after his burial, in the exact centre of Madison Square Garden, there was a prizefight and a ceremony. The ceremony was simple: Jack Dempsey climbed through the ropes; the lights went down; a bugler played taps. Presently the lights went on and Jimmy McLarnin beat Joe Glick, Brooklyn tailor.

Before his death, Tex Rickard, having made professional boxing into a sport more spectacular than any since the wild animal shows of the late Roman Empire, was faced with the difficult task of preserving its pomp and magnitude. Gene Tunney had retired, still champion. Since it is regarded as essential that there should always be a World's Heavyweight Champion, it was necessary to discover immediately who this should be. Dempsey who, judged by the eminently suitable criterion of gate receipts, had never lost the heavyweight championship, was reconsidered for the honor. Accordingly, Rickard went south to Miami Beach, Fla. and began arrangements—with some hope of booming his own and his friends' real estate property—for a bout between Jack Sharkey and Young Stribling, the winner to meet Jack Dempsey for the championship.

Just before negotiations had crystallized into contracts, Tex Rickard died. Jack Dempsey took over as promoter. One possibility for a future heavyweight champion is Maximilian Siegfried Victor Schmeling, who was once the champion of Germany, has fought twice in the U.S., is 23 years old, looks like Jack Dempsey and is being taught to fight like him.

MARCH 18 **STANDARD FOOTBALL:** To the attention of the Intercollegiate Football Rules Committee it came that unprincipled footballers have been blowing up their balls in strange shapes—with irregular snouts that might be used as handles in passing; with fat sides to make punts fly short and crookedly. The committee announced last week that a new apparatus will be used in future to measure pigskins put in play and make certain they conform to the standard shape.

Jack Dempsey. Financially, he has never lost the heavyweight crown.   *Gar Wood. Unbeatable on water (93 m.p.h.), he yearns for competition.*

APRIL 8 **FLASH:** A small, wiry, grey-haired millionaire drove a leaping spray-plumed power boat up and down Indian Creek in Florida at the average speed of 93.123 m.p.h. The achievement broke two world's records: the salt water mark of 80.567 set by the same man, and the fresh water mark of 92.834 set by his brother last summer in Detroit. The man was Garfield Wood, Gar Wood for short. With his record hung up, Gar Wood stepped out of his boat, and set to work designing another boat to go even faster.

In 1912 he invented the hydraulic hoist truck which made him a millionaire and gave him the money and time to indulge his hobby. He now has an income of perhaps $1,000,000 a year, four homes, a fleet of cars, a 15-passenger airplane, a wife and a ten-year-old son. But his is a lonely hobby; Gar Wood is unbeatable on water. He longs for competition.

AGAIN, BASEBALL: New consignments of fat sausages, clink- APRIL 15 ing cases of fizzy drinks moved through the land this week in preparation for the opening of the Big League baseball season. Once a national pastime, now a Big Business, baseball still remains the same old-time game. Unlike football, its authorities seldom countenance changes in the rules. This year they rejected a radical plan for ten-man teams (the tenth man to bat for the pitcher.)

General interest this year centres in efforts to crush the dominance of the New York Yankees, undefeated in the last two World Series. To fill in at shortstop, Yankee Manager Miller Huggins bought the services of one Lynford Lary from the Oakland club for a reported $75,000. Florida sunshine, however, revealed serious faults in Lary's fielding. What to do? A young man on the substitute bench, Leo Durocher, had the answer. Durocher is 23. He did not cost one-tenth of $75,000. Huggins liked him because he was alive. When the oldtimers "rode" Durocher he talked back. He will now play shortstop, and a long step it is for a youth of 23.

BIGGER & LIGHTER: A difference in diameter of $6/100$ in., MAY 20 and in weight of $7/100$ oz., was authorized for standard U.S. golf balls last week by the U.S. Golf Association. The difference may engender international complications next year because the Royal & Ancient Society of St. Andrews, high court of British golf, has refused to change the present standard ball.

The new ball is said to make lies better, putting straighter, drives shorter by five or six yards. Because it has more surface and less weight it increases the errors of hookers, slicers.

BRITISH OPEN: Walter Hagen's caddie was nearly blown off a green by the stiff wind, but Hagen sank his putt. A camera clicked when Leo Diegel was putting. He missed by a foot. That is almost the whole story of the British Open Championship which Hagen won for the fourth time (second in succession) last week in Muirfield, Scotland. Diegel [also an

American] had a chance, but Diegel, as he usually does, blew up. Hagen, cautious as a cat, steady as a locomotive, did not blow up. That is usual too. Hagen's winning score was 292, the same as last year. There was more wind than usual, even for Muirfield. Once it blew a Hagen putt, which had stopped short, the last needed inch.

JUNE 3 **IOWA OUSTED:** The "Big Ten" became the "Big Nine" last week when the University of Iowa was ousted on charges of professional athletics. Iowa, stunned, threatened exposure of professionalism in other "Big Ten" universities.

Leo Durocher, 23, talks back to Yan-kee oldtimers, takes over at short. *Helen Wills. After missing the first ball, she defeated her father.*

JULY 1 **WIMBLEDON:** It was Wimbledon time, and in town for the occasion was Helen Newington Wills, 23, from California, who is perhaps the world's best amateur woman player. Tall, gaunt William Tatem Tilden II once hurt his finger on his right hand while he was at the height of his career. It was characteristic of him to walk down a theatre aisle holding the injured member aloft so that all might see. Miss Wills, from the opposite edge of the U.S., is just the opposite.

In 1918 Dr. Clarence A. Wills took his quiet, pig-tailed daughter to a sunny tennis court in Berkeley, Cal. and handed her a racquet which she swung at first like a nightstick. She missed the first ball. She changed her grip and hit the next one. Within a month she could defeat her father.

Masculinity characterizes the Wills game. No woman hits a ball so hard. Whenever she can she practices with a man, because "it is the best training; the men are naturally more strong, though not always so deft." She is seldom seen without her mother whom she calls "Cass," a young-looking woman with soft blue eyes, who does not play tennis.

For nearly four years as an escort not far distant from the Wills ladies has been Frederick Schander Moody Jr., tall, dark-haired son of a San Francisco broker. Last year the Moody-Wills engagement was announced. No tennis expert, he occasionally runs after a ball. They have set no date for the wedding. She does not know housework, nor will she learn. Last week she said: "I intend to do everything just the same when I am married—my tennis, my painting—and I want to take up golf."

WIMBLEDON: It was the first all-U.S. women's finals in the JULY 15 history of Wimbledon. Fifteen thousand people watched Helen Wills defeat her California neighbor, Helen Jacobs, 6-1, 6-2. Helen Wills knows that the best Jacobs shot is a cross-court backhand. Rarely was Helen Jacobs able to use it. Helen Wills played, in all, twelve sets of singles, losing none, dropping only 16 games.

William Tatem Tilden II, 36, was defeated last week. Four games he won in the first set, only one in the second. In the third Henri Cochet (of France) was leading him 5-1. Suddenly, for a moment, returned the Tilden touch. His serves streaked into the court, bounded far out of reach. His drives skimmed the net, his kills were invincible. But when the score was 5 to 5, Tilden's last fling was over. Valiantly he fought but Cochet took the next two games, the match. Francis T. Hunter and Helen Wills won the mixed doubles. Of the five Wimbledon titles, the U.S. won three, England one, France one.

BASEBALL, MIDSEASON: Baseball (largest commercialized JULY 29 sport) passed its mid-season mark in the Big Leagues. Familiar to "fans" (short for "fanatics"), many a fact about the 1929 season has now become visible to laymen:

¶ *Lively Ball.* Experts have become convinced that the "lively" or "rabbit" ball is the cause of a rise of 50 points in batting averages during recent years, of multifarious home runs, of double-figure scores. A.G. Spalding & Bros., official manufacturers, maintained that the "lively" ball is a myth, that no change had been made since 1909, when the cork centre was introduced. When the New York *Telegram* produced cross-sections of a 1919 ball and of a 1929 ball to show that the 1929 ball contains a layer of rubber not found in its 1919 ancestor, Spalding's president wrote: "Let me assure you that the life of the ball has not been changed since 1920." He left the inference that it *had* been changed between 1919 and 1920.

There is no argument but that the game has changed since "Home Run" Baker made his name knocking 12 home runs during the season of 1913. "Babe" Ruth knocked 60 in 1927. In the old days, the good average hitter batted about 25% perfect (.250 in the tabulations). Today an average of .285 is only fair. About 116 batters in the two Big Leagues have surpassed .300 this year.

¶ *Pitchers.* The pitchers have been having a hard time. Where once it was something of a disgrace for a pitcher to be batted out of the box, it is now a matter for comment when a pitcher lasts the full nine innings. "Best" pitcher of the year has been Robert Moses Grove of the Philadelphia Americans. His record up to last weekend was 16 won, 2 lost. A huge young man, Pitcher Grove propels the ball at such speed that few batters are able to time it correctly, and no matter how "lively" a ball may be it will travel no distance when the batter misses it.

¶ *Batters.* The hitters have been thoroughly enjoying themselves. Last weekend "Babe" Herman of Brooklyn was leading both leagues with an average of .404. Just before bat touches ball he takes his right hand off the handle and is swinging only with his left arm at the moment of contact. In the American League the batting leadership has varied between Heinie Manush of St. Louis and Jimmy Foxx of the Philadelphia Athletics.

¶ *Youth v. Age.* In the American League, the Athletics are so far ahead of the Yankees that they appear almost certain winners. This year Connie Mack (Cornelius McGillicuddy), 66-year-old manager of the Athletics, had relied on his youngsters, notably James Emory Foxx. A versatile youth (just past 21), Foxx can play any position except the pitcher's, was used at third base (his favorite spot), in the outfield and at catching before settling down in his present position at first base. Foxx, a 180-pounder just under six feet, has a chest expansion of $6\frac{1}{2}$ inches. "I worked on a farm," he says, "and I am glad of it. Farmer boys are stronger than city boys. I used to lift a 200-pound keg of nails without letting the keg touch my body—but I never realized then it was helping me train for the Big Leagues."

ALEXANDER THE GREAT: Grover Cleveland Alexander, 42, AUG. 19 old-time National League Pitcher, stalked last week to the pitcher's box in Baker Field, Philadelphia. It was the eighth inning of the second game of a double-header between Philadelphia and St. Louis. Philadelphia had won the first game. Philadelphia was leading now, 9 to 8.

Philadelphia, for whom he had pitched well for seven years, had in 1918 released Pitcher Alexander to Chicago, whence in 1926 he went to St. Louis. But there was another, keener reason why Pitcher Alexander wanted to pull this game out of the fire, which he proceeded to do by holding Philadelphia scoreless for four innings while his St. Louis clubmates made three more runs. It was Pitcher Alexander's 373rd winning game in his National League career, breaking the longstanding League record of the late great Christopher Mathewson (New York "Giants").

A RUTH RECORD: At Cleveland, George Herman Ruth propelled the 500th home run of his American League career. To a country youth who retrieved the ball he gave $20 and a new ball autographed.

WORLD SERIES: In Chicago, and then in Philadelphia, the OCT. 21 Chicago Cubs played the Philadelphia Athletics for "the baseball championship of the world." In the fifth game with the series at three games to one for the Athletics, President Hoover was getting up to go when Philadelphia's "Mule" Haas came up to bat in the ninth inning and knocked a straight pitch over the right field fence, tying the score.

By slaps and gesticulations, since words could not be heard over the roar of the crowd, Cubs tried to make Pitcher Pat Malone feel better. But his nerve was gone. He took a long breath, got rid of Mickey Cochrane on a grounder; burly Aloysius Harry Simmons doubled. Cub Manager Joe

McCarthy signaled to pass Foxx. While the crowd was hooting this, Edmund John ("Bing") Miller's two bagger brought the run that won the championship and $6,000 for each first-string Athletic; to each Cub went $4,000.

OCT. 28 **BROBDINGNAGIAN:** On the S.S. *Olympic* in Southampton, England, last week, carpenters went to work on a bunk. They tore out the end of it, put a row of thick struts under it. The White Star Line took these precautions, not because it had accepted an elephant as a first class passenger, but because a prospective passenger named Primo Carnera, an Italian pugilist, was journeying to the U.S. Fighter Carnera is 6 ft. $11\frac{1}{2}$ in. high and weighs 280 lb. with nothing on. His shoes are size $21\frac{1}{2}$ and weigh $7\frac{1}{2}$ lb. apiece. His collars are size 24, his hats $12\frac{3}{4}$.

He switched to boxing from wrestling because he could find no one willing to wrestle with him. He has fought a year and one-half, won 14, lost none.

NOV. 25 **FORCING v. VANDERBILTING:** In a quiet, smoky room in Manhattan, 32 of the foremost bridge-players of the U.S. met in fours last week to play for the Harold S. Vanderbilt Cup. Expert Sidney S. Lenz was sick [with arthritis] and could not play.

But present were Ely Culbertson and his wife, Josephine, famed as the most dangerous married couple in bridge. All felt that the occasion was significant for something beside the trophy at stake. It was a contest between two basic theories of contract bridge.

In recent months the "Vanderbilt convention"—a bid of one club to oblige Partner to declare strength or weakness —has been losing caste. Replacing it has emerged a new convention, a "forcing" system in which the initial bidder, wanting stronger indication of his partner's strength, bids two in any suit.

After much ice-water had been sipped from black goblets, the Vanderbilt trophy was presented to the team of the New York Bridge Whist Club. The winners had used the new forcing system. So had the teams which came in second and third. Of all the teams in the room, only the one on which Mr. Vanderbilt played used his convention. It tied with another team in fifth place.

LOST CUP: The Professional Golfers Association used to give a silver cup to the player who won their annual tournament. This year they put up a radio phonograph with a bronze plate for the winner's name. Nobody knew where the cup was. Walter Hagen had won it so often that he got careless about it and forgot it one day. Hagen's manager was asked where the cup was. "I don't know," he said. "It's hard enough getting him out of bed in the morning without picking up after him."

MILESTONES

MARRIED: Fannie Brice (real name: Borach), 37, famed comédienne, one-time wife of famed bond-thief "Nicky" Arnstein; and Billy Rose (real name: Rosenberg), 29, Manhattan song writer (*Barney Google, Me and My Shadow*); in New York City Hall, by Mayor James John Walker. Songwriter Rose offered the Mayor $1, promised him another if the marriage was successful.

DIED: Briton Hadden, 31, of Manhattan, co-founder of TIME; of a streptococcus infection of the blood stream which became fatal when endocarditis developed. Publisher Hadden was born in Brooklyn, went to the Hotchkiss School and Yale University (class of 1920). After a year as a reporter on the New York *World*, he went with his school and college classmate, Henry Robinson Luce, to be a reporter for the late Publisher Munsey's Baltimore *News*. Having got as far as they could in spare hours with the Newsmagazine Idea, they returned, jobless and with a few hundred dollars, to New York. After more than a year, they issued, under date of March 3, 1923, the first Newsmagazine—TIME. Thereafter to Briton Hadden success came steadily, satisfaction never.

MARRIED: George Herman ("Babe") Ruth, potent baseballer, and Mrs. Claire Hodgson, widowed showgirl; in Manhattan, at 5:45 a.m. The first Mrs. Ruth, long estranged from her husband and living with a dentist of Watertown, Mass., was recently burned to death.

MISCELLANY

In Harmony Grove, Calif., one Henry Van Steenberger sat, on a bet, before ten gallons of wine. He quaffed, guzzled, bibbed, choked down more, sipped, strained, swallowed hard, until only a half-pint remained after three nights and two days of drinking "at one sitting." Then Bibber Van Steenberger lost his bet. He fell over dead.

In Pittsburgh, one O. J. Coats was arrested on the charge that he did steal a trolley car, did go on a long Saturday-night joy ride to West View Park, clanging the gong merrily, all alone.

At St. Petersburg, Fla., one Mrs. S. C. George of Detroit, bathing in the ocean, found herself beyond her depth, cried for help. On the shore, Surf Fisherman S. J. Oakes cast his line at Mrs. George, hooked her in the finger, reeled her in.

In Chicago, Mrs. Helen Johnson sued her Scotch husband, Arthur, for divorce. Claimed she: He would not let her use a vacuum cleaner lest it wear out the rugs; he would wake before the alarm clock's orison to save the spring; on July 4 he bought the children no firecrackers but ran about the house shouting "BOOM!"

$$\boxed{\text{SCIENCE}}$$

JAN. 21   **EINHEITLICHEN FELDTHEORIE:** It means "A Coherent Theory of the Electro-Magnetic Field" and is the title of a five-page paper of highest mathematical formulae which Relativist Albert Einstein worked on for ten years and last week handed to the Prussian Academy of Sciences in Berlin for criticism. Soon it will be published. His relativity theory, which he phrased within only three printed pages, made time & space the creator of matter. Newton believed space independent of time. Some 3,775 books have been written to explain Einstein relativity and its implications in cosmic mechanics. Albert Einstein now applies it himself to explain earthly physical activities—the pull of gravity, the pulsations of electromagnetic waves. Said he in Berlin last week:

"There is no occasion for anybody to be excited about it. There will be only a few mathematicians who will be inclined to read it, and, although I never did make that statement which was ascribed to me that only eleven people in the world could understand relativity, I really don't believe there will be more than a handful of people who will take the trouble to follow its argument."

FEB. 18   **EINSTEIN'S FIELD THEORY:** As 24¢ copies of Albert Einstein's abstruse "Coherent Field Theory" reached the U.S. last week, the man himself, his wife and a daughter plodded about Wannsee, simply hunting rooms at that lake colony twelve miles from Berlin. He looked haggard, nervous, irritable. He sounded querulous. An internal disease, which last summer he feared would kill him before he could complete his newest theory, has made him so. Like so many other scholars, he takes no exercise at all. He works in the attic of a five-story apartment house near Berlin's zoological garden. The room smells of tobacco. He smokes a long-stem briar pipe, into which he tamps tobacco with his thumb. The grand piano in the room is his diversion. A concert is one of the few evening attractions that will entice him out of his flat below his study.

Dr. and Mrs. Einstein are cousins. March 14 he will be 50 years old. Said she of him some time ago: "Professor Einstein is not eccentric. He hardly ever mislays things. He knows when it's time for lunch and dinner."

Sailing was the main reason for the Einsteins' house hunting at Wannsee last week. The lake is a bulge in the Havel River and boats for hire are plentiful. Dr. Einstein likes placid sailing. Once the sails are fixed he stretches out, hands under his head, and idly watches the sky. This he will do for hours.

Men discovered galactic movement, laws of gravity, electricity, magnetism and electro-magnetic waves. Other men discovered that things were not as they seem. They are made up of particles—particles of molecules, molecules of atoms, atoms of electrical protons and electrons, protons and electrons of world waves which meet, get tangled up, unkink and go undulating on again. Only a superb mind could note and keep track of all these people and ideas. Albert Einstein's is such a mind.

In his world nothing stands still. All moves; all changes. Time itself is not a definite thing. There are no straight lines. Everything curves. Intangible forces wave in every direction. Some waves dampen each other's motion until they have no movement left. But their energy is not lost. It goes into other waves which may merge and thereby strengthen each other.

The Einstein world is a great "field" which has height, breadth, depth and time as its elements. Measuring those four elements requires a new kind of geometry—fourth dimensional geometry, Einstein geometry. It is infinitely more complicated than Euclidean geometry taught at high schools and colleges.

Einstein did not develop his conception of the world suddenly. He began by *suspecting* that nothing in the world was privileged, neither matter, nor motion, nor anything else. His suspicion led to the perception that there is one great physical law which describes everything.

To formulate his general theory of relativity he adopted a metric (a measure) with which he could subdivide practically everything that happened in his fourth dimensional world. It was a theoretical measuring unit invented by Georg Riemann (1826-66) which subdivides time, space, undulations, tensions and the other simplest phenomena. But this *general* theory did not account for electro-magnetism. In 1905 Dr. Einstein had shown that electricity and magnetism were different aspects of one activity. Then, in 1919 he showed that gravity was still another activity. It was impossible, Einstein believed, that gravity and electro-magnetism were two distinct world activities. Therefore, his Riemann metric must be inaccurate. So he was obliged to re-examine his whole world and to re-measure it. Both the Euclidean methods and the Riemannian methods of measurement were only approximate.

Working in his study, musing in his sailboat on the Wannsee, Albert Einstein figured out a new metric which lies between the two previous conceptions. It shows that gravity, electricity, magneticism, everything is a logical, not chance, part of the world. It enabled him last week to phrase in mathematical terms a theory by which "everything in the world" can be explained. Perhaps the pull of the Einstein intellect will raise mankind yet higher by the bootstraps.

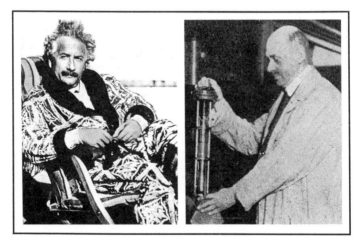

Albert Einstein. His wife says: "The professor is not eccentric."

Robert Goddard. He builds rockets but is no moon man. Page 154.

FEB. 25 **EDISONIANA:** A shrill and crackling hail greeted Herbert Hoover when he joined Thomas Alva Edison's 82nd-birthday party at the Edison estate in Florida last week. It was deaf Mr. Edison yelling: "Hello, fisherman!" On Mrs. Edison's ample table was a big green-&-yellow pound cake. This the old gentleman sliced with skill and raillery. As is usual at his parties, Mr. Edison had an aphorism: "I am not acquainted with anyone who is happy."

Another feature of Mr. Edison's birthday was a gesture of generosity by Mr. Henry Ford. At Dearborn, Mich., Ford's factory town, stands the Edison Institute of Technology and the Museum of American Industries, dedicated to Mr. Edison. The museum contains all Mr. Edison's tools and contrivances, in working order. Mr. Ford last week endowed them both with $5,000,000. At the dedication of the memorials, Mr. Edison, Mr. Ford and a group approached the buildings to enter. Near the door was a fresh-laid sheet of concrete, around which the party started to walk. But not Mr. Edison. Always he takes the short cut and across the concrete he walked. It was soft. His shoes sank into it. Consternation came upon his face, then stubbornness. He plodded ahead, leaving a string of footprints behind. Mr. Ford was delighted and gave orders that the footprints be allowed to harden. Furthermore, he made Mr. Edison take off his shoes and leave them in the museum.

METALLIC MILK: Surprising to scientists as to milk-bibbers is APRIL 1 this large list of metals present in milk: strontium, vanadium, rubidium, zinc, copper, titanium, lithium, calcium, magnesium, potassium, iron, sodium, aluminium, manganese. Also chlorine, iodine, boron and phosphorus.

The presence of some of these minerals in milk has long been known. But that strontium, which makes fireworks burn red, that boron, which volcanoes heave forth, that titanium, which makes war smoke screens, that vanadium, which hardens steel—that such metals of horrendous connotation were also in solution was a revelation made to U.S. householders only last week, from Cornell University. The discoveries were made with a spectroscope. The metallic contents are "small but definite." Now nutritionists must decide what effect those elements have on diet.

HARVARD'S BULLDOG: More than two years ago, three doctors APRIL 29 of the Harvard Medical School did a weird deed which they saw fit to keep secret until last week. Two female English bulldog litter mates were received in the Harvard laboratory. They were observed and found to grow normally. After a month a needle was thrust daily into the belly region of the slightly smaller dog, injecting anterior-lobe extract of cattle's pituitary glands. In a month the smaller puppy had begun to grow faster. Soon the smaller puppy *was* the larger one.

In June of the next year came a scorching day. In the morning, as usual, the dogs scampered out on the laboratory roof. Toward the end of the afternoon the doctors were summoned and there in the sunshine lay a monstrous dead bulldog, by now twice the weight of her litter mate, a dog fit for baying at enormous moons. In the burning heat her heart and lungs had failed to function for her abnormal, overgrown body. Dead though she was, however, she had proved it possible to grow giants in a laboratory.

MAY 13 **EINSTEIN:** Dr. Norbert Wiener, mathematician of Massachusetts Institute of Technology [who was to become famous for his studies in cybernetics—the science of communication and control] last week published some remarks on Albert Einstein. There is as yet no final Einstein Theory, he pointed out; the document published last January is but part of a chain of thought. Also, Einstein has already noticed deficiencies in his latest work, modified it and progressed to further conclusions. "We have this on the basis of direct advices from Professor Einstein himself."

MAY 20 **EASTMAN COLORS:** The problem of making talking movies in natural colors is not yet solved, but last week it was announced that Eastman had evolved a process for tinting whole scenes. The Eastman tinting is described as giving scenes "colors conforming to their emotional content." Talkies will now be available in the following mood colors, among others worked out at the Eastman Laboratories: 1) *Rose Dorée* ("sensuousness and passion . . . amorous . . . exotic"); 2) *Peachblow* ("feminine beauty"); 3) *Firelight* ("mild affection"); 4) *Aquagreen* ("cool lakes in the northwoods"); 5) *Turquoise* ("calm tropical seas"); 6) *Caprice* ("hilarious pink, carnival moods"); 7) *Inferno* ("burning buildings, panic, anarchy"); 8) *Argent* ("grey, everyday life").

JUNE 17 **MOONING:** Far greater than the sum (10,000 francs or about $390) is the honor attached to the annual R.E.P.-Hirsch prize of the French Astronomical Society. Far greater than the practical effect was the imaginative content of the work for which a young German named Oberth last week received this year's award.

Getting to the moon was the object of Herr Oberth's researches. The Society considered that he had actually made progress toward "practical interstellar navigation." The problem begins, and so far has ended, with the forces by which Earth clutches that which is its own. To escape the pull of gravity, an earthborn body would have to take off at terrific speed. Outside the earthly atmosphere, interstellar gases are so rare that they would afford no traction for an airplane's propellor, no buoyance for wings. Most scientists have therefore pondered shooting themselves moonwards in rockets.

Herr Oberth, bearing in mind the desirability of returning, cogitated combining plane and rocket, using the latter for propulsion of the former as has been done experimentally in Germany. He described two kinds of fuses, one using hydrogen, the other of alcohol—which he calculated would drive a plane 13,120 ft. per sec. or about 9,000 m.p.h., making the 240,000-mile trip in some 27 hours. After praising Herr Oberth and giving him the prize, the French Astronomical Society gravely warned that trips to the moon are still wholly impractical. [Hermann Oberth continued his studies, became known as the "father of space travel," and after World War II came to the U.S. to work with the group of German rocket scientists, including Wernher von Braun, whose developments made the U.S. Apollo moon program feasible.]

ROCKETEERING: So unobtrusively does Professor Robert JULY 29 Hutchings Goddard of Clark University, Worcester, Mass. work on his study of the air's upper miles by means of rockets that to many a Clark student he is only a tradition. They call him the moon man, in the inaccurate belief that he is trying to reach the moon with his missiles. Last week, Tradition Goddard detonated very loudly. From a 40-ft. steel tower he fired his latest rocket, a huge steel cylinder 9 ft. long by 2½ ft. in diameter. A new propellant sent it whizzing from the ground. It rose straight up [to about 90 feet]. There the fuel seemed to ignite all at once, instead of in a stream, as planned. The roar sent Worcester ambulances and police hunting for tragedy. They found Professor Goddard and assistants inquisitively studying his rocket shell, which had landed near the site of its propulsion.

Carrying objects, and perhaps eventually persons, by means of rockets is an engineering phase of physics in which Professor Goddard, 47, has been experimenting for 17 years. The principle of rocket motion is simple—action and reaction. Escaping gases act in one direction, the rocket body in the opposite. The ground is not necessary for the rocket gases to push against in order to propel the rocket. Nor is the air. Such action and reaction can take place in a vacuum [like space], a fact which has driven Professor Goddard on his experiments. His objective is not to see how far he can shoot a rocket but to investigate the physics of the earth's outermost blanket of air. [Because of this test, Dr. Goddard—now generally known as "the father of rocketry"—was asked by the State of Massachusetts to cease his experiments for safety reasons. He moved his experiments to the vicinity of Roswell, New Mexico, and continued to perfect his rockets. He died in 1945, but his basic concepts have been used in every liquid-fueled U.S. rocket since.]

OCT. 14   **SPEED AND SAFETY:** Two knowing men last week tangled assertions as to what might be safe speeds for motor cars to operate. Said Paul Hoffman, vice president in charge of sales and one of the four men who operate the great Studebaker Corp: "Whether you like it or not, the public wants speed. Motorcycle policemen should stop chasing fast cars that are imperiling no one and devote themselves to removing the reckless driver from the highways."

Said Louis Dublin, famed statistician of the Metropolitan Life Insurance Co.: "That was the most outrageous talk I ever heard. Mr. Hoffman's doctrine is at the bottom of our troubles. There is no earthly reason for speed higher than 35 miles an hour."

MISCELLANY

In Jackson, Tenn., Herbert Crane told his wife not to put the cat out. She did; he shot her.

In Los Angeles one Gregory Woodford sat with his friend J. A. Pursley in a seventh story hotel window, telling a joke. At the climax Woodford gave Pursley a thrust in the ribs. Both rollicked with laughter, fell out of the window, were killed.

In De Peyster Corners, N.Y., Mrs. Margaret Mason, 58, became despondent at the thought of losing her flock of turkeys at Thanksgiving time, set fire to their shed, died with the birds.

MEDICINE

MONKEY-&-MAN SERUM: At the Harvard Medical School JAN. 7
laboratory last week a hand reached into a cage of monkeys, caught one and drew a little blood from it through a needle. The monkeys crouched in their cages, ignorant that they suffered from infantile paralysis and ignorant that Dr. William Lloyd Aycock and his colleagues of the Harvard Infantile Paralysis Commission had just recently learned how to mix monkey serum with human serum in order to cure infantile paralysis.

Infantile paralysis, so far as is known, occurs only in man and he is the sole source of the infection. Monkeys may be infected in the laboratory. That fact has been valuable in studying the disease (no one yet knows what germ causes it) and in getting a new source of serum. Previously the Harvard Commission, which is doing the most extensive work on the subject in the country, has been obliged to ask cripples for ounces of their blood. The serum derived therefrom was sufficient for doles to only the most promising cases. The new monkey-&-man serum amplifies the supply. [It was not until 1954 that Dr. Jonas Salk produced a polio vaccine on a mass scale.]

KEEN FLAYED: William Williams Keen, witty, venerable MARCH 25
(aged 92) Philadelphia surgeon, lately underwent a minor operation. Afterwards he received a scolding letter: "Why didn't you have the operation without an anesthetic, so you could see how the animals feel that you have tortured all these years? You will have an awful body in the next incarnation. You have one foot in the grave now and the other foot on a banana peel, you old fiend." Remarked Surgeon Keen: "I take it that the letter is from a woman. If so I pity her possible husband. The fun of the thing is that I have never been a research worker. I have never experimented on any animal, not even a mouse or a frog. I shall keep my eye on that banana peel, you may be sure."

APRIL 1 **RADIUM POISONING:** In a hurry to learn what damage radium had done, one William W. Cardow, Waterbury, Conn., motor mechanic, had an autopsy performed on his wife a few hours after her death last week. A Columbia University radium poisoning specialist was summoned by telegraph and he, with a Waterbury pathologist and dentist, took the body apart. They found that its jawbones were decayed, also parts of the skull, a bone in the right thigh, and four teeth. The heart and lungs were sound, but other internal organs yellow with rot. Mrs. Cardow had painted dials for the Waterbury Clock Co. and her death is a social penalty for the public's demand to have night-luminous watches, clocks, gadgets.

Harvard's Dr. Aycock. He seeks a cure for infantile paralysis.

Booth Tarkington: "What a thrill not to see everything." Page 158.

APRIL 8 **TWO OF A KIND:** Identical twins, born of the same egg, are seldom reared separately. Hence Horatio Hackett Newman, professor of zoology and embryology at the University of Chicago, rejoiced last week because he had such a pair under observation: two 19-year-old girls called discreetly A and O. They were born in London, lost their parents at 18 months. A's foster parents raised her in stodgy London, O's in a small Ontario town. Both received similar education. Recently A joined O.

Theoretically and according to previous observations, identical twins should be mirror images of each other. A's and O's conduct agree with this. Both have hasty tempers. They have similar likes and dislikes. They worry about the same things. But mentally Ontario O is two years older than London A.

Their case points answers to two moot points: heredity governs emotions; environment governs intelligence. Couples planning to adopt orphans and concerned with the children's dispositions, by inference would do well to study their ancestral points. Foster parents intent only on raising intelligent children may pick foundlings at confident random.

BLIND & GAY: "It is hard for anyone who has not been blind to realize what a thrill it is not to have to see everything. It is really marvelous not to look at a lot of things and people that you don't want to see." So spoke last week famed Author Booth Tarkington [who had cataracts]. "Someone thanked God who made him blind so that his soul could see. I have come to believe that there is a lot of truth in that. I have done more work during the past year than ever before. I have written a novel, short stories and several essays. It is true that being unable to see is a great aid to concentration. You are not distracted. Half of people's appetite is a result of looking at food. Now that I can't see what I am eating I feel that I could very easily dispense with it."

FIRST SIGHT: Forty-eight years ago a baby was born blind MAY 13 in Montgomery, Ala. Lately, ill, she was taken to the charity hospital at Colfax, La. The doctors told her they thought they might, even now, operate and make her see. Last week the bandages were removed and Mrs. Wagoner did see. Her first remarks were a human document: "I clenched my hands and tried not to scream. I opened my eyes, and I saw. It was his [the doctor's] face. Two eyes and a nose and a mouth, just as I had felt them all these years. I stand at the window and I see automobiles and the wheels turning and smoke coming out of chimneys and people walking around, and I can't believe it. The nurses had to tell me what things were. I would ask: 'What is that long, pointed thing out there?' and the nurse would say, 'That's a church steeple.' I've been going to church all my life and didn't know a church steeple." Although she can now see, she still has the habit of reaching out to touch visitors and passing her hands over objects to determine their size and position.

JUNE 10 **FILIAL LOVE:** To kill his mother at her own pleadings, or to let a painful cancer kill her, was the problem put to one Richard Corbett, intelligent young Englishman. The two, since his father's death, had lived together in southern France. Last November Mrs. Corbett's cancer became unmanageable. Last February doctors decided that radium, X-rays or other measures could neither cure her nor give her surcease from her terrific pain. The son watched her, heard her cries, saw the wrinkles of agony deepen in her face.

She lacked strength and means for suicide. (In France, 40,000 people die each year from cancer; almost half of them kill themselves to end their pain.) She begged him to kill her. She reasoned with him. Her death was certain. He could but bring it to her sooner, and far more mercifully than the cancer was doing. He pondered. Of course, religion forbids good-intentioned murder as well as offensive murder and suicide. But religion is a personal matter. Step by step he puzzled out the logic of his ethical problem: "Has the state, for reasons which are at bottom religious, the right to refuse to incurables the pity which they demand? Has not the individual the right to his liberty? So long as the law is not amended it throws onto individuals the responsibility of the solution."

Richard Corbett assumed the responsibility. He gave his suffering mother a narcotic. Then he shot her through the head. Next he shot himself, but lived. Last week he was in the hospital at Hyères, reluctantly alive and wondering what judgment would be on his matricide. He wrote a long letter to *Le Matin*, outstanding Paris daily, explaining his deed, admitting his "guilt," urging that, come what might to him, the law be changed. "I regret nothing," he said. [He was acquitted.]

AUG. 19 **HICCOUGHS:** For 59 days one Vera Stone, 18, Tennessee girl, hiccoughed. She acked, eked, icked, ooked, ucked until she nearly died. They sought causes and cures, made her gulp cold water and hold her breath. Nothing worked. Last week one shrewd doctor decided that she had hiccoughed so long she had forgotten what it was like *not* to hiccough, was therefore psychologically incapable of helping herself. He gave her a strong, nauseating drug, put her to sleep.

When she awoke her mind was so occupied with her new, counter-irritating misery that she forgot to hiccough, was cured.

QUAIL STUFFERS: To fatten quail for market, Italian and NOV. 11 Polish *gaveurs* (bird stuffers) work in Paris market-hall cellars chewing up grain and fruit into a pap which they let the quail eat from their mouths. The pecking quail abrade the *gaveurs'* lips, noses, chins. The peckmarks become infected, ulcerated; the *gaveurs* sometimes die. So reported the *Journal* of the American Medical Association, ever on the alert for new occupational diseases.

VOLUNTARY PARENTHOOD: Birth Control as an open, organ- DEC. 2 ized movement instead of a furtive, unmentionable practice appeared again last week when the American Birth Control League held, in Manhattan, its first general conference in five years. The calibre of the sponsors suggested a changing social attitude—the wife of Governor Franklin D. Roosevelt, the wife of Morgan Partner Thomas W. Lamont, the Rev. Harry Emerson Fosdick.

The conferees deplored the fact that there are only 29 centres in the U.S. where birth control information is given —four in California (Los Angeles, Oakland, Pasadena, San Francisco), one in Colorado (Denver), eight in Illinois (all in Chicago), one in Maryland (Baltimore), one each in Detroit, Minneapolis, Newark and Cleveland, ten in New York City. The conferees pointed with satisfaction to recent endorsements of Birth Control—by the Junior League of New York City, the Universalist Church, the Central Conference of American Rabbis, the New York City Federation of Women's Clubs, the New York League of Women Voters. (Members of the Pennsylvania League of Women Voters were affronted at their convention in Pittsburgh last week when Manhattan's Dr. James F. Cooper urged them to "have children by choice, not by chance.")

Disclosed for the first time last week to the general public was the fact that Russian experimenters have successfully inoculated women against pregnancy. Four or five doses of serum made from spermatozoa has made women infertile for from five to six months, when further injections continued the temporary sterility.

DEC. 16 **PSYCHIATRIC MEETING:** Some 150 eminent U.S. and European psychiatrists met in Manhattan last week. One subject that was described:

Undoubtedly, the mating of two persons with marked similar talent in music, art or politics will produce offspring endowed with the same talent. But, "clan-bred talent" tends to produce experts with a decided lack of understanding of things outside their own sphere. Such progeny are likely to be dull and stupid, cherishing rigid forms and traditions. Genius, on the other hand, results from the crossing of dissimilar high mental traits resulting in a complicated psychological structure in which the components of two strongly opposing germ plasms remain in polar tension throughout life. This tension exerts a driving force and produces the instability of temperament, emotional pressure and restive impulsiveness which are the earmarks of genius.

MILESTONES

MARRIED: Henry Latham Doherty, 58, self-made public utilities and oil tycoon (Cities Service Co.), "richest U.S. bachelor"; and Mrs. Percy Frank Eames, 40, who had nursed Tycoon Doherty through a nearly fatal arthritis illness. In the luxurious Doherty penthouse apartment in Manhattan, the Doherty bed, at punch of button, moves on rails to a sun porch overlooking the harbor.

DIED: Butcher Matthias Sticz of Kecskemet, Hungary, 506 lbs., "fattest man in Europe"; by suicide. He shot himself because he could no longer afford beef in the quantity (two roasts) which he required at breakfast.

BIRTHDAY: Joseph ("Soso") Dzugashvili, alias Josef Stalin, "Steel Man" Dictator of Soviet Russia, wielder of greater authority over a greater area than any man since Tamerlane the Great. Age: 50. Because of the proximity of his and Christ's birthdays, his parents destined him for the church. Expelled from seminary at the age of 17, he adopted 100% communism as his religion. He has never deviated. On his birthday every newspaper in Moscow devoted its first four pages entirely to Stalin.

MISCELLANY

In Chicago, one William Hoke confessed in court last week that he had placed banana skins on the premises of 45 companies, slipped on them, collected damages. His sentence: six months.

In Boston, one Vincent Featherstone has sold more than one million tickets in his 39 years in the box office. Finally he took one of the tickets, went inside, saw *The Beggar's Opera*, first play he had attended in 39 years.

Around Nogales, Ariz., raged a terrific electric storm. At intervals the blinding flashes revealed a dark horseman, bowed in his saddle, motionless on the plain. When the storm cleared, searchers found the horseman to be Rancher Roy Sorrell. Both he and his mount had been electrocuted, left stiffly standing.

CINEMA

PARAMOUNT'S PAPA: In 1925, when American Telephone & JAN. 14 Telegraph Co. gave a private showing of sound-pictures of people singing, a drummer drumming, officials of the company waited anxiously for the verdict of the man for whom the showing had been arranged—Adolph Zukor, president of Paramount-Famous Players-Lasky Corp. (recognized leader of the industry's "Big Four," closely followed by Loew's, Inc., Warner Bros. Pictures, Inc. and Fox Film Corp.). Mr. Zukor said then: "I'd like to see somebody perfect it. Myself, I can't handle it until it's better." Last week, Mr. Zukor said: "From now on at least 50% of our productions will be sound pictures."

It was an important indorsement. The talkie has caused a crisis. First, it has greatly increased competition in the cinema business. Second, if the talkies become dominant, the U.S. may lose its position in foreign markets because U.S. stars can, at best, speak only one language at a time.

At first, Zukor, 5 ft. 4 in., got along in the fur business. Then he bought a penny arcade in Manhattan. One of the films he showed was *The Great Train Robbery,* a real story that ran for twelve minutes. He started a chain of cinema "palaces" in Newark, Boston, Pittsburgh—empty stores made into theatres with chairs bought second-hand from bankrupt undertaking parlors. He had one real theatre with a piano—the Comedy in Union Square, Manhattan. Zukor had known another furrier named Marcus Loew and had invested in Loew's subsequent theatre business. Neither owned enough houses to keep a "feature" busy all year, so they merged.

Although now a rich exhibitor, he had nothing to do with making pictures. A small, tight trust consisting of ten producing companies handled that. But most of their actors were anonymous. Gambling all his money on his belief that there would be profits in advertising cinema actors like "legit" actors—calling them Famous Players—he fought to break the trust. His wife sold her jewels and friends loaned their savings. He almost went broke, and once the studio burned down. But the idea caught on. Mary Pickford was one of his first stars. And one of his first films, *The Prisoner of Zenda* in 1912, cost a record price of $7,000. Soon he was to make films that cost $1,000,000 and buy out Paramount.

JAN. 28 **VARIATIONS:** Because acting and over-feeding caused brown pouches to appear under his melancholy eyes, the face of King Tut, famed cinema dog, was lifted last week by one Dr. G. M. Eisenhower in Hollywood.

Producer Adolph Zukor: "Half our pictures will be sound pictures."

Clara Bow. The "It" girl is tops at movie box offices.

BOX OFFICE: Theater owners, voting on box-office appeal of cinema people, ranked Clara Bow best of women, Colleen Moore second, Billie Dove third, Mary Pickford sixth, Greta Garbo twelfth. Of men, Lon Chaney was first, Tom Mix second, John Gilbert third.

THE CZAR SPEAKS: Will Hays, "Czar" of the movie industry, said: "Motion pictures are just as necessary in their way as agriculture. Any effort to censor and cut is as great an outrage as to cut the tender tips of newly sprouting corn."

FEB. 18 **"THE DOCTOR'S SECRET"** is Sir James M. Barrie's one-act play *Half an Hour* done as a talking-picture which sticks to the original script in all respects except that the film runs for 60 minutes. The story of the woman who lives through that half-hour—30 minutes from the time she leaves her husband to run away with another man, until, her sweetheart having been killed in a street accident when he went out to get a taxi for them, she is back as hostess in her husband's house—could not possibly be told so well without the sound device. For once, the voices, in spite of still imperfect reproduction, give life to the characterizations. Ruth Chatterton, the faithless wife, was brought from the theatre for sound-cinema, has a long jaw, sly eyes and a good voice.

DOUGLAS FAIRBANKS: MARCH 4

> *"Friends were friends in those brave days—*
> *Porthos, Athos, Aramis, I*
> *Graved our hearts with a mystic phrase,*
> *Bound our lives with a mystic tie;*
> *Come, stir your souls with our ringing call*
> *Of "All for one and one for all!"*

So recites Douglas Fairbanks from the sound-device as prolog to *The Iron Mask,* his sequel to *The Three Musketeers.* The voice, like all filmed voices, creaks a little, but the spirit which the poetry fails to achieve is incorporated in the superb acrobatics of the only living actor who is also a great athlete. He has his best rôle again—D'Artagnan. Under the window ledge a saddle waits; one leap.

Douglas Elton Fairbanks was fired from a Denver office where he filled inkwells because in odd moments he broke furniture, stood on his head. In a stock company and later as a juvenile on Broadway he found that public disorder could be profitable. In 1907 he married the daughter and heir of a soapmaker who stipulated that Fairbanks must supervise his boiling grease-vats. Six months later Fairbanks returned to the stage, was divorced in 1918, married Mary Pickford in 1920. Once, locked out of his room in the Plaza Hotel, Manhattan, he climbed up the face of the building. Social leaders in Hollywood, "Doug" and "Miss Pickford" dance only with each other.

COLOSSAL ENTERPRISE: The announcement, last week, that APRIL 8 henceforth William Fox, head of Fox Film Corp. would produce *only* talking pictures was widely interpreted as "dooming" the silent picture. However, most of the feature pictures now in production are being made with both a silent and a talking version; Universal and Paramount continue to make duplicate prints—one for "wired" and one for non-wired theatres. It is this question of wired houses (*i.e.,* cinemansions equipped to produce talking pictures) that assures the silent film of at least a lingering death. There are more than 15,000 U.S. picture houses, of which only about 2,000 now have sound equipment.

Many Broadway producers were skeptical of the talkie threat. Said Florenz Ziegfeld: "Beauty in the flesh will continue to rule the world." And others point out that what is at present the talkies' outstanding attraction—the fact that a picture can talk—must, after its novelty has disappeared, become their outstanding limitation—the fact that it is *only* a picture that is talking. Even if speaking cinemas lose their present lisp and rasp, the illusion produced by an articulate photograph of John Barrymore as *Hamlet* can never be as satisfying as the illusion produced on the stage by Actor Barrymore himself.

MAY 13 **"INNOCENTS OF PARIS"**—Maurice Chevalier is a French cabaret singer known in the U.S. only to the few who have heard him in Paris. But he has been built into a cinema celebrity with the most expensive advertising campaign ever invested in a foreign actor. In this talkie he plays a poor junkman who pulls a little boy out of a French suicide-river so he can sing to him. Later the junkman becomes the star of one of those French musicals where the girls roll their eyes like Irene Bordoni.

"SATURDAY'S CHILDREN"—The marriage, parting and reunion of Maxwell Anderson's hero and heroine—one of the best of all U.S. plays—becomes heavy and slow in this partly-vocal photograph. Corinne Griffith's voice, heard for the first time, is nasal, unattractive, but somehow memorable.

JUNE 24 **"SHE GOES TO WAR"**—The cinema has had a dreadful time trying to be convincing about the War. This picture is an unreal lyric about a Southern girl who had two sweethearts, one of whom turned out to be a coward. He was drunk when the bugle blew, and when she told him to get out and join the ranks he belched in her pretty face. So she put on his tin

Al Jolson, moody minstrel with a one-sob cinema repertory.

George Arliss as Disraeli. He could double for Dizzy in the House.

hat and got in his place and won a battle for the regiment by shooting a German machine gunner.

EIGHT HOURS: California law forbids children from acting in JULY 8 the movies more than four hours per day. Last week a director needed a child, found Barbara and Beverly Bustetter, twins, cast both for the same part, worked one in the morning, one in the afternoon.

"THE MYSTERIOUS DR. FU MANCHU"—Sax Rohmer's Fu AUG. 5 Manchu stories have been read by schoolboys, financiers and statesmen for nearly two decades. Their fascination lies in the fact that motive is not an element of their plots. It might be terrible to read about a killer who killed for a reason but it is more terrible to read about one who killed for no reason. This picture, though well made, fails to get the flavor of the stories because Fu Manchu is rationalized. He kills Englishmen to get even with them for killing his wife and child in reprisals that followed the Boxer Rebellion.

Warner Oland (Fu Manchu), who used to be an opera singer, makes his cold, tight voice the most exciting noise in the picture.

"SAY IT WITH SONGS"—The sob that rose in Al Jolson's AUG. 19 throat as he sang beside the bedside of Davy Lee in other pictures has grown louder, deeper. Now that sob, heard round the world, constitutes his whole repertory. In this picture Jolson sings well although without burnt cork, which he really needs.

Before he was 20, Asa Yoelson ran away from Washington, D.C., where he had learned to sing in the synagogue with his father, Cantor Yoelson. He got a job barking for a side-show, later went into vaudeville, started blacking his face because he noticed that crowds always laughed at a black man. He was the first minstrel to get down on his knees when he came to the word "Mammy." Now a multimillionaire, he remains capricious, moody, fond of practical jokes. He likes to take long motor trips without planning them, starting at night for some distant point and singing on the way. Last winter he improved his standing by marrying Ruby Keeler, a popular little tap-dancer tutored by "Texas" Guinan.

OCT. 14 **"DISRAELI"**—The efforts of a Jewish prime minister of England in 1875 to buy a public utility for his kingdom have been made into a picture as exciting as a detective story. This is principally due to George Arliss, who has played Disraeli so often on the stage that if set back 60 years he could probably double for him in the House of Commons. He gets across the complicated plot, making you believe in the crafty little minister who loved peacocks, gardening, and Queen Victoria, and whose servants were all Russian spies. Best shot: Arliss making the Governor of the Bank of England sign the check that bought the Suez Canal.

OCT. 21 **"RIO RITA"**—RKO's policy of revivifying somewhat shop-worn stars by publicizing them as new discoveries has worked out well with Bebe Daniels. Even her friends never knew Bebe Daniels could sing. But for 20 years she has been doing everything that any scenario required her to do. In the old Pathé comedies she used to get plastered with dough, tossed in blankets, dumped into ponds. Then she graduated to wearing silver wigs in Cecil B. DeMille's period pictures. One winter there was a popular song called "Bebe, Be Mine," and even now when she goes to a cabaret the orchestra leader usually recognizes her and starts to play it. Bebe Daniels likes all games, but likes best of all to drive a fast car fast. She is seldom arrested.

"THEY HAD TO SEE PARIS"—Always uncomfortable when he is being photographed, Will Rogers tried to create the easy atmosphere of the legitimate stage during the filming of this picture by extemporizing wisecracks and routine not specified in the script. Usually his antics, having mixed up the cast and irritated the director, were halted and the scene shot over again. In the finished film Rogers' unassumed self-consciousness helps to make sharper his portrait of an Oklahoma oil man who takes his family to Paris to get culture.

NEWSREEL THEATRE: The six or seven minutes of newsreel NOV. 18 exhibited in ordinary program houses are selected from many reels of current events. In Manhattan William Fox, in collaboration with Hearst Metrotone, found what to do with the discarded reels. He took over a Broadway theatre (Embassy) and changed its program from a $2 show twice a day to a continuous 25¢ show. He made the program all newsreels, to run for an hour.

You saw a murderer confessing his crime. You saw Prince Umberto of Italy riding in a Brussels street at the moment when an anti-Fascist took a shot at him. Lighter events relieved such stern episodes. The Embassy Theatre became so thronged with patrons that its backers announced they would start a chain of such theatres through the U.S.

"THE TAMING OF THE SHREW" by Shakespeare is Douglas DEC. 9 Fairbanks' first all-talking picture and the first picture in which he has ever appeared with Mary Pickford. His lusty voice, individual because it has never been trained, makes the voices of the schooled actors who play with him seem prosy and lifeless. He has a fine time swaggering in Petruchio's pointed shoes, but his wife outplays him. She is Katherine from head to heels—a stormy, pretty vixen with just a shadow of pout left to tell you that she was once called "America's Sweetheart." [In 1929 Mary Pickford was 36.]

"THE VAGABOND LOVER" reveals once more Rudy Vallée's painful discomfort when required to do anything but croon love songs or play the saxophone. But his voice registers smoothly when he croons "If You Were the Only Girl in the World." The film is helped by the presence of Marie Dressler in a comedy role written specially for her and having little to do with the plot. Best shot: Marie Dressler's idea of how an aristocratic lady handles a chiffon handkerchief.

Hubert Prior Vallée avoided working in his father's drugstore in Westbrook, Me., by playing the saxophone in New England cabarets and theatres. He transferred from the University of Maine to Yale (class of 1927) and played at nights to pay his way. When he got out he went on earning $60 a week, then organized an orchestra of his own. He began to broadcast. Soon thousands of letters a week arrived for him, many from young women: "Dearest Rudy . . ." and he began to make $10,000 a week. Incisive, businesslike, he has no hobbies, works hard. He plays till early in the morning in his respectable Manhattan night club—Villa Vallée—sleeps for a while, gets up to make records, broadcasts at noon. Besides this routine, he works in vaudeville or cinema house appearances. His hair is reddish.

MILESTONES

MARRIED: Douglas Fairbanks, Jr., 19, cinemactor; to Joan Crawford (real name Lucile Fay La Sueur), 21, cinemactress; in Manhattan. Said Fairbanks: "Our affair was a sweet and romantic one." Too busy to honeymoon, they returned to Hollywood to resume work. Neither has been married before.

DIED: Jeanne Eagels, 35, legitimactress, cinemactress; in Manhattan; of an overdose of chloral hydrate. At a private sanitarium, to which she had gone in haste for a neural treatment, she took off her coat, sat down on a bed, fell over dead. On her body policemen found some $300,000 worth of jewelry. After trooping with tent shows, she reached Manhattan in 1911. Meteoric was her success as Sadie Thompson in Somerset Maugham's *Rain* (1922), which ran for some five years.

MARRIED: John Dos Passos, 33, author (*Three Soldiers, Manhattan Transfer*), and a Miss Kate Smith; at Ellsworth, Me. Because to him the married state is not an awesome thing, he did not publicize his wedding, could not remember exactly when it happened.

MISCELLANY

In Manhattan, Professor Huber, manager of a troupe of fleas, conducted his performers from a burning building to the street with the loss of only one, J. Caesar, who did the gladiatorial act. Said a bystander to Professor Huber: "You must treat them gently to make them so obedient." Said he: "They're artists. I treat 'em gentle or I treat 'em rough according to their nature."

In Louise, Ky., Hardy Hay, 60, farmer-nominee for a county office, set out astride his mule to canvass for votes. For a week his family waited his return. On the eighth day the mule appeared, riderless. A posse set out, hunted two counties, finally found the body at the bottom of a 30-foot cliff. On a scrap of paper dated a week before, Farmer Hay had written how he fell over the cliff, broke his thigh, despaired of help. In the last paragraph was his will.

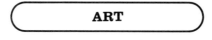

ART

HAVEMEYER COLLECTION: For some time past, the bouquets FEB. 4
hurled in the direction of the Metropolitan Museum of Art
have been of the variety vulgarly known as Irish. Harsh
words have been spoken, epithets employed. Among the
multifarious ailments reported has been the predominance
of academic works, the paucity of moderns. Last fortnight
the Metropolitan found itself raised to unexpected glory
when it inherited the famed H.O. Havemeyer collection,
which includes, besides masterpieces of earlier schools, the
very finest specimens of French impressionism. This single
gift, valued at many millions, is perhaps the greatest contribution the Metropolitan ever received.

When Louisine Waldron Elder was a young girl, she liked
pictures. Particularly did she like pictures by Edgar Degas of
bedraggled and rhythmic danseuses stretching their weary ten-
dons upon the ballet rack, pirouetting with a one, two, three
and a *pas-de-bas.* Louisine saved her pin money, watched it
swell to $100, took her hoard to Mary Cassatt who bought
for her a Degas, the first to enter an American collection.
"I sadly needed that money," said Degas.

In 1883, Louisine Waldron Elder married Henry Osborne
Havemeyer (American Sugar Refining Co.) and started to
collect pictures in earnest. A few years later, she could walk
into her private museum, gaze upon Veronese, Rembrandt,
Hals, Rubens, El Greco, Goya, Monet, Manet, Renoir,
Corot, Cézanne, Mary Cassatt and Degas.

On Jan. 6, 1929, Mrs. Havemeyer died. To the Metropolitan Museum were bequeathed all objects in the collection
except Persian potteries which were given to her son, Horace
Havemeyer. Frequently in the past, Mrs. Havemeyer gave or
loaned pieces from her collections, always, however, with
the stipulation that her name be not mentioned.

DUVEEN ON DA VINCI: "The right eye is dead," said Sir FEB. 18
Joseph Duveen, dolefully. "Dead," he intoned, "very dead."

Sir Joseph Duveen casts doubts on a reputed masterpiece (right).

"La Belle Ferronière." A Leonardo— not a copy with a "dead" eye?

Surely Leonardo da Vinci had never painted a "dead" eye. But there was another consideration: if the jury should decide that Leonardo *had* been the painter, Sir Joseph's remarks might cost him $500,000.

During the War, Capt. Harry J. Hahn, Kansas City auto salesman, met and married Mlle. Andree Lardoux. Her dowry property included a painting of a gentle faced brunette that had been acquired by the Lardoux family from an aide of Napoleon Bonaparte. In the Louvre was the famed *La Belle Ferronière* (The Blacksmith's Daughter), most often attributed to Leonardo and almost identical with the Lardoux portrait. In 1916, George Sortais, French connoisseur had pronounced the Lardoux painting in writing to be the work of Leonardo. Thus his dictum implied that Leonardo had painted this subject twice. Actually, apart from dogmatic critical opinions, there was no evidence that Leonardo had painted either *Belle*.

In 1920 Captain Hahn took his wife and her picture to Kansas City. The Kansas City art museum favored the reputed Leonardo. A sale seemed likely; the price, of course, would be in six figures. None heard the rumors more quickly than stalwart, ruddy Sir Joseph Duveen, who is unquestionably the most potent name in art marts of both hemispheres. When asked for his opinion of the Lardoux painting, Sir Joseph's crisp moustache twitched and his mobile eyebrows performed a scornful ascension. "The picture," he declared, "is a copy." The Kansas City museum did not buy the painting. Mrs. Hahn sued Sir Joseph for $500,000 libel.

Then for eight years the trial was held in abeyance while both sides collected ammunition. Expert minions of Sir Joseph and Mrs. Hahn went to the Louvre, peered, compared, microphotographed, gathered historical data. Back to Sir Joseph came favorable reports. Back to Mrs. Hahn came favorable reports. Her experts were rumored to have discovered telltale thumbprints. (Left-handed Leonardo often rubbed his pigments with his curiously burned right hand.)

Last week the trial began. The jury was chosen for its ignorance of Leonardo. On an easel stood the Lardoux painting. For the first few days Sir Joseph was constantly in the witness box. First salvo for the prosecution was a statement of intent: "We hope to show that Sir Joseph has a strangle hold on the picture business. He is the man who is going to sell all the paintings." Sir Joseph volleyed: "The neck [of the painting's subject] is a clumsy cylinder of flesh." He pointed to "poor" shadows, "faulty construction, faulty anatomy."

As the trial wore on, the absence of absolute evidence grew obvious. There was a deadlock between the connoisseur, foiled by the need to express nebulous impressions in concrete language, and the shrewd lawyer, facetiously impaling but hampered by lack of the factual material of law. To some spectators it seemed wise to let Leonardo da Vinci lie quietly in his undiscovered grave by the sunny river Loire; to sell pictures for whatever they may bring.

A HUNG JURY: After 21 days of trial, 590,000 words of testimony and 14 hours of deliberation by the jury, the Manhattan trial of Sir Joseph Duveen came to naught. The jury deadlocked at nine votes for Mrs. Hahn, three for Sir Joseph. Mrs. Hahn had been unable to prove that her heirloom painting was a Leonardo, or that Sir Joseph was guilty of slander when he pronounced it only a graceless copy. He, on the other hand had failed to impress the jury with his opinions, could not feel the pride appropriate to an international art tycoon. MARCH 11

MEXICO'S RIVERA: In Mexico it is wise to carry a pistol. Most Mexicans do it. In Mexico City there is a man who MAY 6 stands, peaceably enough, on a scaffold and paints pictures of his countrymen on walls and ceilings. Sometimes even he carries a pistol, a very large one with a commensurate cartridge belt. But this pistol is not a weapon. It is an artist's symbol.

Artist Diego Rivera believes in revolution, so he dresses the part. He is, however, no ferocious cinema "greaser." He is genial, cultured, industrious. His repute grew when last week he was awarded the annual Fine Arts Medal of the American Institute of Architects. Artist Rivera's concept of revolution has nothing to do with bombshells. It might be described as a patient communism, and it is reflected in his art. For him, art is a proletarian function, growing out of the hot little huts of *peons,* expressing their lives.

His frescoes are devoted to the laborer, miner, country school teacher, market place, burial, festival, harvest, battle. Most of his work is a sympathetic tale told with figures that have the bare graphic form of Giotto and the incandescent coloring of the South. Now in his 40's, he was born in a mining town. His middle-class parents gave him Spanish and Aztec blood. Like most young artists, he looked first to the Old World, lived in Paris, married a Russian. He returned to Mexico shortly after the Obregon government came into power. The government, socialist-labor, saw the virtue of popular art, commissioned native artists to decorate government buildings in a way that peons could understand. Diego Rivera has emerged as a leader.

Like Michelangelo in the Sistine Chapel, he mounts his scaffold and paints, as the fresco process demands, directly on the wall. A huge man, he sometimes works 16 hours without ceasing. Once, overcome from exhaustion, he toppled, split his head. He delights in inviting lady lionizers to help him work. He uses a collection of jars and tin cans filled with paint for a palette, mixes his colors on a tin plate. He has refused lavish offers from the Russian government for paintings in Moscow. His religion is completely unorthodox, a private affair. He believes in People, and their ghosts.

JULY 22 **DEATH OF HENRI:** As it must to all men, Death came last week to Robert Henri (pronounced Hen-Rye), 64, outstanding U.S. artist. Robert Henri was not an elegant, sensational painter like the late John Singer Sargent, nor a trenchant controversialist. Insurgent, he did not crusade. He taught instead. In his insistence on vision rather than style lay his greatness as a teacher. His protegés included Rockwell Kent and the late great George Bellows. "Every stave in a picket fence," he wrote, "should be drawn with wit, the wit of one who sees each stave as new evidence about the fence. The staves should not repeat each other. A new fence is stiff, but it doesn't stand long before there is movement through it, which is the trace of its life experience."

NATIVE SCHOOL: Critics have said that the most artistically SEPT. 2 significant things in U.S. architecture are not skyscrapers or state capitols but grain elevators, barns, oil-cracking stills. Because the grain elevator is not plastered with irrelevant decoration, because the barn was not preconceived in Paris or Athens, because these buildings are simple, sincere and to-the-point, they are Good.

Now Condé Nast, eastern smartchart publisher (*House & Garden, Vogue, Vanity Fair*) has promised $2,500 per year for three years for unique traveling fellowships—unique because the students of architecture will do all their traveling, not among European chalets, châteaux and cathedrals, but in the U.S. among barns, grain elevators, oil-cracking plants.

MODERN MUSEUM: Like a great mausoleum the Metropol- SEPT. 16 itan Museum of Art is full of many tombs—tombs of Egyptian Pharaohs, of exalted bric-a-brac, of Art. In the art tombs are laid away examples of the work of the great painters and sculptors of other times. Progressive artists throughout the East have long given up hope of modernity in the Metropolitan. Few of them ever visit its vaults. Scathingly they view it only as a trysting place for shop-girls and their beaux, a shelter for nurse-girls and babies on rainy days, a "point of interest" for out-of-towners.

Last week art circles were stirred by news that Manhattan is to have a U.S. Luxembourg. (The Luxembourg in Paris is a testing ground for pictures. After ten years a picture *may* be transferred to the august Louvre.) A committee of art collectors and patrons planned and announced a Museum of Modern Art, to open in October. The committee has leased a gallery-sized room. For two years they will show the pictures of contemporary European, Mexican and U.S.

painters and sculptors. Then the Modern Museum plans to build its own building. Pledged for generous donations are many patrons who are waiting to see "if the thing is a success."

OCT. 7   **GENIUS, INC:** Strange and condoned has been the existence of Architect Frank Lloyd Wright. Erotic and impulsive, he deserted his wife and six children to live with a Mrs. Mamah Bostwick Cheney and her two children, family of a Chicago businessman. For himself and them he built a splendidly original home on a rocky hill at Spring Green, southern Wisconsin. A thin-lipped Barbados Negro, their butler, one day chopped Mistress Cheney, her children and four neighbors to death with an axe and burned down the house. When Architect Wright rebuilt it, Miriam Noel, English sculptress who had fallen in love with his picture, joined him first as mistress, then as wife. She left for a "vacation" and her husband promptly took an ad interim companion. There followed divorce, his marriage to a Montenegrin dancer, a second burning of his hill house, a third rebuilding thereof. *Who's Who In America* this year dropped him from its roster of reputable notables.

Widely condoned have such episodes been, for Frank Lloyd Wright is rated a very great and original architect, although personally impulsive and improvident. Last week certain of his Chicago friends decided that they could at least overcome his improvidence. They made him become an institution with a charter. Frank Lloyd Wright, Inc. has issued $50,000 worth of preferred stock. He himself is no stockholder.

Architect Wright was born in 1869 on a Wisconsin farm where he spent his childhood tending sheep. With no formal education he informally studied engineering at the University of Wisconsin. Although he received no degree he became unusually proficient in that profession and twenty years ago his reputation in architecture was world-wide.

The basic philosophies of his buildings are: 1) They, especially homes, should be constructed as integral parts of their landscapes and of the materials of the neighborhood. His thrice-built home at Spring Green [called "Taliesin"] seemed a rocky outcropping of the hill itself: 2) Buildings should interpret the spirit as well as suit the use of their occupancies. This has created blocky, mechanistic, "modernistic" structures. His best hotel is the Imperial at Tokyo, famed for octagonal copper bathtubs and "skyscraper" furniture. People for whom he builds homes yield to his artistic bullying.

RIMA: Wandering in a haunted Venezuelan jungle, a natu- OCT. 21
ralist once heard a trilling note, birdlike, clear, unearthly. He sought its source for days, but it always eluded him. One day by accident he came upon the triller. It was Rima, a bird-girl. In his famed *Green Mansions*, Novelist William Henry Hudson described the graceful Rima thus: "Her figure and features were singularly delicate. . . ."

In 1925, three years after Novelist Hudson died, London bird-lovers dedicated to his memory a bird-sanctuary decorated by Sculptor Jacob Epstein, situated in Hyde Park. Sculptor Epstein's panel represented Rima, arms outstretched, succoring two birds of prey. But to the consternation of the bird-lovers and the embarrassment of then Prime Minister Stanley Baldwin who unveiled the statue, Epstein's Rima was a strange, bovine character with tremendous, sagging muscles. She was called grotesque, horrible. The protests culminated in a student uprising in which the bird-girl was painted green. Londoners today point out with chagrin her quiet nook, declare she "scares the birds away." Last fortnight a London "bobby" noticed something amiss. Rima was almost invisible beneath tar and feathers.

Sculptor Jacob Epstein and his "Rima." She was called grotesque and horrible at her unveiling, and now some protestor has tarred and feathered her.

NOV. 11   **MODIGLIANI'S MODE:** From the death of Michelangelo to the present day, good Italian painting has been practically non-existent. But in 1884, a sickly boy was born in the Ghetto at Leghorn, Tuscany, to Flaminio Modigliani, son of a Roman usurer. The boy was named Amedeo which means "love of God." When he was 14 he had typhoid fever and in his delirium raved about his longing to become a painter. His mother, impressed, promised that he should go to art school.

In 1906, after a few years of study with mediocre landscapists, Modigliani went to Paris where he delved into the cubism and Negro sculpture which preoccupied his new friends, Picasso, Matisse, Derain and Braque. He became alcoholic and consumptive, affected voluminous trousers, a gay scarf, a wide-brimmed black hat. He was known as the poorest man in Paris. Meanwhile he painted steadily and achieved a personal style.

When the War broke out in 1914, Modigliani coughed too much to be drafted. He stayed all night in the cafés, sketching for drinks. When an unusual cold wave struck in December 1920 he died of influenza with the words "Cara, cara, Italia!" (Dear, dear Italy) on his lips. A few days later his mistress threw herself from a window.

Friends of the painter wired his brother in Italy that he had died a pauper. The reply was: "Bury him as a prince." Modigliani was carried to his grave by the celebrities of Paris.

Last week in Manhattan the first one-man show of Modigliani was held. Among the 37 canvases, mostly portraits of his Paris friends, was his last canvas, a large nude. The aura of respectability at the exhibition might have amused the little, consumptive painter. People who would not have been seen talking with him now pay $20,000 for his canvases, eulogize him as a great genius. In his day derisive fingers were pointed at the elongated necks, piggy eyes, distorted sloping shoulders characteristic of the Modigliani manner. Laymen's fingers are still pointed. Others admit the distortion but defend it by saying that the Egyptians distorted, as did El Greco. The merits of Modigliani, they add, are many: his color is finely schematic; his line is sensitive and delineates the sitter's character with wit and insight; his best canvases show the feeling of a real primitive.

MUSIC

AGAIN, MASTER MENUHIN: No child prodigy today can rival JAN. 7 in fame young Yehudi Menuhin, 11-year-old violinist. A year ago he went East from California, astounded Manhattan with his masterly conception of the Beethoven concerto. Last week he went again, again played with the Philharmonic Orchestra, this time the Tschaikovsky concerto. Although now he plays on a full-sized fiddle and has a reputation which might well be the envy of many a full-sized fiddler, his performance last week suffered in comparison with the younger Yehudi's. As before, critics marked his amazing virtuosity, but many detected signs of a precocious vice: striving for effect.

SEGOVIA'S RETURN: Andrès Segovia is to the guitar what Casals is to the cello, Kreisler to the violin. Last year his U.S. début was one of the major events of the season. Last week he played again, without accompaniment, music by Händel, Bach, Haydn, Albeniz, with such skill and understanding as to hold his Manhattan audience rapt.

ROSE CAVALIER: Richard Strauss' *Der Rosenkavalier* has be- JAN. 14 come for many one of the world's great operas. One reason why performances of it are rare in the U.S. is that it is hard to find among the eccentric ranks of the sopranos any who are capable of filling, but not bursting, the trousers of the handsome Count Octavian, who masquerades as a woman through much of the action and is thus played by a woman. There is one such at the Metropolitan, the great Jeritza; but she, uncomfortable in trousers, does not like the rôle.

Who, then, last week, was to sing *Rosenkavalier*, already once postponed, when Soprano Greta Stueckgold fell sick? Who but Jeritza, although she had already been billed for the first *Carmen* of the season. She asserted that if the Metropolitan found suitable costumes she would be Count Octavian. Manager Gatti Casazza rubbed his hands with happiness. Wardrobe Mistress Pangoni put pins in her mouth and took up shears. Jeritza stood impatiently, while the pretty but uneasy clothes of the count grew up around her like the scaffolding of a superlative statue. "I like to show Gatti I can work," she said. She sang *Rosenkavalier* one evening, prowling happily through Strauss' high notes. The next afternoon she was Carmen.

Maria Jeritza (with wardrobe mistress) dons pants for "Rosenkavalier."

Walter Gieseking: tall, hulking, bold and great.

FEB. 4 **GIESEKING:** A tall, hulking man walked on to the stage at Carnegie Hall last week, bent himself into an awkward bow at the piano, and played superbly Bach's Partita No. 2, three Scarlatti sonatas, Schumann's C Major Fantasia and the first book of Debussy preludes. He was Walter Gieseking, come from Germany for another extended tour.

Three seasons have passed since Gieseking made an inconspicuous début in Aeolian Hall. "His European notices were so superlative," said Manager Charles Wagner afterward, "I knew no one would believe them so I decided to let his music speak for itself." His music spoke so eloquently that Sunday afternoon that members of the audience told their friends. No one had ever played Bach like Gieseking, and they rhapsodized over an amazing technic, a style that was as fluent and easy as it was immaculate. His Debussy was surely the essence of poetry. He is, critics say unanimously, a great musician.

Many a first name has been dropped with fame. Kreisler needs no Fritz for identification, no Mister for his dignity. Neither does Paderewski need his Ignaze Jan, nor Gieseking now his Walter. He practices little because once after a long tramp through the Alps he found he played just as well without having touched a piano for six weeks. Now he memorizes much of his music away from the piano. He does not smoke, play cards or eat butter. He is 33, quite bald, and the father of a 17-months-old daughter named Jutta.

"LES NOCES" —Igor Fedorovitch Stravinsky is always "good MAY 6 box-office." Last week his half-hour ballet, *Les Noces* (first U.S. production) drew a $25,000 audience to the Metropolitan Opera House. Stravinsky's power of attraction lies in his reputation for being "primitive." He is "primitive" no longer; but *Les Noces* is a perfect example of what used to be meant by that term.

Written for percussion instruments, piano, four soloists and a chorus, it was given last week under the enthusiastic baton of Philadelphia Conductor Leopold Anton Stanislaw Stokowski. On one side of the stage a bride is being prepared for her wedding night, her long hair is being combed. On the other one sees the anointing of the groom. Then comes the departure of the bride, to the lamenting of her parents. Finally the nuptial celebration described by Conductor Stokowski in the program note: "Svacha takes off bridal veil. . . . Father of bride strikes bride with whip (ancient ritual, symbol of submission) and then passes whip to groom. Girls and bride dance to ancient folk-song—the whole company becomes increasingly intoxicated. . . . Groom strikes bride with whip (symbol of possession). Bride and groom embrace. . . . Father of bride sings the final eloquent phrase, interrupted by bell-like crashes from the orchestra."

ROBESON'S RETURN: A big, bronze-colored man, magnifi- NOV. 18 cently built, scrupulously dressed, walked on the stage in Manhattan's Carnegie Hall last week and waited quietly for his audience to settle. Then he began in a voice the color of his skin to sing "I Got a Home on a Rock, Don' You See." It was Paul Robeson, athlete-actor-baritone, making his first U.S. appearance after a three-year absence in Europe.

The youngest son of a schoolteaching mother and a Methodist minister, he was educated first in the public schools of Princeton, N.J. His record won him a scholarship at nearby Rutgers College. An average of over 90% in all his studies won him a Phi Beta Kappa key in his junior year. He was considered Rutgers' best debater. He won his R in football, baseball, basketball and track. The late Coach Walter Camp called him the "greatest defensive end that ever trod the gridiron."

Paul Robeson meant to be a lawyer. He took a two-year course at Columbia, earned his degree. During that period, however, he performed in a Y.M.C.A. play which Playwright Eugene O'Neill happened to attend. O'Neill went backstage and begged Robeson to act in *Emperor Jones*. Robeson consented, made a name as a big actor. Singing came naturally then; his voice had always been splendidly full and smooth. In 1925, he gave his first recital of spirituals—another success. Then he went abroad.

Paris, Berlin, Vienna, Prague, Budapest all hailed his concerts. Famed were his performances in *Show Boat* in London. Because he was a Negro, he was asked not to enter the Hotel Savoy dining-room. He handled the situation with grace and dignity.

Robeson's returning recital was a modest repetition of spirituals he had sung before—"Water Boy," "Joshua Fit

Paul Robeson, athlete-actor-baritone with a voice of bronze.

Arturo Toscanini. He warns Stokowski not to catch cold. Page 182.

de Battle ob Jericho." Critics complained, as in 1925, that such a program tends to monotony, that Robeson's range is too limited to offset it. But the lay audience received him ecstatically. In January he returns to London to play the Moor in Shakespeare's *Othello*.

MAESTROS: Last week one of Arturo Toscanini's concerts DEC. 2 with Manhattan's Philharmonic-Symphony Orchestra was attended by Leopold Stokowski, conductor of the Philadelphia Symphony, who went backstage to congratulate Toscanini during intermission. The Italian is near-sighted. He peered blankly at his famed Polish visitor, who said:

"Don't you recognize me, Maestro? I am Stokowski."

Said Toscanini: "Then put on your hat or you'll catch cold."

ITURBI: During recent years Spain has sent the U.S. many an expert musician. 'Cellist Pablo Casals and Soprano Lucrezia Bori led the procession. And now comes José Iturbi, famed throughout Europe and South America as Spain's greatest pianist. Sailing up Manhattan harbor on his arrival, Iturbi wept. He went to a hotel chosen for him by his manager, rang for tea. But, knowing no English, he failed to make the waiter understand. Shrugging his shoulders, Iturbi sat down at the piano, played *Tea for Two*, got what he wanted. When Iturbi finished his recital at Carnegie Hall, no one left. Many rushed forward to watch his square fingers more closely, called for encore after encore. The Brahms technical difficulties were topped at a speed which was never bewildering. Debussy, despite its mistiness, had structure, clarity.

Now that he is a success, there will accompany him on tour the kind of press stories the public most eagerly devours. Many will be interested to know now that he spent his first Manhattan night in a Harlem cabaret listening to brazen jazz which he adores, that he likes apples, oysters, caviar, plays good tennis, boxes, dances, does subtle imitations of Charlie Chaplin, Lon Chaney and Pianist George Gershwin.

EDUCATION

MAY 6 **AGE IGNORED:** Last January, Robert Maynard Hutchins was 30. Last week he was made President of the University of Chicago. Going from Yale, where he is Dean of the Law School, he will duplicate and improve upon the feat of Chicago's first President, William Rainey Harper, who made the same journey for the same purpose at the age of 35. (Other famed young college Presidents: the late Dr. Charles William Eliot, President of Harvard at 35; Dr. Clarence Cook Little, President of the University of Michigan at 37; Dr. Glenn Frank, President of the University of Wisconsin at 38.)

A normal prodigy, neatly dressed in New Haven-tailored suits and plain neckties, Robert Maynard Hutchins was made Secretary of Yale University in 1923, while he was still in law school. Then he said: "I get so sick of hearing that I am young. I wish that I would suddenly grow up and get bald-headed. People come into my office and when they see me they laugh. President Angell said that Yale had robbed the cradle to get a secretary, and I replied that I wanted every one to know that I had a birthday last week and am now 24 years old."

Last week he was saying: "It is difficult being so young and presiding over men much older and more experienced. But I have gone ahead ignoring my youth and generally there is nothing to remind me of it except occasions like this when there is nothing much to be said except that I am only 30."

Ignoring his youth will be more than ever necessary for President Hutchins of Chicago. He will command educational machinery used by nearly 15,000 students. Physically the University is among the hugest in the U.S. In the libraries are stacked more than 1,150,000 books. Last fiscal year its assets were $77,812,221.26. Looming in the University's financial background are Julius Rosenwald and John D. Rockefeller, Jr.

PRAISED FOR SNOBBERY: The mellow pathos of commence- JUNE 10
ment tide, the sentimental verbiage of commencement
speeches were missing last week at the Massachusetts Institute of Technology. At a graduating class banquet Prof.
Robert Emmons Rogers arose and shattered whatever mood
of revery or reminiscence was present.

"I am going to talk to you," said he, "on the necessity
of being a snob . . . a gentleman belonging to the ruling
class. You have got to take the rule away from the bootlegger, the politician and the man who came up from one
suspender button. Put on a front. One of the reasons for
Harvard's greatness [Professor Rogers was a Harvard graduate, class of 1909] is that in all her 300 years she has put
on a big front. Harvard never apologizes, never argues, never
listens to criticism, but goes on calmly putting on her front
and gets publicity for that very reason. What applies to the
corporation applies also to the individual. You cannot go
on the assumption that you are as good as the rest of folks.
You should take the attitude that you are a damned sight
better."

*Robert Hutchins, a university president   J. P. Morgan, caught munching a
at age 30. Page 183.   bun at his 40th Harvard reunion.*

REUNION: Most prominent of U.S. college graduates who JULY 1
did not attend their June college reunions was President
Hoover. Citizen Calvin Coolidge marched in the Amherst
commencement parade last week, and Banker John Pierpont

Morgan, who last fortnight was given a Princeton honorary LL.D, returned to Harvard for the 40th reunion of his class. He lunched with President Abbott Lawrence Lowell at a private table in the "yard," was caught by a cameraman munching a bun. Banker Morgan, eschewing costume, wore a black cutaway, grey trousers, panama hat. He left early to board his huge black yacht, the *Corsair*, to go and inspect his new 343-foot yacht, a-building at Bath, Maine.

The distinction of having Banker Morgan among its visitors mitigated and contrasted with the ignominy of another Harvard occurrence last week. The Senior class had elected one Edward Fuller Fitzhugh, Jr. of Boise, Idaho, to write the Baccalaureate hymn. That was a sad selection. Poet Fitzhugh wrote four quatrains of lofty, Harvardian sentiment to be sung to the tune of "Ancient of Days." The lines were published. Not until then, last week, was it discovered that the first letters of the lines in each quatrain spelled a four-letter word. Amid guffaws and embarrassment, Author Fitzhugh was expelled. Said he: "I guess I never did grow up."

DEC. 16 **GOUCHER'S DIGNITY:** "At the homes of friends, according to the will of the hostess," at resorts to which young Baltimore men friends escort them, privily, by stealth, Goucher College girls have usually smoked if they wanted to. Keeping in stride with other pragmatic women's colleges, last week Acting President Hans Froelicher announced that as long as smoking did not "interfere with routine class work" or create fire hazards, henceforth Goucher girls might smoke when, where and as much as they pleased. Said he: "It was found that enforcement of the rule required snooping and tattling, incompatible with the dignity of the college."

RELIGION

BATTLE OF THE BOOTHS: General Bramwell Booth of the FEB. 25
Salvation Army was quick to appreciate the talents of Edward John Higgins. The Higgins rise to power was therefore swift-winged. In the U.S. he helped Commissioner Evangeline Booth (the General's sister). In China he helped natives. Ten years ago he started helping the General most efficiently. Today he *is* General. Unfortunately, so is General Booth.

In England last week gathered the High Council of the Salvation Army. Their faces were dolorous for they were going to depose General Booth [who was too old and ill in their view to continue his leadership]. They had done it once before and it had done no good. This time they meant to mean business.

The General's daughter, Catherine Booth, was there hoping for speeches and emotion. But the High Council was grimly silent. Sister Evangeline Booth also was there. She had often toyed with the idea of being herself elected General. But when the Council elected Commissioner Higgins she was not disappointed. General Booth has worn no other suit but the Salvation Army uniform for 54 years. It seemed likely last week that he would battle to the last court not to change his clothes.

PASSOVER: There should never be starch in napkins, dresses, MAY 13
shirts, for starch is *Chometz*, which is leaven. The night after the feast a father or a grandfather may tell the little ones to say only half their prayers, for that night "God is nigh to his people." Thus may begin the holy feast of the Passover, symbolic of liberty, memorial to the exodus, and to the night when the Lord's angel slew the Egyptians' first-born but passed over and left unbereft the homes of the Israelites.

Throughout the world last week all Jews celebrated the last day of the Passover feast. In New York City homes, where live nearly half the U.S. Jews, unleavened bread (now largely made commercially) was eaten and the ancient ceremonies were observed in huge, modern temples. Looming in the minds of good Jews was the distracting thought that William Henry Cardinal O'Connell, dean of U.S. cardinals, had criticized and darkly accused today's foremost Jew, Dr. Albert Einstein.

Said his eminence: "What does all this worked-up enthusiasm about Einstein mean? I have never met a man yet who understands in the least what Einstein is driving at. . . . I very seriously doubt that Einstein himself really knows what he is driving at. . . . In a word, the outcome of this doubt and befogged speculation about time and space is a cloak beneath which hides the ghastly apparition of atheism."

Last fortnight Dr. Einstein indirectly answered the Cardinal, declared his religion in a cable to Rabbi Herbert S. Goldstein of Manhattan. Said Dr. Einstein, "I believe in Spinoza's God, who reveals himself in the orderly harmony of what exists, not in a God who concerns himself with fates and actions of human beings."

Jews were not altogether comforted by the Einstein reply. Some recalled that Spinoza had been excommunicated by the Jewish Orthodox Church. The Holy Roman Catholic Church officially condemned as heresy his writings. In the Bronx, Rabbi Jacob Katz thundered: "Cardinal O'Connell would have done well had he not attacked the Einstein theory. Einstein would have done better had he not proclaimed his non-belief in a God who is concerned with fates and actions of individuals. Both have handed down dicta outside their jurisdiction." Less bitter Rabbis pointed out that although Spinoza had once been called "this famous atheist," he had also been called the "God-intoxicated man," that time has now granted reverence to his name, that to believe in his philosophy might not mean to deny the God of Israel.

AUG. 19 **"SCANDAL, DISGRACE":** The Protestant church is not only split by sectarianism, but suffers the further weakness of conflict between the sects. Many Protestant preachers realize this but avoid the subject as unpleasant. Many others are busy adding to the confusion. Not so Dr. Harry Emerson Fosdick, curly-headed, fat-cheeked, dynamic pastor of Manhattan's Park Avenue Baptist Church. Last week he made one of the direct, unequivocal remarks which distinguish him from so many divines, which fill his church to overflowing. "Our Protestant denominationalism," he said, "with over 150 sects in the U.S., has become utterly obsolete, so far as modern significance is concerned, and is now a public scandal and disgrace!"

"CONSTRUCTIVE CHRISTIANITY": Horse-racing is a multi- SEPT. 2
million-dollar industry in Kentucky. When, in 1923, reformers threatened the industry by trying to repeal the law legalizing parimutuel betting, the industry's chief defendant was no julep-sipping blue grass gentleman, no raucous paddock tout, but the Rev. Thomas Leven Settle, rector of the Church of the Good Shepherd (Episcopalian) of Lexington. The Legislature, awed by the unfamiliar spectacle of a churchman defending racing, listened to his arguments that repeal of the law would result in worse evils, and were convinced.

At the time, the Church of the Good Shepherd was small, its congregation nondescript. Soon subscriptions for a new church came from grateful horsemen in all parts of the country. At Saratoga Springs, N.Y., a blooded horse was auctioned, the proceeds donated to Dr. Settle. In Lexington, turfmen deserted conservative churches they had attended all their lives, went to the beautiful new $225,000 edifice.

Last week the rich congregation heard that Dr. Settle was resigning. He was going back in the mountains to the little

Evangeline Booth wanted to be a Salvation Army general. Page 186.   *The Rev. Settle of Kentucky, the Parson who saved horse-racing.*

mining town of Harlan. Already he had aided Harlan by raising $9,000 toward a new $18,000 church. The bishop had agreed to let him go. Explaining, the Parson Who Saved Horse-Racing said: "It means a real sacrifice but has great opportunities for constructive Christianity. The future of the State lies in the mountains of Kentucky. Our church must bear its part in the development."

SEPT. 23 **CHESTERTON v. WELLS:** England's three greatest publicists are George Bernard Shaw, Gilbert Keith Chesterton and Herbert George Wells. At a Roman Catholic Congress in London last week, Mr. Chesterton [a staunch Catholic] ignored Shaw's recent sarcastic statements concerning sex and elected to assail Mr. Wells, evolutionist. "An atheist," he boomed, "is much more difficult to emancipate than anyone else because he is, above all people, the narrowest and most completely captive." But Mr. Wells was not even an atheist, explained Mr. Chesterton. He is merely anti-Christian, which requires less logic, courage or consistency than being an atheist. "They [the Wells type of thinkers] talk about believing in a purpose in things and tell you they don't believe in a divine person in whom a purpose resides. I cannot imagine anything like a purpose wandering around the world without any person to belong to. H. G. Wells used a phrase like this: 'Life will use me for its purpose.' That appears to me exactly like a man jumping from the top of Westminster Cathedral and saying, 'The force of gravity will use me.'"

SEPT. 30 **JIM CROW RECTOR:** If an Alabamian refused to admit Negroes to a public meeting he would surprise nobody. Neither would a Virginian who refused to attend a church where Negroes were worshipping. Last week in Brooklyn the Rev. William St. John Blackshear, Texas-born rector, asked Negro members of his Congregation to go elsewhere to church. A lot of people were surprised.

"The Episcopal Church provides churches for Negroes," he read out from his pulpit. "Several of these churches are within easy reach of this locality. Therefore, the rector of this parish discourages the attendance or membership in this church of members of that race." As the startling words fell, embarrassed white members of the congregation looked from the corners of their eyes at the Negroes. One young

Negress hurried out of the church crying into her handkerchief.

Son of a cotton planter, Mr. Blackshear became Rector of St. Matthew's Protestant Episcopal Church in Brooklyn last June. The congregation knew that he had been trained at the Virginia Theological Seminary and had done graduate work at Oxford and Harvard, that he was a captain in the War, cited for bravery. What they did not realize was that like any true southerner Mr. Blackshear believes Negro and white civilization can at the best be parallel, never equal.

First and most vehement of the subsequent protests was made to the Vestry of the church by the National Association for the Advancement of Colored People. An open letter said: "For them to be publicly and insultingly expelled is not only contrary to the teachings of Christianity but is a gross violation of . . . common decency and courtesy. If it has your sanction, God help you!"

The Rev. Blackshear of Brooklyn asks his Negro members to go elsewhere.

The late Priest Power. His grave is credited with miracles. Page 192.

Bishop Ernest Milmore Stires of Long Island was pained, but explained that the Episcopal Church leaves the individual parish practically autonomous. He declined to express any public opinion except this: "Personally I have the greatest affection and a warm paternal feeling for our colored brethren."

Rector Blackshear stuck to his announcement. Reasons he gave were: "I do not wish to take support from the two churches for colored people in the neighborhood. In these congregations Negroes can develop their power of leadership, whereas in white congregations they are bound to be subdued."

A particularly irate objector was Columnist Heywood Broun of the New York *Telegram*: "I have a grave suspicion that the Rev. Blackshear has somewhat mistaken his function. Seemingly he has begun to assume . . . that the Lord's house which he tends is one of the better country clubs. There is no record that Jesus Christ ever said, 'Suffer the little Caucasian children to come unto me.'"

The following Sunday only one of the five Negro members of Mr. Blackshear's congregation appeared. But nine new Negro faces were there. Six detectives eyed them suspiciously while Dr. Blackshear preached that "hate is the cancer of the soul." After the service the Negroes lingered, were congratulated by several white worshippers.

OCT. 7 **SUNDAY SCHOOL BIBLE:** When the patriarch Abraham was 99 years old the Lord told him that his wife, Sarah, would be the mother of nations. Hearing this, the patriarch fell upon his face, roared in laughter shouting: "Shall a child be born to him that is a hundred years old? And shall Sarah, that is ninety years old, bear?"

Last week the National Sunday School Union of Great Britain printed a Bible which gave what the Lord told Abraham but carefully omitted the aged man's merriment and doubt. Both Old and New Testament had been carefully revised and expurgated of all things that might bring evil thoughts to the young. Discussion now turns chiefly on how the editing has been done.

When Joseph was 17, to take another example, he was brought from Canaan into Egypt, sold to Potiphar, a captain of the guard. Then, during the warm, dry days when Potiphar was with his troops, his wife desired the lusty young slave, said to him, "Lie with me." When he refused and fled from the house, leaving his cloak in her hands, Potiphar's wife cried out that she had been attacked, caused Joseph to be jailed. Such is the story the Bible tells with artistic realism. Carefully the National Sunday School Union substituted "tempted him to do evil" rather than give the exact words of Potiphar's wife. Question: Does the substitution help?

MIRACLES IN MALDEN: Flocking, pushing, stepping on toes, NOV. 25 upsetting policemen, trampling shrubbery, scores of thousands of Roman Catholics moved in a long line which surged all week long—not to get into a football stadium, but to see and if possible touch the tombstone of a priest, the Rev. Father Patrick J. Power in Holy Cross Cemetery at Malden, Mass.

Father Power died at 25, some 60 years ago. About 30 years later rumors crept about that his grave held miraculous powers of healing.

Fortnight ago the rumors grew and flew. From all over came the sick, the halt, the blind, the faithful, the curious; also quick-lunch vendors, trinket peddlers, troublemakers. Boston's Mayor-elect James Michael Curley came with his son to kneel beside the shrine. The estimated audience last week was 250,000.

Many were the miraculous cures reported; many were the reports denied. Some allegations: Morris Goldstein, 14, paralyzed, walked for several yards. Vincent O'Neill, 7, born blind, cried: "I can see, grandma, I can see people!" Gardner Jackson, onetime chairman of the Sacco-Vanzetti defense, made investigations and reported that Vincent O'Neill was never stone-blind. Said his father, "He has a cataract over one eye. The other eye has perfect vision."

MALDEN'S MIRACLES: "Please do not kneel. Please, *please,* DEC. 2 PLEASE, lady, don't kneel there! Touch the stone and pass along. That's all that is necessary. Pray in the chapel. Move along, now. Move along. . . ."

All last week policemen on duty in Holy Cross Cemetery at Malden, Mass. had to keep moving the great throngs who came to touch the lowly tomb of Patrick J. Power. Attendance in the third week totalled well over a million. So overrun was the cemetery that other graves were sadly desecrated, other funerals made impossible. Finally, William Henry Cardinal O'Connell, Archbishop of Boston, twice a visitor to the grave, decided to call a halt. The gates of the cemetery would remain closed except for funerals, pending an investigation.

AERONAUTICS

JAN. 14 **QUESTION MARK:** Endless circles and arcs, endless glissandos of flight. Over Southern California droned the Fokker cabin monoplane *Question Mark*. At the dawn of the new year five U.S. Army flyers had swooped into the air from Los Angeles. Their resolve was to shatter all existing records for endurance flights, to stay in the air until men or engines succumbed. Experts had allowed their three Wright Whirlwind motors 400 flying hours before bearings splintered and poppet valves ceased to pop. The flyers seemed infallible.

Back and forth they swept. Every so often the *Question Mark* took on fuel. This required uncanny air jockeying. Only 15 feet directly above the *Question Mark* flew a fuelling plane. From this plane dangled a thin rubber hose. While the planes zoomed at 75 miles an hour, Lieut. Harry Halverson aboard the *Question Mark* reached out, grabbed the hose, thrust it into the tanks. Once there was bungling. Gasoline was spilt. Major Carl Spatz, the commander, was burned. [He later doubled the "a" and, as "Tooey" Spaatz, a four-star general, commanded the U.S. Air Force.] Lieut. Elwood Quesada was overcome by fumes. [Quesada became a lieutenant general and commanded the 9th Tactical Air Force in World War II.] Later a swinging rope conveyed Zinc oxide, balm for Major Spatz. Lieut. Quesada recovered. Other ropes were swung, provided oranges, oatmeal, coffee. The larder of the *Question Mark* was stocked at the start with roast chicken. Bridge was played, innumerable cigarets were smoked. One motor began spurting oil. Sergeant Roy Hooe pussyfooted along the slim runway leading to the spewing machine, did some windy tinkering.

The flyers broke the U.S. record for re-fuelled flight (37 hours, 15 min., 14 sec.). They broke the international re-fuelled flight records (61 hr., 7 min. set by Belgium in 1928). Shortly afterward fell the world's record for heavier-than-air sustained flight (65 hr., 31 min. set by Germany in 1928 without refuelling). There remained but two records to pass, that for lighter-than-air sustained flight (the French dirigible *Dixmude*: 118 hours, 41 min.) and the distance record (non-stop distance record of 4,475 miles set by Italy in 1928).

And so the *Question Mark* flew until the seventh day. On the seventh day it rested. After 150 hours, 40 minutes, 16 seconds aloft, the plane came to earth. Out of the fuselage stumbled the crew. For Quesada, a dish of ice cream; for Major Spatz, a shave; for them all and for the *Question Mark* the acclaim which they had won by snatching from the clouds all existing records.

"MISHAP": The reporters at Valbuena Field, Mexico City, knew that a colossal story was coming their way—in fact, well nigh into their laps. There in the air was the cabin monoplane *City of Wichita*, in which could only be Col. Charles Augustus Lindbergh and his fiancée, Anne Spencer Morrow. It was apparent from the naked axle on the right-hand side that the Colonel had lost a wheel. It was a story with a hundred possible endings, any of them momentous.

Col. Lindbergh circled above the field several times, making preparations. The windows were put down to avoid flying glass, and Col. Lindbergh undoubtedly packed cushions around Miss Morrow. On touching the ground, the plane ran along, neatly balanced on its one wheel, for a few seconds. Then the wheel-less axle struck the earth. The plane dragged 30 yards, suddenly flopped over on its back. Col. Lindbergh's right shoulder, dislocated five years ago in a parachute jump, was redislocated. Miss Morrow, though badly shaken, was uninjured.

Col. Lindbergh said: "It was a mishap, not an accident." Miss Morrow, perhaps without realizing it, gave out a long-sought-after tidbit of news when she said: "Augustus will speak for me." The cause of the accident was narrowed down to a cotter pin, which one of the mechanics at Valbuena Field had forgotten to replace after greasing the landing wheels that morning. The wheel, Col. Lindbergh said, fell off after a stop for luncheon.

Early next morning, Col. Lindbergh and Miss Morrow climbed into a small yellow biplane, made three short flights. Col. Lindbergh handled the plane deftly with his left hand. Again the press whooped for heroism, but the hero and all other airmen knew that he had merely taken the cure prescribed by the U.S. Army Air Service—that a pilot who has cracked up must make another flight at the first possible moment, to restore self-confidence. There was no need, however, for Miss Morrow to take the cure—except to be sporting and to do aviation a great and good turn.

Charles Lindbergh survives "a mishap, not an accident."

Amelia Earhart: "Women get more notice when they crash." Page 210.

APRIL 1 **ANTARCTIC WIND:** Commander Richard Evelyn Byrd sat sombrely in his snug Antarctic base last week, thinking of Laurence McKinley Gould, Harold J. June and Bernt Balchen, who the previous week had flown to the Rockefeller Mountains, 128 miles away. By radio they had reported their arrival there, then fallen silent for days. After dog teams had started for the mountains, Commander Byrd with Malcolm Hanson and Dean Smith chanced a flight to what disaster they knew not. They found the first party miserable but safe in a wind-ripped, snow-clogged tent. A 150 m.p.h. gale had blown their heavy plane away together with their radio set.

The men had hugged the ice, dug knives into it to keep from blowing away. "The wind bellowed and shrieked at us," wrote Harold June. "Pieces of snow, big lumps, began to hit us. They were pieces of packed snow from the mountain two miles away." At 150 m.p.h. (by their indicator) the wind sounded thin and high. It sucked at the plane, whirled her backwards for half a mile. The three men could only wait wet and miserable for rescue. It came.

DETROIT SHOW: At Detroit's second All-American Aircraft APRIL 15 Show last week, planes ranged from the tricky little Heath at $975 which only the best of pilots dare handle, to the $67,500 Fokker, for which, with its ornate fittings, Cadillac's President Lawrence P. Fisher just paid $75,000. In between were sturdy one and two-seater open cockpit monoplanes and biplanes. Most models, however, were "closed jobs."

Inherent stability is what every exhibitor claimed for his plane. As a safety factor practically every plane carried a stabilizing apparatus which might be fixed to prevent it from suddenly going into stall, tail spin, or nose dive. Another protective device fixed in most planes nowadays is a broad canvas belt to be strapped across the passenger's lap. It keeps him from being tossed out of an open plane and, in case of crash, from being hurled the length of the cabin. When necessary, he can unfasten the belt in less than one second.

AIRPORTS: Aviation still does not know what it requires in APRIL 29 fields. Flyers consider Croydon, near London, and the Tempelhof, near Berlin, at present the best equipped fields in the world. Croydon's chief merit is that planes have a 1,400 yd. runway in any direction. Practically all the field is grass-covered. This permits comfortable landings and takeoffs, except in rainy weather. Then the planes tear up the sod. To remedy that fault Croydon officials are considering putting a paved strip all around the field. Like so many U.S. airports, Croydon is far (12 mi.) from the centre of the community. But the English air lines provide comfortable automobiles between airport and metropolis.

EAGLE SPEAKS AGAIN: Col. Charles Lindbergh was induced to MAY 13 fly to Washington last week, to tell a joint committee of Congress what sort of airport the capital ought to have. Col. Lindbergh laid down the following specifications: 1) A field at least one mile square, having hard surface runways; 2) As near to the heart of the city as possible; 3) A good hotel and restaurant at the field; 4) Tunnels underground so that passengers could cross the field without danger of being run down. "We will be able to land on a field we cannot see," Lindbergh predicted. "Fog flying is hazardous now, but I expect that within the next few years we will be able to fly through almost any kind of weather. For landing we will, I think, be able to use intersecting radio beams, sonic altimeters and other instruments."

FASTER, FASTER: The night-flying transcontinental airmail got under way last week. On the new schedule, letters posted on either coast one evening are delivered at the opposite coast two mornings later. This has been made feasible by flood-lighting the route's western terminus, Oakland Municipal Airport. Until the Rockies were flown at night, the shortest air mail trip across the continent was performed in one day, one night, one day. Now it is done in one night, one day, one night—saving one business day.

MAY 27   **ON THE MAP:** Two years ago last Monday, Charles Augustus Lindbergh flew from New York to Paris. Before the flight, Lindbergh was a sober boy of 25, with four parachute drops from troubled planes as his outstanding feats. This week he is a serious young man, with character hardened against flattery and cajolery, intent on founding a family and consolidating his fortune.

The afflatus which he gave to U.S. aviation has in the two years become a mighty thing. A two-hundred-million-dollar air industry has developed. The air-mail has been systematized. Passenger traffic has become a more significant phenomenon than air-mail or air express. The first passenger in a heavier-than-air machine was one Charles Furnas, employe of the Wright Brothers. The longest air line and at present the only transcontinental one is the Boeing Air Transport. William Edward Boeing, 47, founded it. He entered the transport business to make money out of mail, express and passengers, but more especially to have sure buyers of the planes he was making at Seattle. He got into plane-making literally by accident. One day in 1917 he grew angry because his private plane cracked up with him. He decided that he could build better ones. A rich lumber and mining man, he could and did put vast wealth into the industry. His factory is now rated the largest in the U.S. devoted exclusively to the manufacture of airplanes. His transport systems are the largest in the world.

Appended is a timetable whereby the air traveler may calculate the distances, time, stops, costs of U.S. air journeying. Inspection has shown that schedules are closely kept.

U.S. AIR TIME TABLE

Route	Miles	Hours	Stops	Fare
Boston-New York	220	1:45	2	$25
New York-Washington	201	2:15	1	$30
Chicago-San Francisco	1,943	22:30	10	$200
Chicago-Salt Lake City	1,319	14:30	6	$146
San Francisco-Los Angeles	379	5:00	3	$45
Miami-Havana	261	2:15	1	$55
El Paso-Dallas	575	7:00	5	$71
Seattle-Los Angeles	1,099	14:00	7	$125

ZEPPELIN'S FAILURE: "You should have better sense," cabled Mrs. Henry J. Pierce to her husband in Manhattan. He had pleaded with her not to sail on the *Graf Zeppelin* from Friedrichshafen. She did sail, early one fair morning last week, with Susi, female gorilla, 17 male passengers and the Zeppelin's crew of 40 (Dr. Hugo Eckener commanding). En route to Gibraltar the crankshaft of one of her five engines broke. Near Cartagena, Spain, Commander Eckener turned her back towards Friedrichshafen.

And then began a night and day of struggle. Two more engines went out of commission. The ship reached the Rhone. Rushing down and against her went the mistral, the draft which comes from France's coolish central plateau and ends over the warmish Mediterranean. The *Graf Zeppelin* bucked the mistral. The wind tossed and whirled the ship. A fourth engine went dead. Only one remained to drive her and that was not enough. Commander Eckener headed her south and floated with the wind.

At Cuers-Pierrefeu, about ten miles from Toulon, there is the mooring mast of the lost *Dixmude*, France's only dirigible, and her hangar. A company of Senegalese troops pulled the ship to earth and walked her into the hangar. Passengers, weary, pretended unconcern over their dangers. Most of them declared that they would wait until the ship's motors were replaced and she would start again for the U.S. That, it was apparent, would not be for several weeks.

AGAIN, MITCHELL: William Mitchell [better known to his- JUNE 10 tory as "Billy"], the Brigadier General who talked himself down to the rank of Colonel and out of the Army by criticizing the War and Navy Departments' post-War air policies [at a court-martial in 1925], this week began fresh repetition of his criticisms, in current issues of *Aeronautics* and *Liberty*.

As many a lover of word-fights may have forgotten, Col. Mitchell has clamored for almost a decade for a Department of Aeronautics separate from the War and Navy Departments. His experiences during and immediately following the War persuaded him of the need. He was the first U.S. officer to fly over the German lines, was chief of the U.S. air service in the Argonne offensive, and shared in practically all the major A.E.F. operations. He was in more engagements than any other U.S. officer. He has a great battery of ribbons and medals.

Now he has trained upon a target whom he dared to attack only by indirect fire during his Army service—President Coolidge. "I recommended in 1925," he now writes, "that a board of disinterested persons be convened by the President to determine how the aeronautical problem should be handled in this country. President Coolidge 'stuffed the deck.' He appointed persons well known to be hostile to the independent development of aviation. Instead of creating a department of aeronautics separate from the Army and Navy as the English, French, Germans, Italians, Russians and Spanish have, they merely appointed an additional secretary in the Army, Navy and Commerce Departments which entrenched the bureaucracy more firmly and gave an opportunity of passing plums to friends. A great cry was made all over the country through Coolidge's controlled press that air power was being assisted and developed. Nothing of the kind was done, as it was still made the tail of the dog."

Shortcomings of the U.S. as an airwise nation which General Mitchell considers important include lack of through transcontinental air lines, lack of transoceanic lines, the vulnerability of warships to planes ("battleships have become so top-heavy and useless that if they get a good crack below the waterline, they just turn over and sink of their own accord"), the impossibility of protecting cities from air raids, the poverty of the Army and Navy in fighting planes.

LARK: One of the strangest experiences that the crew of the *Los Angeles* (the U.S. Navy's only big dirigible) ever had was when, last September, a man ran out with a shotgun as the ship sailed over Layton, N.J., and fired a charge up into the big silvery bag. The buckshot tore only small holes in the ship's fabric, but it might have struck machinery, caused disaster. Had the *Los Angeles* been inflated with inflammable hydrogen instead of inert helium, she might have blown up.

Last week Carpenter Merton Hankins, the lilliputian gunner, was tried for assault with attempt to kill. It was just a "lark" for him, he said. He and four other men had been shooting at a target in a backyard. They drank some New Jersey stuff and decided to go hunting deer. They sighted the *Los Angeles*. Merton Hankins wanted a ride. He waved his hands. He shouted. He turned capers. The crew of the *Los Angeles* paid no heed, so Merton Hankins fired his shotgun at the ship, he said, "just to attract attention." The jury found Merton Hankins not guilty of assault, evidently because his reputation as a larkster was well established. Two years ago, when a club refused to let him fish in its privately stocked trout pools, Jokester Hankins opened the dam, let out the water, killed most of the fish. For that he was fined $200.

WOMEN FLYERS: Amelia Earhart was vexed last week. The JUNE 24 cause: a $10,000 air race "for women only" had been proposed from Santa Monica to Cleveland. But when Miss Earhart and others with a taste for prize money and *kudos* asked for details, the details were vague. The female air derby was, it appeared, but an idea. Men flyers were scoffing at it. Miss Earhart, the first woman to "fly" the Atlantic [in 1928] went along only as a passenger, some men pointed out. Women's records mean nothing. Women lack nerve. They have no stamina, no perseverance. The implication was that women could not endure the 2,500-mile flight from Santa Monica to Cleveland. The scramble for prize money might become a shambles.

Suggestions were made to ease the rigors—that a man pilot accompany each woman racer to extricate her from difficulties, that the race be from Omaha to Cleveland—over level country. The scornful remark was even made that "none of them will be able to get over the Rockies."

Vexed by such gibes, Aviatrix Earhart spoke out: "Women *are* less expert than men in flying. But that is not because they are women. A man has mechanics thrown at him from the cradle. Women haven't. They must pay for everything. Tradition and training, as well as other factors, militate against their becoming bus drivers, officers on ships or locomotive engineers. Yet some women can fly. They do get more glory than men for comparable feats. But, also, women get more notoriety when they get cracked up."

JULY 29 **INSURANCE:** When Prizefighter Gene Tunney flew a year ago in a Sikorsky Amphibian the 150 miles from Speculator, N.Y., to New York City, his insurance company charged a premium of $1,000 to insure his life for $300,000 and the plane for $30,000 during the single, short trip. Another company might have charged more, another less. No one knows what is a fair rate for aviation insurance risks.

Igor Sikorsky, after only six years in U.S. aviation, a great success.

Jimmy Doolittle. When his wings fell off, he bailed out. Page 203.

SIKORSKY TO UNITED: Sikorsky Aviation Corp. was sold last week to United Aircraft & Transport Corp. for about $2,500,000. The deal lines up one of the best planes in the world, the Sikorsky Amphibion (Sikorsky's preferred spelling), with other United subsidiaries—Boeing, Vought, Pratt & Whitney motors, Boeing Air Transport.

Inventor Igor I. Sikorsky was in Europe when the deal was announced. If any one had told him six years ago when, a Russian immigrant, he founded his U.S. company, that in 1929 it would bring $2,500,000, he would have believed it. He has never lacked self-confidence. In Tsarist days he was his country's foremost aeronautical engineer. He designed the world's first successful multimotored plane (a four-motor job, 1913), flew the first multimotored seaplane (his own design, 1914), enabled the Russians to make the first heavy air bombardments of the War.

GRAF ZEPPELIN, AGAIN: The gorilla and the chimpanzee were AUG. 12 glum, the 600 canaries fidgety, the 19 passengers restless aboard the *Graf Zeppelin* as she rushed across the Atlantic last week on the second transoceanic commercial voyage. [The first was in October, 1928.] She reached Lakehurst, N.J., from Friedrichshafen, at the German-Swiss border, in 95 hrs., 23 min., without trouble, having averaged 60 miles an hour—about twice as fast as the S.S. *Bremen*. There were discomforts aboard—prohibition against smoking because of the inflammable hydrogen which kept the *Graf Zeppelin* aloft, restricted space for exercise.

INDISCREET PASSENGERS: As Joseph Bogan was landing his taxi plane at Chicago with one hand, he kept bashing at his two passengers with a fire extinguisher in the other hand. Reason: The passengers tried to take control from him in mid-air when he would not stunt them. Police arrested them for disorderly conduct.

CLEVELAND RACES & SHOW: The City of Cleveland repaired SEPT. 9 highways running west to Cleveland's municipal airport. Citizens hung out flags. Janitors painted directional arrows on roofs. Thus opened the Cleveland air races and show. The industry sent 1,200 planes to race, stunt, skeedaddle. Army, Navy, Marine Corps and Canadian military flyers demonstrated their maneuvers. Cynosure of the acrobatics (from the Greek meaning literally "high goings on") was lanky Colonel Lindbergh. He and his wife flew together to the airport. He took off each day with Naval Lieutenants F.O. Kivette and Frank O'Beirne dogging his tail. They snapped together over the field, rolled together, looped together, scooted towards earth together, never losing their formation. Then alone the antic colonel would take the sky, twirling about, flying upside down.

So dumbfounding that it caused the laughter of relief was

Juan de la Cierva's Autogiro [a propeller-driven plane that had both wings and helicopter-like vanes] which he drove himself. He landed in a 20-ft. chalked circle, a simple feat for his machine. The Army's best flyer, James Harold Doolittle [the famous "Jimmy" Doolittle who would lead the first bombers to Tokyo in World War II] flew the wings off a plane in which he was practicing inverted dives. He jumped safely with a parachute, and at once put a duplicate plane through the same stunts. The human cost of attracting public attention to the Cleveland show was high: five were killed, five injured.

SEPT. 16   **CITY OF SAN FRANCISCO:** Like the wreck of the *Titanic,* the crash of Transcontinental Air Transport's *City of San Francisco* in New Mexico last week was relatively one of the world's great commercial disasters. It was the first bad one on a U.S. Transcontinental line. The great tri-motored Ford with five passengers and crew of three flew west from Albuquerque into an electrical storm and oblivion.

ZEPPELINING: "Speaking frankly," said Dr. Hugo Eckener, "the *Graf Zeppelin*'s voyage around the world was to demonstrate the expediency of her mode of travel, to intensify public interest." The trip served its purpose. It led last week to banker negotiations to provide Dr. Eckener with money for four more Zeppelins.

Except for brief electrical storms, navigation was simple for Capt. Lehmann on the *Graf*'s final leg to Friedrichshafen. He detoured over Santander, Spain, to salute King Alfonso and Queen Victoria. This was a prudent courtesy, because Spain is building a dirigible hangar at Seville which will be useful when the Germans establish their Europe-South America Zeppelin line. Some passengers were vexed at the delay. Their nerves were jumpy because one Frederick S. Hogg, retired Mount Vernon, N.Y., businessman, had smoked a cigar in the ship's lavatory. One spark might have blown her up. Some of the other passengers wanted Passenger Hogg imprisoned. Capt. Lehmann only reprimanded him, took his cigars and pocket lighter ignominiously away.

The *Graf Zeppelin* was built for demonstration purposes. It is aerodynamically imperfect. Because it is a cylinder with conic ends, air does not flow smoothly over it. It will never be put on a commercial line but will be used as a training ship for crews and for sight-seeing trips.

As soon as mail contracts are signed, U.S. money will be forthcoming and the four commercial dirigibles will be rushed into construction. The Germans will establish a line between Europe and the U.S. with two ships running each way weekly. The U.S. base will be near Baltimore, Washington, or Richmond, Va., because the weather there is more even than points farther north. The Goodyear-Zeppelin Corp. [a U.S. firm owned jointly by the rubber company and the German Zeppelin works] will run its ship, or ships, from the Pacific Coast to Hawaii, later to the Philippines.

357.7 M.P.H.: Fast went England's supermarine Rolls-Royce SEPT. 23 seaplane for an average speed of 357.7 m.p.h. (The fastest lap was 368.8.) That was man's fastest authenticated travel. The plane had gone even faster in practice spins.

DOOLITTLE: The Army Air Corps has a questionnaire which SEPT. 30 flyers must fill out after accidents. Last week, newspapers had fun printing Lieut. Doolittle's report on his Cleveland mishap. The phrases were as short and compact as their author. His "description of method of leaving plane" was two words: "Thrown out." His "complete and accurate account of the causes for the jump," was two more words: "Wing broke."

TRANSPORT INDUSTRY: Three-quarters of a billion dollars are now invested in the entire aviation industry. Forty-five companies are transporting mail, express and passengers over 75,000 miles daily. This year the number of passengers will approximate 150,000. (Last year the total was 52,934.) But passenger traffic does not yet pay its way. Only between San Francisco and Los Angeles and between New York and Boston do ships frequently have all passenger seats sold.

Mail contracts, which represent the U.S. government's way of furnishing essential subsidies, almost pay the operating expenses of most of the carriers. But not all expenses. No one yet knows if passenger, freight and mail air rates are fair to both the public and the operator. Air carriers dislike excess baggage and want to restrict free baggage to 25 or 30 lbs. on single-motored planes, to 50 lbs. on multimotored ones. (Mrs. Charles Augustus Lindbergh generally travels with only one evening gown and no extra wrap. Just after a recent landing Col. Lindbergh scolded her for not wearing a petticoat.)

OCT. 7   **BLIND FLYING ACCOMPLISHED:** Totally blind flying, solely by the aid of navigating instruments, became an accomplished fact for the first time last week. Lieutenant James Harold ("Jimmy") Doolittle, 33, "best Army flyer," did it at Mitchel Field, L.I. Blind flying, where nothing of the ground or horizon can be seen, is the terror of aviation. At the speed of plane flight (100 m.p.h. usually) a pilot loses his sense of balance. At night or in fog, where he cannot orient himself against ground objects, he flies to one side, his wings tilt, the plane goes up, down, or, happily, level. He does not know. His instruments go "hay wire." He is helpless.

Experienced professional pilots, particularly on the night mail routes, often set their planes at neutral, take their hands off the controls, fold their arms and apathetically wait to get out of the fog, or to crash. Three new instruments developed during eleven months' work made Lieutenant Doolittle's work possible. They provide visual radio direction, indicate an artificial horizon, and by a barometer altimeter show to within a very few feet how far above the ground the plane is at all times.

A two-seater, dual control biplane was equipped with these new instruments. Harry Frank Guggenheim, 39, president of the Guggenheim Fund for the Promotion of Aeronautics, [which helped finance the system and borrowed Doolittle from the army to test it], had an argument with Lieutenant Doolittle at the field. The lieutenant wanted to fly the plane alone. Mr. Guggenheim, a flyer himself, insisted that Lieutenant Benjamin Kelsey, who had assisted in the research, occupy the front seat to take control in case accident happened. Piqued, daring Lieutenant Doolittle consented.

He crawled into the rear cockpit, hauled an opaque cloth entirely over himself and instruments, gave the plane the gun. Off were the two men, Lieutenant Kelsey with his arms resting on the gunwales, Lieutenant Doolittle completely shrouded. Fourteen miles in all he flew, seeing nothing but his instruments. Certainly, assuredly, he made an excellent three-point landing within a few feet of his take-off.

POLAR BYRD: A cold green horizon cheered the Byrd Antarc- DEC. 9
tic Expedition. It meant clear flying weather toward the South
Pole. Into their grey Ford transport climbed Commander
Richard Evelyn Byrd, Pilot Bernt Balchen, Radioman Harold
June and a photographer. The fuselage door slammed shut.
There was a smooth take-off with the three motors howling.
Commander Byrd's mind "shot back to an exactly similar
scene in the Arctic spring, May 9, 1926, when Floyd Bennett
and I arose from the snow at Spitzbergen and headed North-
Pole-ward." Wrapped in a U.S. flag which the explorer had
planned to drop over the South Pole was a stone from Floyd
Bennett's grave [he died in 1928 of pneumonia].

For 450 miles they flew due south over the great ice plain
called Ross Shelf. Then they were at the Queen Maud Range.
For three steep miles the Antarctic wall rises. The loaded
plane could not mount so high. Commander Byrd, navigating, found a nick in the icy wall of which the late lost Roald
Amundsen had written. But Byrd had to dump three months'
supply of food to let the plane rise upward—and over.
Hours later a radiogram left the plane: "We have reached
the vicinity of the South Pole. We can see an almost limitless
polar plateau." For a few minutes they romped around the
polar point, then scurried—for gasoline was getting low—
to the plateau's rim. A landing at the cliff foot for fuel stored
days before. A scoot for Little America. Exuberant radio reports to the world. The flight made Byrd the first man in history
to fly over both poles.

AT CHAGRIN FALLS: As National Air Transport's Thomas P. DEC. 16
Nelson headed west for Cleveland last week, thick snow
flurries hid him from the ground. At snow-blown Cleveland,
Pilot Nelson was late, by minutes, hours, days. Col. Lindbergh, onetime flying companion of the missing man, flew
his own machine over the treacherous Alleghenies to join
25 other planes in a systematic search of northern Ohio.

Three days after the disappearance, a rabbit hunter found
Nelson 25 miles east of Cleveland near Chagrin Falls. He
had jumped just before crashing. (Presumption was he was
forced down by ice forming on his wings.) The jump apparently stunned him. Unconscious, he froze to death, hard by
the busy Cleveland to Pittsburgh motor road, the tenth mail
flyer to die on the New York-Cleveland route.

DEC. 23 **DIRIGIBLE ANCHORAGES:** In Manhattan, onetime Governor Alfred Emanuel Smith (part owner of the New York "Giants," board chairman of the County Trust Co. and president of the Empire State Building Corp.) announced that the plans of the Empire State building, world's largest, world's tallest, on the old Waldorf-Astoria site on Fifth Avenue, would include a mooring mast as dirigible way-station, 1,300 feet above the street.

MILESTONES

MARRIED: Playwright Eugene Gladstone O'Neill, lately divorced, to Carlotta Monterey, actress. In a prenuptial contract, Playwright O'Neill agreed to lease for 13 years the great Château de Plessis, 25 miles from Tour, with a 600-acre game preserve. Miss Monterey also required installation of a roof garden, gymnasium, swimming pool.

DIED: B. V. Vickers, English arms maker (machine-guns); at Bakewell, Derbyshire; of a gunshot wound received when his hunting dog snapped at his gun-loader, who flinched, discharged a gun accidentally.

ENGAGED: Nelson Aldrich Rockefeller, 21, Dartmouth senior, second son of John Davison Rockefeller, Jr.; and Mary Todhunter Clark, 22, of Cynwyd, Pa., Foxcroft graduate, granddaughter of the late President George B. Roberts of Pennsylvania R.R.; at Philadelphia.

PROMOTED: Commander Richard Evelyn Byrd, polar explorer; to the rank of Rear Admiral, U.S.N., retired; by act of Congress.

MISCELLANY

In Los Angeles, Lucio Godino, Siamese twin, was arrested for traffic violations. Judge William M. Northrup suspended sentence because the innocent brother, Simlicio, pleaded that he should not be jailed for Lucio's offense.

In Chicago, 52 civil service aspirants appeared at City Hall where they were undressed, were measured, answered questions on law, diplomacy, U.S. history, the number of dogs in Chicago. This procedure eliminated all but 21 who were sent into another room, made to chase imaginary dogs in a hypothetical backyard. One Philip Keafta, who had chinned himself 45 times, held his breath 45 seconds, ran about the room, tripped on a taut wire hazard, fell and broke his ankle. He was qualified, however, and when he emerges from the hospital will be City Dog Catcher, salary $2,200 a year.

In Chicago, one David Petros, Persian frankfurter vendor, went to the police station, moaned through an interpreter that his equipment had been stolen. "Write the name of the man you suspect on this dotted line," said the desk sergeant. Puzzled by the interpreter's translation, Petros wrote his own name, went home. There a police officer met him, took him to jail, locked him up for the night.

In Africa, telegraph linesmen, long mystified by the destruction of wires over the veldt, discovered that languid giraffes use them for head rests.

In Peabody, Mass., police raided a cemetery chapel, found a night club going full blast, arrested 36 people, confiscated 38 quarts of alleged beer.

One of the strange facts about 1929 is that though it has gone down in history as the year of the great stock market crash, there was really very little evidence at the time that the nation was headed for the great depression that followed. Despite some warnings to the contrary, the nation's mood was primarily one of hopefulness and optimism, not only before and during the crash, but afterward as well. Indeed, TIME *could report a month later that the taxes levied by New York State on the heavy sales of stock during the market slump were a blessing, and that the money might be used to "build broader bridges to bear the increasing traffic of U.S. prosperity." During the remainder of the year there was news of business as usual—of mergers and expansion, and of booming sales in expensive motorboats. It was as if the nation had not yet discovered what was happening to it.*

MAN OF THE YEAR: Last July, in a matter of fact sort of way, JAN. 7 Walter P. Chrysler offered the public a new automobile called the Plymouth. Early in August, Mr. Chrysler brought out another new car, called the De Soto. In autumn came the news that Walter P. Chrysler was going to build the world's tallest skyscraper, a 68-story colossus towering more than 800 feet above Manhattan. The doings of Walter P. Chrysler, already prodigious, now became fabulous. Mr. Chrysler carefully explained that his building had nothing to do with his automobile business, that it was a separate enterprise. "I like to build things," he said. "I'm having a lot of fun going thoroughly into everything with the architect."

With the arrival of the new year, Mr. Chrysler announced that the name of the Chrysler Corp. was changed, significantly, to Chrysler Motors. A new competitive set-up began to appear. In 1928, the centre-ring automobile battle was Ford *v.* General Motors. The issue: Could the Model "A" check the growing threat of Chevrolet and General Motors? Now the issue is enormously complicated by the injection of Chrysler Motors. Can Chrysler challenge General Motors? Undeniably, Mr. Chrysler had been the outstanding businessman of the year.

Mr. Chrysler does not ignore the lead with which General Motors starts the contest. But he sees no limit to the markets over which the two motor-monsters can struggle. "It devolves upon the United States," he said last September, "to help motorize the world."

"Walt" Chrysler was a Kansas boy. When he was 17 he got into the Union Pacific shops as an apprentice machinist, glad of 5¢ per hour and a chance to learn. Mechanical engineering became his life, not his profession. When he wanted a shotgun, he made one.

He set out to see what other railroad shops were like. At the age of 33 he was superintendent of motive power of the whole Chicago & Great Western system. "W.P." they called him. His mechanical curiosity was aroused by the two or three horseless thing-a-ma-jigs that sometimes moved through the streets, especially on Sundays, kicking up dust with a maximum of noise and a minimum of grace. He went to the Chicago automobile show of 1905 (the city's fifth show) and stood entranced in front of a beauteous white Locomobile. The salesman said it cost $5,000 cash. Mr.

Walter P. Chrysler: the U.S. must "help motorize the world."

Edward H.H. Simmons: "The Stock Market is safe." Page 213.

Chrysler had $700 in the bank. He borrowed $4,300 and shipped it home. Mrs. Chrysler was not very much pleased, especially when she discovered her husband did not mean to get some good out of so much extravagance by driving it around. Instead, what did he do but take it all apart, put it all together and take it all apart again.

In the years since, he has been the greatest rebuilder of automobile companies that the industry had ever known. In view of the present movement of Chrvsler Motors *v.* General Motors, it is important to recall that the Buick company was the first automobile company Mr. Chrysler ever took in hand. He had it in hand from 1911 to 1919. He jacked up its production from 40 cars per day to 550 and established its name as a synonym for soundness.

From 1915 to 1920 he was in charge of all General Motors production. Later he overhauled the Willys-Overland company from hubcaps to stockholders, and in the midst of that task, undertook the same job for Maxwell. It was perhaps an accident, perhaps an earned result, that when the Prince of Wales visited Long Island in the summer of 1924, he drove a smart roadster that was so little known the newspapers felt justified in mentioning its name—Chrysler.

FEDERAL WARNING: Toward Wall Street last week the Fed- FEB. 18 eral Reserve Board shook a threatening finger, spoke a warning word. With loans to brokers standing at $5,669,000,000, the Board felt that too much money was being absorbed by the stockmarket, that other interests were being forced to pay too much for money they borrow, that industry as a whole was suffering from diversion of funds to brokers and speculators. Taken at face value, the statement would mean refusal of loans for speculative purposes, plus a rise in the rediscount rate, which in turn would mean a stock market afflicted with scarce money and falling prices.

Meanwhile, however, speculators were inclined to feel that the Reserve Board's big words were larger than any big stick it might produce, that it was perhaps talking chiefly for the moral effect which its speech actually did have upon a nervous and inflated Exchange.

FEDERAL RESERVE *v.* SPECULATION: Into Congress last week FEB. 25 overflowed the financial argument between Federal Reserve

Board and Wall Street. Ponderous Senator James Thomas Heflin of Alabama bellowed that Wall Street was the hotbed and breeding place of the worst form of gambling that ever cursed the country—worse than the Louisiana State Lottery which slew its hundreds while the New York State gambling exchanges were slaying hundreds of thousands.

The outstanding development of the week was the fact that, without taking any radical measures, the Federal Reserve Board, aided by frontpage publicity, succeeded in scaring Wall Street into a liquidation movement. A definite obituary on the bull market might, however, be a little premature.

MARCH 18 **WARNING:** If the Stock Market is on the way to running over a steep cliff into the sea, why have not the bankers endeavored to cast out its speculative devils? One reason, say cynics, is that the brokers are excellent customers of the banks. Last week, however, one U.S. banker did speak his mind on inflation, flayed not only the Market but also the newly organized investment trusts, which he called "incorporated stock pools." This banker was Paul Warburg, Chairman of International Acceptance, which recently merged with Bank of the Manhattan Co. A member of the Federal Reserve Board from 1914 to 1918, Mr. Warburg was eminently qualified to discuss stocks and money.

The Federal Reserve Board, said Mr. Warburg, has lost control of the money situation by failure to take decisive action before inflation reached its present strength. He blamed "structural defects" rather than the System's personnel. Action cannot be prompt or decisive when it depends upon 120 men in twelve separate boards working with a central board of eight men "who may be wide apart in their views and bewildered by political influence."

DAVID BUICK: "If I'd only got into the automobile business on the ground floor, what a millionaire I'd be today! I'd be sailing a yacht around the world right now. Those guys got a break."

So, to himself, ruminates many a U.S. man-in-the-street. But such envious persons might well harken to the story of David D. Buick. He was in on the ground floor. He died in Detroit last week, obscure, impoverished. And when he went to work he walked. The Buick he had helped build was a good car. (He was working on it before the Ford Motor Co. was incorporated, and the two millionth Buick was produced in the fall of 1928.) But there arose arguments, disputes, misunderstanding in the company he had founded. And after three years as general manager, he left it with a block of stock which would soon have made him an exceedingly rich man.

But David Buick seemed to have no affinity for money. Disappointed in motor cars, he went to California and organized an oil company. To finance it he sold much of his stock. Then title litigation wrecked the oil company—expensive litigation that consumed the remainder of the stock. With what he saved from this disaster Mr. Buick went into real estate and became partner in a company that controlled many acres. Unfortunately, they were Florida acres. [The boom in Florida land had collapsed disastrously in 1926.]

In 1924, Mr. Buick went back to Detroit. He had no money. He was 69. Finally he was put at the information desk of the Detroit School of Trades. He was a thin, hunched little old man who peered at questioners through heavy glasses. Mr. Buick died of cancer. Shortly before going to the hospital he said: "I'm not feeling sorry for myself or worrying about the past. It was the breaks of the game that I lost out."

CRASH: On Tuesday, March 26, came the biggest stock APRIL 1 market crash in Coolidge-Hoover history. The banks had withdrawn 25 million dollars from the market, a mere bagatelle. Money opened not at 9% (of the day before) but at 12%. It rose to 15%. Another selling wave set in—especially in coppers. The amateurs fled even faster than the day before and hundreds who did not flee were sold out, adding to the casualties. Money still rose, up, up, to 20%.

AGAIN, ZOOM: Possibly unchastened, but certainly cautious, MAY 6 the Stock Market last week edged its way back across the Four Million Shares a Day mark, succeeded in maintaining a bullish, though still rather bilious, complexion. Yet only the memory of its recent crisis, plus the still large loans to brokers, could have kept the Market from lowering its horns to another bull stampede. For of bullish portents there was no end:

A.T.&T. became a three billion dollar corporation; New Haven Railroad stock crossed par for the first time since 1913; U.S. Steel Corp. production went from 96% of capacity to 100%; General Electric's first quarter broke all records in sales, orders and net.

MAY 20 **CAPITAL v. CREDIT:** A onetime medical student made a speech last week and within 48 hours received requests for 40,000 copies thereof. The speechmaker was Edward Henry Harriman Simmons, who has been president of the New York Stock Exchange since 1924—longest term in history. The speech was defense by attack. Outstanding points: Almost the entire increase in loans to brokers came not from banks but from private corporations which the Federal Reserve could not control, that the more the Federal Reserve Board scolds and harries the Stock Market the higher the interest rates go because the capitalist, filled with terror, has put his money not into stocks but into the call money market—"the safest form of investment known in this country." Thus the Reserve Board has, against its own intentions, continually forced money into call loans and away from other employment.

Always attacking, never merely defending, Mr. Simmons next argued that to divert "the enormous masses of capital today invested in stock market loans" into "commercial business" would "produce a huge rise in commodity prices, inflation of inventories, and an artificial business boom . . . which could only end in a colossal smash." In other words, if business in general had the money now in brokers' loans it would swell up and burst. There is more capital extant "than the country knows what to do with." The safe place for this capital is in the Stock Market—a kind of financial safety valve in which surplus funds may harmlessly be blown off.

MAY 27 **HOOVER COMMITTEE:** There are, according to the Hoover Economic Survey [started in 1921 under Secretary of Commerce Herbert Hoover], some 17 million U.S. citizens engaged in playing the Stock Market. Most of these investors are new, small, ignorant. They speculate to double their capital rather than invest to get a steady increase. They are motivated by faith.

"1929 and All's Well" was, indeed, almost the gist of the lengthy report. Stock market absorption of credit was regarded with misgiving. But the keynote, ringingly struck, was that there is no limit to the capacity of the U.S. consumer to consume. Thus was observed a non-vicious circle in which the manufacturer constantly produced more merchandise, the consumer constantly consumed more merchandise, and out of the horn of plenty came gifts for all.

STILL STRONG STEEL: The steel business is the best index of JULY 29 U.S. prosperity. As steel goes, so goes the country. Steel has lately been going at record pace. Best second quarter earnings since the war. Unprecedented third quarter generally predicted. Industry operating at 95% of capacity.

BEAR FRIDAY: Speculators chewed ragged cigars last week, AUG. 19 conferred past midnight, lost their sleep. Thursday's stock market had closed strong when the Bank of England did not raise its rediscount rate. Then, late in the afternoon, came announcement that the Federal Reserve Bank of New York had raised its rate from 5% to 6%. Wall Street was caught unprepared. Tycoons rushed to telephones, brokers called up bankers. Long after the dinner hour two Rolls-Royces still waited outside the austere House of Morgan.

Detached observers were inclined to view last week's rise as an adjustment to the high rates on call money already established. But when the gong sounded on Friday, trading began with clamorous confusion. Ten thousand shares of A.T.&T. were sold at 266, 15 points off. The New York *Times* averages showed a decline of $9.66 compared to the record May 22 decline of $8.12. But Saturday saw gains in the general list. By Monday the rise, although not universal, bore up many stocks. U.S. Steel reached a new all-time high.

"SIMPLE MEN": What happens to bankers who drive their bank over a cliff and leave depositors with n cents on the dollar? Last week a Federal judge provided an answer. Just six weeks after Clarke Bros., private bankers, failed in Manhattan, James Rae Clarke, senior partner, was sentenced to eight years in the overcrowded Atlanta penitentiary. Philip L. Clarke, John R. Bouker and Hudson Clarke, Jr. each received a sentence of one year, one day.

The sentences were no heavier because the bankers gave up their entire personal property for the benefit of the depositors and it was acknowledged that the junior partners had gained little or nothing personally from the crash, which was attributed mainly to bad banking. Said Federal Judge Anderson: "I don't believe a set of as simple men as you ever before carried a banking institution to destruction. No brains or ability has been shown by any of you."

Hudson Clarke, Jr. received a suspended sentence on his promise to lead "an honorable life" and try to support his crippled father and the families of the others, who are left destitute. He walked from the court, free, with $1.27 to start life over again. Angry depositors, told that they might eventually receive 20¢ instead of 5¢ or 10¢ on the dollar, added four more items to the sum of what happens to bad bankers. Each item was an egg thrown at the three manacled convicts on their way to jail.

OCT. 14 **THE BUYERS:** An indication of the background of many a stock purchaser was seen in the inquiry received by a broker from a customer as to whether Cuba Cane [largest of the Cuban sugar companies], was or was not a corporation dealing in walking sticks, crutches.

Stocks in general went down last week more than in any other week for a year, then made a come-back. In Chicago, many gangsters, known to be heavy speculators, received margin calls, left brokers' offices muttering threats. Dynamite was thrown into the home of one brokerage credit manager. Stench bombs were tossed into three brokerage offices. "A new form of wolf has invaded La Salle Street," said the deputy police commissioner, "the racketeer who responds with a bomb when he is called for more margin."

NOV. 4 **BANKERS v. PANIC:** John Davison Rockefeller, Jr. was in Detroit attending Edison celebrations [the 60th anniversary of Thomas Edison's incandescent bulb]. It was said that he had been quietly liquidating for some weeks. Promptly at 10 a.m. on Thursday Oct. 24 sounded the gong of the New York Stock Exchange and 6,000 shares of Montgomery Ward changed hands at 83—its high for 1929 having been 156. For so many months people had saved money and borrowed money and borrowed on their borrowings to possess themselves of the little pieces of paper by virtue of which they became partners in U.S. Industry. Now they were trying to get rid of them even more frantically than they had tried to get them. Even in a panic-market, someone must buy the "dumped" shares, but stocks were dropping from 2 to 10 points before a buyer could be found. At around noon there came the no-bid menace. It looked as if U.S. Industries' little partners were in a fair way to bankrupt the firm.

Then at 1:30 p.m., a popular broker and huntsman named Richard F. Whitney strode through the mob, made swiftly for Post No. 2 where the stock of U.S. Steel Corp., most pivotal of all U.S. stocks, is traded in. It was now at 190. If it should sink further, Panic might surely take command. Loudly, confidently, Broker Whitney made known that he offered $205 per share for 25,000 shares of Steel. Soon tickers were flashing the news. More and more steel was bought until 200,000 shares had been purchased. Other buyers bought other pivotal stocks. Brokers and traders agreed that the man who bid 205 for 25,000 shares of Steel had made himself a hero. [In 1938, Richard Whitney, by then a former president of the Stock Exchange, went to prison for stealing from his clients.]

Despite the rapid Thursday afternoon recovery, the low point of the swinging pendulum cut off many a speculative head. Wild were the rumors of ruin and suicide. Roaring was the business done by downtown speakeasies. Soundly anticlimactic was the remainder of the trading week.

But the now successful Bears made Monday, Oct. 28, a day of fresh disaster. Over the weekend many an investor had fully realized the necessity for an immediate exit from the market. Thus the session, opening with an accumulation of selling orders, was hopeless from the start. Again Broker Whitney haunted Post No. 2, but this time Steel broke through 200, reeled down to 186. A.T.&T. fell 24 points; General Electric, 47; Eastman Kodak, 41, etc., etc. etc.

By Tuesday morning the suspicion that there might be a panic had turned to the apprehension that there *was* a panic. Tuesday brought a quota of cheerful utterances. President Hoover said that U.S. Industry was on a sound basis. But the almost incredible number of 16,338,000 shares were dumped that day as if they were so much junk.

Would the nightmare, to many tragically cruel, never end?

NOV. 11   **FAITH, BANKERS & PANIC:** Someone had to show faith. The first to do so was the president of the Sun Life Assurance Co. of Canada, who said that his company was not selling stock but was buying. From Washington the Assistant Secretary of Commerce radioed to the nation that its business was sound, that only 4% of U.S. families were affected by the break. William Wrigley, Jr. announced that he was buying stocks. In Chicago Philanthropist Julius Rosenwald, board chairman of Sears Roebuck & Co., guaranteed the margin accounts of all his employees. Chicago public utility tycoon Samuel Insull announced that he would do the same thing. But the climax came when the wizened little man who lives in the fortressed home in Pocantico Hill, N.Y. (John D. Rockefeller, Sr.), said: "My son and I have for some days past been purchasing sound common stock." Thus did the men whose names are known strive mightily to alter a national psychology.

Stock Exchange Governors ordered the Exchange closed after 1 o'clock Wednesday, Thursday, Friday; all day Saturday. Tuesday was election day. Thus was further rest insured. Clerks who had passed many a sleepless night returned to clean up the greatest amount of work they had ever had in so short a time. In the hurly-burly many an error had been made. The clerks had to rectify them. It was the most nerve-wracking crisis in U.S. business history.

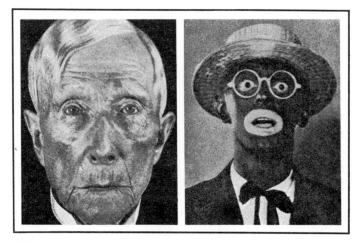

John D. Rockefeller: "My son and I have been purchasing stock."

Eddie Cantor asks for a job as a Sears Roebuck office boy. Page 218.

MARKET "LESSON": Why the crash came on Oct. 23, 1929, is NOV. 18 as mysterious (and as unimportant) as why the World War chanced to begin on Aug. 4, 1914. If some trace the War no further than to an archducal assassination, then others might trace the Crash to a wide variety of specific moments. Vital point is the undermining of popular confidence that ended in the crash.

Causes of this undermining were several: Warnings from the Federal Reserve Board and other prophets of disaster—warnings which, scoffed at when given, nevertheless filled the Market with a conviction of sin. The September slump (currently almost ignored in favor of the peculiar theory that the Market crashed without warning) was of tremendous importance in its indication that a Market which could survive only by constant rises had reached the limits of its climb.

Slowly the Market began to realize that 1929 might be an abnormal, high-water year instead of one more level in a rising tide. The Market had mortgaged itself with the future as its security. If that future did not continue rosy, the security had disappeared.

HEROES, WAGS, SAGES: To all things must come an end. Last NOV. 25 week there came an end to the almost uninterrupted panic of selling that has fermented U.S. stock markets since Oct. 23. An extra dividend of 30¢ was declared by General Motors Corp. There even came a time for some jokes. Actor Eddie Cantor confessed that when he had heard of Mr. Rosenwald's offer to protect his employes' accounts, he had wired for a job as office boy at Sears Roebuck. Other gags: From the Ritz jumped two men hand-in-hand (they had held a joint account); hotel room clerks asked each new arrival whether he wanted a room for sleeping or jumping.

But there was sad news. Suicides, long rumored, became facts. Most prominent of suiciders was James J. Riordan, president of New York's County Trust Co. In Philadelphia, Brokers Frank S. Palfrey and W. Paul Brown shot themselves. In Chicago Herman L. Felgenhauer, grain broker, took gas. One of the few gainers in the wild selling was New York State, which netted $4,884,427 in October from its 2¢ a share tax on stock sales. Thus can the state build better roads, broader bridges to bear the increasing traffic of U.S. prosperity.

BOOKS

APRIL 1 **"DODSWORTH"**—Sinclair Lewis. Samuel Dodsworth was, perfectly, the American Captain of Industry, believing in the Republican Party, high tariff, and, so long as they did not annoy him personally, in prohibition and the Episcopal Church. He did not split many infinitives. He sometimes enjoyed Beethoven. He was none of the things which most Europeans and many Americans expect in a leader of industry. He was not a Babbitt, not a Rotarian, not an Elk. He never slapped people on the back. His wife was poised and luminous. She talked occasional babytalk to Sam, tolerated his lovemaking. Her time was filled with clubs, committees, charities and bridge.

But when Sam sold out his business and was temporarily free, she insisted upon being taken abroad. Before long, Fran had managed to have a series of affairs. In Italy Sam found the improbable Edith. On the steamer, westward bound, Fran took Sam for granted. Sam finally balked, took the return steamer to Edith.

Less important than *Babbitt* or *Arrowsmith*, kinder and more accurate than *Elmer Gantry*, *Dodsworth* is as shrewd a piece of reporting as any of the others. Red-headed, gaunt and cadaverous, Super-Reporter Lewis sniffs atmosphere with a long, peculiar nose, pierces actuality with swift sharp glances.

APRIL 22 **"THE WORLD CRISIS—1918-1928"**—Winston S. Churchill. The first volume of Mr. Churchill's *The World Crisis* was dedicated "To All Who Tried," this latest and last, "To All Who Hope." That is a strange title to give a pessimistic climax like this: "The story of the human race is war. . . . The War stopped as suddenly and as universally as it had begun. . . . In a thousand arsenals, men pulled themselves up with a jerk. . . . Their projects were put aside, unfinished, but their knowledge was preserved; their data, calculations, and discoveries were docketed 'for future reference' by the

War Offices in every country. . . . It is in these circumstances that we entered upon that period of Exhaustion that has been described as Peace."

Mr. Churchill, British Minister of War during "the" war, describes it in terms of exasperation, cynicism. His opinion of the whole Peace Conference fiasco is violent. He grills the whole U.S.: "After immense delays and false hopes, Europe was left to scramble out of the world disaster as best she could; and the United States, which had lost but 125,000 lives in the whole struggle, was to settle down upon the basis of receiving through one channel or another four-fifths of the reparations paid by Germany to the countries she had devastated."

Winston Churchill: a blast at the U.S. after Europe's war.

Erich Remarque: feverish horror in "All Quiet on the Western Front."

"A PREFACE TO MORALS"—Walter Lippmann. **"MID-CHANNEL** MAY 27 **–AN AMERICAN CHRONICLE"**—Ludwig Lewisohn. In the chorus of U.S. philosophizing, somewhere between the deep notes of John Dewey and the loud guggling of the Menckens, two voices are raised—Walter Lippmann's, young and clear, Ludwig Lewisohn's, old and sad. The two have much in common. As Jews, both men can claim rich philosophical heritage. As conscious Americans, both incline to intense modernism. As intellectuals, both prescribe an adaptation of Greek philosophy.

"I want God—the absolute," says Mr. Lewisohn. "There

is none. Very well. Then something to take his place: permanent values somehow embodied and so to be served." Says Lippmann: "What most distinguishes the generation who have approached maturity since the debacle of idealism at the end of the War is not their rebellion against the religion and moral code of their parents, but their disillusionment with their own rebellion. It is common for young men and women to rebel, but that they should rebel sadly and without faith in their own rebellion—that is something of a novelty." In his vision of what the heart should desire, "the evidence converges upon the theory that what the sages have prophesied as high religion, what the psychologists delineate as matured personality, and the disinterestedness which the Great Society requires . . . are all of a piece, and are the basic elements of a modern morality."

In formal philosophy, Walter Lippmann has had sound training: he assisted George Santayana at Harvard, consorted with William James. When he was 23, Lippmann fused his experiences with his years of abstract studies, produced a brilliant *Preface to Politics* which Freud hailed as the first political treatise to be based on Freudian psychology and which Theodore Roosevelt brandished as a textbook of the Bull-Moose campaign. Enthusiastic, Roosevelt encouraged Lippmann to found *The New Republic*, progressive weekly. His memoranda elucidating Wilson's Fourteen Points lay on the table at the Peace Conference, were daily consulted. At 39, this last February, he gained the title of Editor of the New York *World*. Most earnest have been his editorials in support of Alfred Emanuel Smith in the late campaign. He virtually dictated the 1928 platform of the Democracy.

JUNE 17 **"ALL QUIET ON THE WESTERN FRONT"**—Erich Maria Remarque. England's august Manchester *Guardian* has called this German work "the greatest of all war books." "We" are the soldiers. We feel the Front in our blood. Shells whistle, our senses sharpen. We feel the animal in us, we want to hide in the earth. An uncertain red glow spreads along the skyline before us. Shells howl, pipe, hiss. Searchlights sweep the dark sky, halt, quiver on a black insect—the airman. A bell rings—Gas! I remember the gas patients coughing out their burnt lungs in clots. I don my mask. Like a big, soft jellyfish the gas floats. Suddenly the noise ceases. We run out.

The French storm-troops are 100 yards away. It is not against these men we fling our bombs. It is against Death, now visible, hunting us down.

The net effect is feverish horror. There is a vivid, merciful unreality about the book. To be permeated by horror is to be destroyed spiritually. That is how the book tells, simply, "of a generation of men who, even though they may have escaped the shells, were destroyed by the war."

The author, 31, is a French-German. In 1916 he left school for the Western front. When peace came, he carelessly turned his hand to whatever offered. Money won at roulette enabled him to travel. Money gone, he wrote this book. The War destroyed the comrades to whom he was devoted; destroyed, too, his youth and spirit. He does not forgive.

"A FAREWELL TO ARMS"—Ernest Hemingway. This story of OCT. 14 Lieutenant Frederic Henry, U.S. ambulance officer on the Italian Front, of the Lieutenant's affair with Catherine Barkley, an English nurse who died in childbirth, is infused with the chaotic sweep of armies and tenderly quiescent love. In its sustained, inexorable movement, its throbbing preoccupation with flesh and blood and nerves rather than fanciful fabrics of intellect, it fulfills the prophecies that his most excited admirers have made about Ernest Hemingway.

His mannered style may still be annoying to some, but its pulsing innuendo cannot be denied. His man and woman stand incoherently together against a shattered, dissolving world. They express their feelings by an endearment as trite as "darling." And as they make their escape from Italy, later gaze at each other in torment by the deathbed of Catherine, their tiny shapes on the vast landscape are expressive of the pity, beauty and doom of mankind. The boredom and inertia so frequent in *The Sun Also Rises* never occur in *A Farewell to Arms*. He has gone back to the cause of that weariness—the desolating conflict of nations.

Numerals in italics indicate a picture of the subject mentioned.

PICTURE CREDITS

PRODUCTION STAFF FOR TIME INCORPORATED
John L. Hallenbeck (Vice President and Director of Production),
Robert E. Foy, Caroline Ferri and Robert E. Fraser
Text photocomposed under the direction of Albert J. Dunn and Arthur J. Dunn

QUOTES OF THE YEAR

Henry Ford *(on enforcing Prohibition — p. 15):* "Nobody wants to fly with a drunken aviator."

Al Capone *(on being sentenced to a Philadelphia prison 16½ hours after his arrest for carrying concealed weapons — p. 64):* "They work fast here."

Florenz Ziegfeld *(commenting on the future of movies — p. 165):* "Beauty in the flesh will continue to rule the world."

Thomas A. Edison *(on the occasion of his 82nd birthday — p. 152):* "I am not acquainted with anyone who is happy."

Herbert Hoover *(in his Inaugural Address — p. 13):* "I have no fears for the future of our country. It is bright with hope."

The Prince of Wales *(on seeing living conditions of British miners — p. 82):* "This is ghastly!"

Calvin Coolidge *(on the chore of packing to leave Washington — p. 10):* "It is easier to get into the White House than out of it."

ANSWERS TO PICTURE QUIZ— 1: Walter P. Chrysler; 2: Albert Einstein; 3: Walter Hampden (as Cyrano); 4: Princess Elizabeth; 5: New York Mayor Jimmy Walker; 6: Senator Reed Smoot; 7: Helen Wills; 8: Zeppelin Commander Hugo Eckener; 9: Eva Le Gallienne; 10: Ramsay MacDonald; 11: William Wrigley Jr.; 12: Jimmy Foxx; 13: Max Schmeling; 14: Samuel Insull; 15: Mrs. Herbert Hoover; 16: Henry L. Stimson.